EXTRAORDINARY MIRACLES IN THE LIVES OF ORDINARY PEOPLE

Inspiring Stories of Divine Intervention

by

Therese Marszalek

Harrison House
Tulsa, Oklahoma

13 12 11 10   10 9 8 7 6 5 4 3

Extraordinary Miracles in the Lives of Ordinary People:
Inspiring Stories of Divine Intervention
ISBN 13: 978-1-57794-825-4
ISBN 10: 1-57794-825-4
Copyright © 2007 by Therese M. Marszalek
PMB 111
3327 W. Indian Trail Road
Spokane, WA 99208-9153
www.breakingoutministries.com

Published by Harrison House, Inc.
P.O. Box 35035
Tulsa, Oklahoma 74135

CONTENTS

DEDICATION

I dedicate these pages to my heavenly Father, the God and Father of our Lord Jesus Christ. Your continual demonstration of unconditional love throughout my life is the greatest miracle I've ever known. I also dedicate this collection to my earthly father, Gene Preston, who entered his eternal reward in heaven March 5, 2006. I will forever thank God for the privilege of being your daughter.

PREFACE

When the Lord downloaded His plan for *Extraordinary Miracles in the Lives of Ordinary People* into my heart, He whispered, "I've handpicked exactly fifty miracle stories for you to proclaim, some which have not yet taken place. It will be a work of My Spirit, not of your flesh. In My divine timing I will connect you with those I ordained for this project."

Extraordinary Miracles in the Lives of Ordinary People came to pass just as God said. Like a box of delectable chocolates, it includes such a vast spiritual spread that you may be tempted to read your way through the entire book in one sitting! Each contributor gives their own sweet taste of the Master of Miracles. I have included a contact section in the back of the book to encourage you to connect with these people as you are led by the Holy Spirit. Whether for ministry or personal reasons, I believe God-ordained relationships will be birthed through this book, helping us all to fulfill the master plan of the Master of Miracles.

It is no surprise that the Lord directed me to include exactly fifty stories, as "Pentecost" is translated from the Greek word *pentekoste,* meaning "fifty" or "fiftieth."* Seven Sabbaths passed after the resurrection of Jesus, and on the fiftieth day the Holy Spirit was poured out on the waiting church. I encourage you to read again the entire book of Acts, as it describes the miracles that took place on and after the Day of Pentecost.

God birthed this book as I walked through a fiery season of trial. He directed me to collect miracle stories from across the globe through interviews, phone conversations, and personal visits—all which became intimate encounters with Him. I wrote, spoke, and proclaimed God's wondrous miracles during an extended period of great personal need. Yet, as trials intensified, my hunger for God intensified and led me to a deeper intimacy with my heavenly Father. Afterward, I realized that He used the miracles He had orchestrated for this book to strengthen and release my faith and trust in Him for the miracles I needed.

I believe that is exactly what He's going to do for you as you read this book. Whatever looks impossible and feels insurmountable in your life will be overwhelmed and eventually overcome by the miracle-working love and power of your heavenly Father. May a mighty outpouring of the Holy Spirit saturate your heart and transform your life as you read these *Extraordinary Miracles in the Lives of Ordinary People!*

---

*James Strong, *Exhaustive Concordance of the Bible,* "Greek Dictionary of the New Testament," (Nashville, TN: Thomas Nelson Publishers, 1984), #4005.

1

WHEN WE DON'T LIMIT GOD
by Suzanne Pillans

Therefore, since we are receiving a kingdom that cannot be shaken, let us be thankful, and so worship God acceptably with reverence and awe, for our "God is a consuming fire."

HEBREWS 12:28,29

I was talking on the phone to Angela, the secretary of Eurovision, when she asked pointedly, "Will you go to Malawi, Africa, for one believer?"

"If Jesus says so, I will go," I said.

Putting down the telephone receiver, I asked, "For one believer, Lord?"

"Yes," He replied, "even for one believer." I booked my airline ticket to Malawi.

On December 4, 2004, Pastor Duncan Nyozani met me when I arrived in Blantyre. We stepped into a small truck, so crooked I wondered how it could possibly drive straight. Three and a half hours later we arrived in the village of Migowi.

The dusk sun sank behind the Maluzi Mountains, casting its last rays of light on the grass roofs of the mud huts. We walked the last half hour to Duncan's hut, as there were no roads. After giving me a grass mat to sleep on, he showed me to a small room with a tiny window. I spread the mat on the mud floor then arranged my sleeping bag and mosquito net.

"Lord, how will You do it this time?" I prayed, trying to get comfortable. The Lord always has a plan!

At 6:00 the next morning, I welcomed daylight and was glad to arise. It was just as well—four guests were waiting for me at the door. On their way to the market, they were suffering too much pain to complete the journey.

"The witch doctors haven't been able to help us," they explained. "We heard that you were coming to tell us of a man called Jesus who can heal us, so we have come. Can you tell us where we can find Him?"

"You can find Him right here!" I answered. "You see, Jesus gave His life for you and me. He was crucified on a cross two thousand years ago to save mankind from their sins, sickness, and all bondage from the devil. Three days later He rose from the dead in total victory over every evil power. After ascending to heaven He sent His Holy Spirit down to continue His work on earth through His believers. They are the ones who accept Him into their hearts and are reborn in His Holy Spirit. Jesus is with us now because His Spirit is in me, and He can heal you right now!"

"Please pray for us!" they pleaded. When I laid hands on them, the two with severe arthritis received healing instantly. Another woman was healed of sore knees. Alina White, who suffered from AIDS, saw all symptoms vanish in a moment. Her chest and stomach pain left. From that moment on she started gaining weight, and two years later she remains healed.

These four newly healed ladies ran to the market with great excitement, telling everyone that Jesus had healed them. By 9:30 Duncan's garden was full of people. That morning God healed thirty-five more people of blindness, high blood pressure, sleeplessness, arthritis, and stomach and chest pains—just to name a few. Seventy of these people became Christians.

The next morning I found a group of people waiting outside the mud hut door to receive healing, and again God healed them. By 2:00 P.M., the scheduled time for the crusade to begin, word about Jesus had already spread far and wide. Hundreds of people travelled over the low rocky hills with their colorful sun umbrellas, carrying blankets so they could sit on the ground.

Because the surrounding area was in the midst of a devastating drought, three people in the community had already died of starvation. After preaching about believing and trusting God, I asked, "Has anyone prayed for rain in this drought?"

No one had considered praying, as none were Christians. So I asked, "Would anyone like to become a Christian?" Marvelously, about four hundred people rushed forward, and I led them in prayer to receive Jesus as Lord and Savior. How those new believers prayed!

"They're praying now for rain," Duncan whispered.

"Oh!" I replied. When they were finished, I told them to sit down. "Is anyone sick here?" I called out. "Come forward now!" About three hundred people rushed forward, nearly squashing me against the mud hut wall in their urgency. "Lord, this is too many!" I prayed.

"Tell them to stand back," the Lord commanded. "I will heal them where they are."

"Stand back, everyone," I ordered. "The Lord told me He will heal you where you are. Lay your hand on your sickness or pain and receive your healing now in Jesus' name." Sudden squeals and shouts rose from the crowd as they received instant healing. Exhilaration spread through the crowd.

After telling those already healed to sit down, I said, "Those not yet healed stand in a line." As I prayed for those in the line, they received their healing then headed to the microphone to testify of deliverance of various sicknesses, including arthritis, malaria, and stomach and chest complications. The people jumped up and down, praising God.

Looking to the mountains, I noticed a wind springing up, blowing clouds that moved their shadows over the sun scorched mountains. Within minutes the sky darkened, then rain began to pour. The crowd screamed in excitement.

Duncan told the people that the meeting was over and encouraged them to race home before the hard rains came. I quickly told the people, "Those who are still sick, come to Duncan's hut tomorrow, and the Lord will heal you!" Then I rushed to cover with the others.

An elderly leper named Bendicto, to whom Duncan had introduced me the night before, was the first to arrive at 6:30 the next morning. The Lord instantly healed him of leprosy. It was a wonderful sight to see him walk without his crutch and free of pain. Others came and received their healing as well.

Since the rest of the community was out planting their seeds, no more crusades were planned for that week. I felt disappointed at first—all this way from England for a one-hour crusade. But the following day I read a note from the village chief that said, "I never saw anything like Wednesday's crusade. The Lord God healing the sick and answering my people's prayers for rain within the hour! I am a very happy man and so is the whole community."

Duncan and the chief told me that because God answered the people's prayers for rain and healing, the whole community had become Christians—about two thousand people! Only then did I realize what God had done. I bowed before the God who led the Israelites through the Red Sea to the Promised Land to show them that He alone is God—there is no other. I had witnessed this same God show Himself to this small rural village by answering their prayers for rain.

I left Duncan with two hundred pounds and returned to England, though as time passed I regretted not leaving him with more money. I knew their food would soon run out. On December 29 I told God that I was concerned that I had only left enough money for two weeks of food and could not get money to Duncan. In response to my prayer, the Lord told me to phone John Gee, a farmer in England. I obeyed. The farmer knew someone in Blantyre who could deliver food to the people if I put the money in his account in England.

Two days later sacks of corn were delivered to a very surprised Duncan. The Lord continued to prompt His people in our local churches to give monthly until the village's successful harvest. Then a letter arrived from Duncan.

"Dear Mum Suzanne, I eventually received the two hundred pounds you sent by post, but I did not need it because food kept arriving every time we ran out. Please can you use this two hundred pounds to buy a piece of land so we can build a church?"

The whole community joined together, making bricks and drying them in the sun, to build a large church, pastors' rooms, kitchen, and ablution block. A year later the church was packed with people at every service.

In December 2004 Duncan invited me to conduct a weekend crusade in their new church. I managed to get diarrhea when I arrived, but I was determined to preach. Feeling weak and dizzy, I made my way to the lectern, spoke what came into my mouth, then sat down next to the lectern. I could not remember one word I preached. Then I said, "Anyone sick come forward now." Thirty people came forward. "Lay your hand on your sickness or pain and, when you are healed, put up your hand high in the air." Within a minute and a half every hand went up—every person was healed. I told them to sit down.

Duncan then introduced twelve pastors I had not seen sitting behind me. As the pastors introduced themselves, I discovered that two of them had travelled over one hundred kilometers to hear me speak. Duncan, knowing I was not feeling well, released me to go back to my room. I played back my mini tape recorder and listened to the message I had just preached. To my amazement I discovered that despite the challenges I had faced physically, it was the best sermon I'd ever given—and ideal for pastors!

The next day I returned to Blantyre and suddenly began to realize that having symptoms of illness forced me to trust God for healing all the more while praying for the healing of others. It taught me to rely completely on God. I understood, "Less of me, more of God; none of me, more of God." I had been too weak to give anything of me in that talk, therefore releasing the Lord to work through me in greater power and healing. In my weakness, He became strong.

The Lord spoke to my heart and said, "Do not limit Me. Let Me be God."

"How have I limited You, Lord?" I asked.

He told me to read 1 Kings 18:30-39 and said, "If Elijah had not soaked the sacrifice with water three times and filled the trench with water, he would have limited My miracle."

The next crusade was held on the Mozambique border with Rev. Sydney W. Murijah of the Jesus Christ Church. When fewer than twenty-five people showed up, I preached the gospel despite my feelings of disappointment. "Don't limit God" kept running through my mind. Suddenly I knew what the Lord wanted me to do. "Go find the sickest person in the village and bring that person here tonight," I commanded. "Then invite the whole village to come and watch Jesus heal that person!"

That night the church was packed with people, including the sickest person in the village. Seriously ill, she appeared to have AIDS. She had been bedridden for two years and unable to stand up or walk. Pointing to her, I commanded, "Sickness, leave in Jesus' name! Body, be healed in Jesus' name! Strength, come back in Jesus' name! Now, in the name of Jesus, stand up!"

She stood. "Now, in the name of Jesus, walk!" And she walked. "Now, in the name of Jesus, run down the aisle and back."

She looked at me in horror.

"In Jesus' name you can!" I said. Then instantly she took off and ran down the aisle and back totally healed. All present became Christians and worshipped the Lord until three o'clock in the morning!

The next day group after group came to receive healing and to receive Jesus into their hearts, including two chiefs and two girls, Judith, fourteen, and Maria, twelve, who were born deaf and dumb. Jesus healed them both— they could hear. Soon they learned to talk and eventually attended school.

Back in England the Lord showed me how the people in the West limit Him by unbelief, lack of commitment, lack of prayer, and by putting other things before their relationship with Him. He showed me Judas receiving thirty pieces of silver. The moment Judas received the silver, he loved the silver more than he loved Jesus. The Lord showed me that many of His people love their money, homes, holidays, jobs, promotions, sports, lifestyles, and even their ministries more than they love Jesus. So, how can He move in with revival?

The Lord said, "Preach repentance." Everywhere I have gone since January of 2005, I have preached this message. When I do, the entire congregation repents and many are in tears. I have realized that repentance is the first step into the presence of God. I encourage people to go further into His presence by thanking Him for all He has done for them, especially through the Cross. I encourage them to praise God for who He is. Then we enter into a charged, expectant, active silence, enjoying His glorious presence. Suddenly something unexpected happens. Squeals, cries, and worship break out as people are healed in their seats, set free, and delivered—all, often without the laying on of hands, as the Holy Spirit comes in power.

When we truly put God first, as the commandments say we should, we can rejoice because people receive healing left and right, and line up to testify about their healings. This is happening wherever I preach this message. When we don't limit God, He answers with fire, with His presence, with His healing power, and with His delivering power. He answers by showing up as God.

When we serve God we need to live a life of prayer and trust Him totally. We know that He will answer us because Jesus is alive. We can become spiritually equipped for spiritual work by approaching God as the source of our strength and wisdom, praying as Jesus did, and He did nothing apart from the Father. (John 5:19.)

We need to become well acquainted with Jesus through prayer and the Word so we can walk in the authority of His name and be empowered to do the works He did. We need to be filled with His Holy Spirit daily in order to succeed in the tasks He gives us and to not limit the glorious work He desires to do on earth. If we come to Jesus daily and get equipped to do His work—without limiting Him in any way—THEN revival will come to the land.

Put Jesus first in your life, above everything else, and watch Him turn up in power!

Suzanne is an ordained minister, who graduated from the Bible Institute of South Africa. She and her husband, Wilifred, operate Standlake Equestrian Centre and Christian Ranch in England. Ever since Suzanne travelled to Israel in 2000 and the Lord anointed her with a healing ministry, she has been invited to speak in different countries as a healing evangelist. She is an affiliate evangelist with Eurovision, concentrating mainly on Africa. In various parts of Africa Suzanne's ministry equips pastors and evangelists with bicycles, megaphones, and Bibles to reach remote villages that have not heard the gospel. In 2000 Suzanne helped to build Bala Orphanage in Kenya, a Christian school housing about three hundred orphans. Suzanne and Wilifred have been married since 1983 and live in Oxford, England, with their daughter, Rebecca.

2

ONE MIRACLE BEGETS MANY
by Niki Anderson

Then the woman, seeing that she could not go unnoticed, came trembling and fell at his feet. In the presence of all the people, she told why she had touched him and how she had been instantly healed. Then he said to her, 'Daughter, your faith has healed you. Go in peace.'

LUKE 8:47,48

*M*any people would agree that a single miraculous healing is adequate for a lifetime. But the night I received my healing, the God of abundance let me witness the miracle abound to others.

It began when I was between eight and nine years old. I began suffering from chronic bladder and urinary tract infections. A sick child is a harassed child, and I recall feeling both discomfort and perplexity. Telling my caring mother about my symptoms was natural, but undergoing the physician's intrusive exams was humiliating and painful. I dreaded every appointment.

For months the doctor monitored my condition, and once a week I walked blocks from our home to a pathology lab, where I delivered a specimen in a jar that Mom concealed in a brown paper sack. The problem persisted through antibiotic treatment and other medical recommendations. Various medications failed to arrest the stubborn infections. The doctor moved forward by advising an exploratory surgical procedure. An injected dye would enhance his observations and assist him in making a diagnosis.

My mother prayed. She was troubled by the thought of her little girl facing the possibility of surgery, or worse yet, an incurable disease. Realizing my need for a miracle, she turned to the God she had always portrayed as loving, willing, and powerful.

The night before the scheduled procedure she noticed a newspaper advertisement announcing a series of meetings at a church where a missionary was slated to speak and pray for the sick. Mom packed my older brother and me in the car, and the three of us made the long drive through greater Los Angeles to attend the service.

As we stepped into the narthex of the church, I felt the presence of God. How does a child identify this Presence? The change in atmosphere from outside to inside the church was like stepping from a cold, air-conditioned building into the warm sunshine of a perfect summer day. The sanctuary was charged with a sense of God's beneficent characteristics—peace, strength, joy, assurance, and power. My older brother would later say to Mom, "I *liked* that church. Can we go back?"

A few pews in the center front were reserved for those who would request prayer for healing at the conclusion of the service. My mother guided us to the last pew of that section. The rest of the congregation was seated behind us.

While listening to a lively piano prelude, I felt a tap on my shoulder and turned to see who it was. I saw Jesus' love in the face of a soft-spoken, middle-aged woman. Her 1950s coiffeur was tidy and feminine, and her features beautiful—none upstaging the other. Her complexion was flawless. Her happy eyes, her clear voice, and her gentle tap were all part of the divine encounter. I presumed she was a member of the congregation.

She asked me, "Why have you come? Are you ill? Do you want prayer?"

At times Jesus also questioned seekers. Of the blind and mute man He probed, "Do you believe I am able to do this?" (Matt. 9:27). Of blind Bartimaeus He inquired, "What do you want Me to do for you?" (Mark 10:51).

"Yes," I told the woman. I needed healing and had come for prayer. She smiled, and as her eyes met mine I felt a surge of compassion and faith fill my body. The sensation was mild but unmistakably holy. At that moment, as my faith connected with the compassion of Jesus I beheld in the face of the believing woman, I was healed.

I sat reverently, silent, not telling even my mother what I had just felt in the brief exchange with the lady behind us. But the drama continued. Within the hour I watched God's healing virtue pass to others. I still marvel at the power, faith, and virtue that flowed from person to person.

The missionary minister stepped to the pulpit and shared God's Word. Following his message, those in our pew were the first group ushered forward to the prayer line. Nothing visibly spectacular happened until I came forward. When he laid his hands upon me, he began exclaiming, "I'm healed, friends! It's *me* that's been healed!" He began skipping about on the platform, waving his arms, laughing, and praising God.

"I've had bleeding ulcers and was hardly able to preach this evening," he explained. "I argued with God about coming tonight. But He promised to touch my own body if I would pray for others. When I put my hands on this girl I felt His power rush through my body."

I needed no more than childlike reasoning to understand what had occurred. The curative power of God's Spirit was still abiding in my body. That same healing virtue reached into the diseased stomach of the missionary when he placed his hands upon me. The surge of blessing continued as others went forward for prayer and experienced deliverance from sickness and disease.

The next morning my parents waited outside the operating room as a team of medical personnel performed tests and conducted the exams my doctor had prescribed. Sooner than expected the physician entered the waiting room and signaled my mother and father.

"Mr. and Mrs. Williams, I have no explanation for this, but we found no inflammation and no indications of anything abnormal. There's nothing to cure, no need for surgery. It's strange but we can only be pleased."

My mother was quick to reply. "God touched her, doctor. We prayed. She was healed last night and this confirms it." He consented with a twinkle in his eye. His knowing expression was a hint that perhaps he had heard similar testimonies that pointed to God.

That previous night marked the end of my infections. It also marked the point in time when I learned that miracles really do still happen. The foundation was laid then and there for my lifelong conviction that God surely does heal and mend broken bodies.

Niki Anderson is an author and speaker. Her books include bestseller, **What My Cat Has Taught Me About Life** *(Honor Books),* **Inspur-r-rational Stories for Cat Lovers** *(Honor Books), and* **What I Learned from God While Gardening** *(Barbour Publishing, Inc.). She lives in Spokane, Washington, with her husband of thirty-one years and Myles, her red tabby.*

3

MY REFUGE AND MY FORTRESS

By Therese Marszalek

He will cover you with his feathers, and under his wings you will find refuge; his faithfulness will be your shield and rampart.

PSALM 91:4

*M*y spirit flipped when Janice Wood, the pastor's wife from Moses Lake Assembly in Moses Lake, Washington, called in October 2004 to invite me to speak at their December women's event. Although my planner indicated a conflict, I sensed a need to adjust my schedule for this special event.

"Is there a special theme you'd like me to develop the message around for this gathering?" I asked Janice.

"Yes," she said, "we'd like you to speak on the subject of miracles."

I changed my schedule with ease, confirmed the December engagement with Janice, and started praying and preparing my message.

My heart had been stirred about God's miraculous signs and wonders for several years. The excitement I sensed in my spirit intensified as I interviewed people who had experienced miracles. I spent increasing time before the Lord with my face in the carpet, crying out for a demonstration of His power through miraculous signs and wonders.

I had blocked off several days, including November 16, to pray and prepare for ministry in Moses Lake. I had just interviewed Art and Olita Pope two days earlier, which further energized me on the subject of miracles. Art had shared his testimony of God replacing a completely deteriorated knee with a brand-new knee (chapter 18).

Unfortunately, November 16 didn't go as planned. My son James called after he arrived at Shadle Park High School. "Mom, I forgot the paperwork I need for basketball tryouts," he said. "Could you bring them to school before the end of the day? Today's the cut off."

"Sure," I said, sternly reminding him to be more responsible. "I'll drop it off this time."

Driving to the school, I practiced my stack of scripture "recipe" cards that included a Bible reference on the front and the verse on the back. I had developed a habit of using driving time to memorize Scripture.

Instead of flipping through the cards rapidly as I normally did, I got stuck on Proverbs 3:7-8, "He holds victory in store for the upright. He is a shield to those whose walk is blameless. For he guards the course of the just and protects the way of his faithful ones."

I rattled off the scripture, placed it at the back of the pile, and continued with the next verse. But I couldn't focus on the next scripture because the last one remained illuminated. I brought Proverbs 3:7-8 back to the front of the pile and repeated it again and again. I meditated on this scripture on the way to the school and all the way home. "Thank You, God," I said, pulling into the garage. "You are *my* shield."

My rumbling stomach reminded me I hadn't eaten lunch. Since my husband, who works from a home office, was at an offsite customer meeting, I decided to eat alone. After warming up some homemade soup in the microwave, I sat down to enjoy my meal, still thinking about the scripture from Proverbs.

It smells like something is baking, I thought to myself. I glanced at the stove, then remembered I hadn't cooked or baked anything that morning. *Must be my imagination.* I thought.

Several minutes later a nauseating burnt odor saturated the air. Knowing something was very wrong, I looked again at the stove from the dining area, noticing the back left burner of our flattop stove was set on the highest setting. Directly on the now bright orange burner sat a clear glass baking dish containing a few pieces of leftover "Ooey Gooey Pumpkin Dessert," a scrumptious family recipe.

I ran toward the stove to shut off the burner. About a foot in front of the stove, I reached for the dial when a deafening crack sounded. Shards of glass and pumpkin were strewn everywhere. Panicking, I tried to push what was left of the pan off the burner. At the same time I noticed the sizzling glass that had landed on our new hardwood floors. I attempted to grab the chunks of charred glass but they were too hot to touch. Using a paper towel, I carefully gathered the bigger pieces which had branded black burn marks in the wood.

I scanned the room in awe. When the pan had exploded, jagged glass shot in all directions like fireworks. Scorching, crystal-like shards melted the Saran wrap that sat on the countertop. Shattered glass covered the floor and counters like a crystal blanket. The flattop stove had what looked like a trillion tiny glass bits strewn across the surface, yet the glass top remained intact.

I examined my bare arms and ran my fingers through my hair and across my face to check for blood. Although I had been standing directly in front of the stove when the glass exploded, not one single piece of glass had touched me.

I thought again about Proverbs 3:7-8, "He is a shield...He protects the way of his faithful ones." Knowing the flying hot glass could have slashed my skin or even blinded me, I said, "Thank You, Jesus, for being my shield."

I spent the next two hours picking up the ooey gooey pumpkin dessert, wiping down walls and sweeping up glass. While cleaning the remnants of the accident, I sang praises to God for demonstrating His divine protection and shielding me from harm. I didn't even suffer a minor cut.

When Tom returned home, I told him what had happened. Although not anxious to show him the burn marks in our hardwood floor, I was relieved to see his gratitude to God for protecting me. "The floor can be fixed," he said. "But you're irreplaceable." Tom was stunned when he saw the mountain of glass I had collected from the kitchen and dining room.

Because I didn't ever want to forget God's supernatural protection, I took a picture of the glass piled up next to the burn marks in the floor. The unusual photograph reminds me of the great miracle God performed in my life that day.

As I lay down to sleep that night, I pondered God's supernatural protection. I realized that although I had planned to spend my day preparing a message about miracles, God enabled me to experience a miracle instead.

In addition to authoring Extraordinary Miracles in the Lives of Ordinary People, *Therese is author of* Breaking Out *(Publish America),* Take Her Off the Pedestal *(pending), co-author of* Miracles Still Happen *(Harrison House), and a columnist and freelance writer for publications across the country. Therese is an inspirational speaker, passionately ministering hope and healing through Jesus Christ. She and her husband, Tom, have three children and live in Spokane, Washington.*

4

A GREATER MIRACLE
by Jennifer Rees Larcombe

But while he was still a long way off, his father saw him and was filled with compassion for him; he ran to his son, threw his arms around him and kissed him.

LUKE 15:20 NIV

*T*he phone rang in our home in the village of Mayfield, England, just as I was about to serve up our traditional English Sunday lunch of roast beef and Yorkshire pudding. Crossly I pushed the saucepans to the back of the stove and picked up the receiver.

"Jen?" said a hesitant voice. "I'm not sure I ought to say this, but I had a terrible dream about you last night. You were dying." Perhaps I would merely have laughed if I had not highly respected my friend, a local church leader; and if I had not dreamt the same thing myself the night before.

I was startled but muttered, "I'll pray about it," then hurried back to my cooking.

As the family clustered cheerfully round the long kitchen table, three boys on one side and three girls on the other, a large lump in my throat made eating impossible. Richard, the youngest, was only four, and Sarah, the oldest, was soon to be fourteen. My children were happy, healthy, country children—yet how could they possibly cope without their mom?

At the far end of the table sat my husband, Tony, smiling round at everyone in his usual loving way. How would he cope on his own? No! I could not die. This could not happen to them. These silly dreams were just sent by the enemy to frighten me.

But I was frightened, and during the following week I tried hard to banish those fears by a positive orgy of cleaning. I gutted the garage, attacked the attic, and sorted every cupboard and drawer while fear continued to stalk me. Finally, I realized I had to confront my fears. So while Richard was at his Play Group, I took myself for a walk in my favorite woods.

The last time I had gone there it had been spring. English Blue Bells had carpeted the ground and new green beech leaves had formed an overhead canopy. Now it was February. The flowers and leaves were dead, and the woods were dark and damp.

The solitude provided me opportunity to face my thoughts. I was not afraid of *being* dead, for that meant I would go straight to heaven. What bothered me was the affect my death would have on my children. Suddenly I felt the Lord speaking to me. "You trust Me for yourself, so why don't you trust Me for your children?"

While I struggled to work that through, He spoke again. "Your life has been like these woods in springtime, full of color, laughter, and happiness. But suppose things became bare and bleak like the woods look today. Would you still praise Me?"

"I don't know, Lord," I confessed." How could I possibly know beforehand how I would react?"

A few weeks later I became seriously ill with encephalitis, a brain virus. I was rushed to Kent and Sussex Hospital where my husband was told my chance of survival was small. Dimly I remember feeling my body invaded by numerous tubes, leads, and drips while I was imprisoned behind cot bars. I wondered why I couldn't move my arms and legs and why people talked about me as if I was no longer there (apparently hearing is the last sense you lose). Finally one day I heard the voice of my minister praying for my healing.

He's too late, I thought as my body began to rise from the bed. Up I floated, towards a beautiful soft light, free of pain at last. *I'm going to see what God is like,* I thought happily as I drifted into a beautiful garden.

"Do you want to come on in or go back?" a voice asked. Startled, I looked back and saw my six children huddled together far below.

I suppose I'd better go back for their sakes, I thought rather resentfully.

My minister was still praying as I found myself back in that painful cage once again, and many times during the following eight years I bitterly regretted that decision!

After many months in the hospital I was finally allowed to go home, looking like a skeleton, wearing diapers, and unable to balance, focus my eyes, or grip or feel things with my hands. Sarah was trying to be Mom to the other kids but her schoolwork was suffering, and I could see she was almost at breaking point.

Tony, responsibly trying both to hold down his job and care for me, looked exhausted, and the younger children were running wild. I could do nothing to help them. In fact, knowing I was an added burden made me long to die. I kept asking, "Why did this happen to me?"

For two awful years I wrestled with the dilemma of not receiving my healing. Why didn't God hear the prayers of my church and Christian friends and heal me? Perhaps He was not as loving as I had been brought up to believe, or maybe He no longer had enough power.

Friends took me to numerous healing services, and when their prayers made no difference they offered many suggestions for why God was not healing me. Was I holding on to some secret sin? Perhaps my parents had sinned? Some thought I didn't have enough faith or I wasn't praising the Lord enough. Perhaps I wasn't thinking positively or maybe actually *liked* being ill! I explored all their suggestions, underwent a lengthy deliverance session, and tried every possible kind of prayer ministry—but nothing changed.

Gradually I began to hate my Christian friends and stopped going to church, not realizing I was actually angry with God! Secretly I blamed Him for my pain and misery.

Things became so difficult financially that we had to sell our home in the country and move into town. I loathed the very idea! A couple of weeks before we moved I reached the end of my rope. Sick with a searing sense of loss, I looked out of the window, trying to fix the beautiful view permanently in my memory. Behind me the house was full of packing cases and arguments. Life for the children had felt like hell for the last two years, and I could see that Tony was drifting away from me into a cold silent cell. I reckoned it would only be a matter of time before he left.

I wanted to scream, loud and long, but that would frighten the children still more. So I staggered furiously out into the yard on my elbow crutches. It was raining heavily, and the slurry from the cow's field had seeped in through the fence, forming a stinking bog of thick brown muck. Overbalancing, I fell right in! My arms and legs did not have enough strength to get me out, and I knew I would have to wait until someone in the house came looking for me.

"This is what my life is like," I told God indignantly. "You've reduced it to nothing but cow dung and You don't even *care!*" All the anger that I had been silently holding towards Him welled up and exploded in curses I didn't realize I knew! I thought God must surely strike me dead, but I wasn't remotely bothered.

Suddenly I felt God's presence more powerfully than I ever had before. His love seemed to surround me as tangibly as if He had human arms, and He spoke to me. "I know how you feel and I *do* care. Why don't you let Me into the center of your life and let Me take care of your pain and misery?"

I was totally taken by surprise. As a Christian I knew He was in my life, but was He in the center? I realized I had pushed Him out onto the circumference, replacing Him with my many problems. I sat there waiting a long time for help, but spent it asking God back into His rightful place and giving Him my children, my marriage, my home in the country, and my physical and emotional pain.

I would love to say that I was completely healed from that moment— it would make such a good story! I could have made a fortune traveling round the world telling the sick that if they wanted healing they only needed to be baptized in cow dung! But I wasn't healed that day. In fact, I became steadily worse over the next six years. Nevertheless, something had radically changed inside me. Having God in the center of my life brought me a tangible peace and contentment which radiated from me and touched the rest of the family as well.

Our marriage mended, and the children relaxed and began to enjoy life again. Sarah, who had become exhausted caring for us all, had become ill herself and dropped out of school. After our move, however, her health improved and her studies went so well that she went to Oxford University. There, she took a course in history and eventually became a distinguished academic, lecturing at Oxford and Cambridge. We joined a lovely church where Tony became an elder, and the children formed their own personal relationships with the Lord.

Once I was pronounced permanently disabled by the medics, the state gave us various types of practical help, which eased the situation somewhat, but my health remained precarious. The virus kept flaring up, sending me back into the hospital's intensive care unit, and on several occasions they told Tony I would not live through the night. Each acute episode caused more damage to my central nervous system, and soon I was permanently in a wheelchair, dependent on my caregivers for everything. Yet I can honestly say we were a happy family, enjoying the Lord's love and grace. I kept myself busy by writing books on the mystery of healing and the problem of 'not being healed' and soon became quite well-known as a writer in Britain and abroad.

Then, in 1990, everything changed drastically! In March I began suffering from a bad attack of writer's block. I simply could not seem to finish the book I was writing. Tony suggested I take a few days retreat on my own with the Lord and took me to a place near the sea in Sussex.

Early on the first morning I felt God say, "I want to heal you." Firmly I dismissed the thought, believing that healing was medically impossible after eight years of deterioration. AND, I did not want to start looking for a miracle again only to be disappointed. So I tried to focus on my book, but concentration was impossible because I kept hearing that inner voice say, "I want to heal you."

For twenty-four hours I fought a huge battle of faith in my mind. Could I actually believe that God wanted to heal me after all these years? Did I even want Him to now that life had become so safe, comfortable, and satisfying? And how would my many disabled friends feel if God picked me out, giving me some special favor I knew I did not deserve?

"You'll just have to show me for *sure* this is *You* speaking and not the enemy or my imagination," I told God crossly.

At dawn the following morning I awoke feeling that the Lord had something important to say. Opening the flyleaf of my Bible I found myself writing, "March 13, 1990: You must wait quietly until I send you someone out of the blue who will tell you that I want to heal you and then pray for you."

I sensed my battle was over as I added a sentence of my own. "I thought You wanted to use my life from a wheelchair, but I now give You permission to use it any way You like."

Those two sentences remain in the front cover of my Bible to this day and feel like a sacred contract. I went home at the end of the week, fully expecting to be healed at once, but nothing happened. I felt that the words "wait quietly" meant that I should tell no one about that word from God, not even Tony. I said nothing and waited quietly, but I think the hardest thing God ever asks us to do is to wait!

Three months dragged by, and I began to doubt that the Lord had spoken. Perhaps I had imagined the whole thing. Every time the doorbell rang I hoped it was some big name person in the healing ministry coming to bring me God's message—but no one came.

Because of the books I had written, sometimes I was asked to speak in churches or conferences. One of those occasions was planned for June 13, but I was having a hard time facing it. I felt too disappointed with God to talk to a church full of strangers on the subject, "Why Does God Allow Suffering?" The night before the conference I could not sleep, as I was dreading the ordeal so much. About 4 A.M. I got up to sit in my chair.

"What am I going to say, Lord?" I prayed miserably. Suddenly I seemed to be sitting in front of His Great White Throne surrounded by the women to whom I would be speaking later that day. They looked emaciated as they desperately held out wooden begging bowls. Before the throne a figure was kneeling in prayer, interceding for each of them by name. As He rose and came towards us I realized it was Jesus. He approached each woman in turn, putting something in each of their begging bowls. I could not see what it was, but I knew it was exactly what each individual most needed. As He looked down into their upturned faces, I saw the compassion in His eyes. His love flooded into each of them. With such joy in His face, He did not look like many artists have depicted Him. I will never forget the laughter lines around His eyes. I cannot remember Him coming to me before the vision faded, but He certainly filled my bowl later that day!

My minister's wife took me to the conference along with my wheelchair, surgical collar, diapers, and painkillers. I know I made a mess of the morning talk because I was in too much pain to think straight, but just before we broke for lunch someone in the front row interrupted to ask a question.

"What is the name of your illness?"

"Encephalitis," I replied briefly and tried to hurry on with the talk.

"I'm so sorry," she continued, looking terribly embarrassed. "I'm only a new Christian, but I feel God is telling me to tell you He wants to heal you."

After a dead silence in the church, I could see my minister's wife looking extremely annoyed. However, I knew this was the person for whom I had been waiting. It was exactly three months to the day since I had written God's message in the Bible I now held in my lap.

Completely overwhelmed with joy I burst into tears. Someone hastily stood up and announced a hymn, and the meeting finished abruptly. In vain I looked for the girl who had sat in the front row, but I was soon engulfed in a swirling crowd of women asking for healing prayer and lost sight of her. I could only hope she would return for the afternoon session.

To my relief I later saw her sitting in the congregation for the afternoon session. I made up my mind I would not let her escape a second time! As soon as the benediction had been pronounced I shot my wheelchair in her direction.

"Please, pray for me," I asked her breathlessly.

"Oh no!" she replied, horrified. "Didn't I tell you I'm only a new Christian? I can't pray out loud, and I've never read any books on healing." Just then a lady with a tray of teacups pushed between us and the girl disappeared again! I could hardly hold back the tears of disappointment.

However, she had only gone to the minister's office to persuade him to come and pray for me.

"No," he said firmly, "God wants *you* to pray."

"But you know I can't!" she protested. While living in South Africa she'd had several illegal abortions and enjoyed numerous promiscuous relationships. She knew Jesus had forgiven her past, but she always felt He would treat her as a second-class Christian. Truly, I believe God used her to pray for me so He could show her that when He forgives He also forgets. No one is second-class in His eyes.

Most of the women had gone home when she finally came back to find me. Someone urged her to place her hands on my head, and I could feel them shaking with fear.

"Lord Jesus," she stammered, "Jen's been ill for eight years. Please make her well now." She quite forgot the "Amen." But inside me I knew I was well. When I opened my eyes she had disappeared again!

"I'm not going out of here in a wheelchair," I told my minister's wife. Then, to her astonishment, I stood to my feet without help, pain, or effort.

We drove home in stunned silence, hardly daring to believe it was true. Tony and my youngest daughter, Naomi, were waiting at our front door ready to take me straight to bed because I always collapsed, exhausted, after an outing. They watched in horror as I jumped out of the car, pulled my wheelchair from the trunk, and carried it up the steps to the house.

Tony said nothing and just left the house. He did not return until dark! Naomi went up to her bedroom and locked the door. Duncan, who was fifteen and a bit of a rebel, sat gazing at me as I flitted happily around, tidying the house without so much as a walking stick. Finally he said, "Mum, if God can do this for you, then He can do *anything!*"

It took ten long days before they all recovered from the shock. Poor Tony had been told so often that I was about to die that he was afraid to let himself believe. He finally trusted that it was true when we took a walk in the country and I leaped over a gate and raced him up a steep hill.

"We have a future together after all!" he said, and I saw the light in his eyes return. Dr. MacDonald-Brown, our family doctor, was equally mystified. As a member of our church, he had *prayed* for us often during those long years. Now he *thanked* God with us.

At first we wanted to keep our news to ourselves, but I was too well-known as a writer for that to be possible. Soon the media were at the door, and our photos were on the front page of magazines and newspapers. Television companies busily arranged programs. I was bothered by all the publicity until I realized that it was a wonderful opportunity to tell the world that God still heals today.

All that happened fifteen years ago, but I will never take my health and energy for granted. I believe God performed a miracle that day in June 1990, which He began when I fell in the cow dung! Happiness is easy when you are healthy and life is going well, but the kind of peace and contentment God gave our family when I was in the wheelchair was also a miracle.

Jen was a happy mom living in the English countryside with her six children and two foster children when encephalitis totally disabled her. For eight years she struggled, then in 1990 her dramatic healing changed everything. She has written many books, including **Unexpected Healing** *(Hodder and Stoughton),* **Turning Point** *(Hodder and Stoughton),* **Journey into God's Heart** *(Hodder and Stoughton), and* **Beauty from Ashes** *(BRF). Jen still lives in the country but now runs Beauty from Ashes, a retreat and healing center for those facing major loss or grief.*

5

JOURNEY TO JOY
by Carol Harrison

This Book of the Law shall not depart out of your mouth, but you shall meditate on it day and night, that you may observe and do according to all that is written in it. For then you shall make your way prosperous, and then you shall deal wisely and have good success.

JOSHUA 1:8 AMP

In 1995 two stale, backslidden Christians and our young son sat Sunday after Sunday in the little church across the street from our home in St. John, Washington, making grocery lists and figuring interest on financial loans during the sermon. The pastor must have thought we took more notes than anyone within earshot. We played our parts well.

My husband, Larry, was chairman of the church board. I taught an adult Sunday school class and occasionally led worship. On a good day forty people attended Sunday school. Our church was small, and all members were used in the service of the church regardless of their credentials.

The fragile shell of our facade began to crack when Larry's admitted greed inspired him to invest a large amount of money into a "can't lose" deal. The funds would supposedly be recovered in thirty days with interest. Without my knowledge he gathered and invested $100,000, then borrowed another $100,000 against our home and invested it with the same individual. Larry said that if the business deal worked, I would never worry about finances again.

I asked the inevitable question: "What if it *doesn't* work?" Larry said we could lose everything, including our home. Yet, he assured me that he was convinced it would work and that in thirty days our troubles would be over.

I had not realized until then how independent we had become in our marriage. On one hand I was frightened, but on the other hand we had been married twenty-one years and had never been in financial distress despite being self-employed. We had never known debt. We owned our home, paid cash for everything, and saved until we could pay for purchases, even vehicles.

The thirty-day deadline came and went, along with the sixty- and ninety-day deadlines. The interest payments became due month after month, amounting to thousands of dollars—and life became uncomfortable for Larry. As the weeks and months rolled on, he slipped into deep depression. He wouldn't get up in the morning. Because he didn't want to eat, he lost thirty-five pounds. Unable to think clearly or function normally, he visited our family doctor, who prescribed an anti-depressant.

Larry's inability to work drove him deeper into depression. I owned a floral and gift shop in our small town of five hundred. While it made enough money to put food on our table and keep the lights on, life was scaled down dramatically.

We knew sin and disobedience had been our downfall, and I trusted God to know how long to let us wallow in the consequences before extending His hand to bring us out. In the midst of our crisis, I saw God's fingertips coming through the dark cloud of despair hanging over our lives.

Living in a rural area made Larry's business of sales, installation, and maintenance of satellite TV systems lucrative for many years. Suddenly, several systems randomly broke down. Although repairs were minor, there were many.

When the first call came, Larry drove to Shannon Gaines' home to check out the system. Shannon noticed that Larry didn't seem to be himself and asked if he was all right. He admitted that he had been struggling with depression and assured her that he was okay.

Shannon told Larry that he didn't have to put up with depression and called her two young sons. They laid hands on Larry and prayed for him. When she invited him to church, Larry told her he already attended church. Shannon told him she didn't want to take him from his church, but that if he was free to attend on Wednesday night, she felt the teaching would help him. He thanked her and went on his way.

When the second customer call came from Laurie Willson, Larry drove to the home. While he worked on the repair, Laurie and her sister Barb Link discussed the great teaching they were receiving at their church. They didn't realize how much their conversation ministered to Larry's broken spirit. Laurie and Barb invited him to church, which was the *same church* Shannon Gaines attended.

Call number three came in from another customer, Scott Kinzer, so Larry drove to his home. After completing the repair work, Scott gave Larry two tickets to his church's Christmas play. Amazingly enough, he attended the *same church as the others!*

By this time Larry was beginning to take notice. He drove to the much talked about church one day, located in a community forty miles from our home. As he pulled into the parking lot, peace came over him like a blanket and he felt as if the depression lifted. Thinking he was imagining things, he returned home.

Despite his encounter with God's peace in the church parking lot, day by day depression took a deeper toll on Larry. When he asked what I thought about visiting this church, I was apprehensive. I had heard reports that they did the Hokey-Pokey during praise and worship, and I didn't want to do the Hokey-Pokey. But for the sake of Larry's sanity, which seemed to be slipping away, I agreed to attend the Christmas program.

The program was beautiful and professionally presented, and the people were friendly. The three recent satellite customers greeted us warmly while introducing us to other church members. We were impressed but not convinced. After all, forty miles is a long way to drive to church, especially when our current church was across the street from our home.

The depression continued and so did the incredible interest payments. Larry and I moved numbly through each day. More challenges came when my father became desperately ill and was hospitalized for almost three weeks. Our son, Travis, was a teenager and needed our guidance and direction, but we were too busy coping with depression, financial pressure, and caring for my father. Life was hard on us all. However, God's hand carefully protected Travis during our crisis. I believe He nurtured our young teenager because we, as his parents, had no strength or time to nurture him. Travis never rebelled and was always kind and affectionate toward Larry, giving all of the love and support he knew to give.

No one from our little church called to check on us even though we were often absent. We became completely isolated. Later, we realized this was part of God's plan. I couldn't burden my parents with our problems. Larry's parents had both passed away. And our church didn't seem interested in helping us. We had only one direction to turn: upward. God threw a net over us and lifted it ever so gently to Himself.

Once again a satellite system broke down. The customer who called was sweet, elderly Inez Broweleit, who said she just couldn't explain what had happened. She said that first a cloud had come over her house. Then a lightning bolt struck her satellite dish and blew out her receiver. Then the cloud moved on. She chuckled, saying she could not quite comprehend how this could have happened on such a beautiful, sunny day.

Although Larry was having a tough day, he agreed to take a look at Mrs. Broweleit's system. Not only did her satellite diagnosis prove correct, but she had been a nurse in her younger years and recognized that Larry wasn't feeling well. He was sweating profusely and seemed somewhat confused, so she gave him a large glass of water and began questioning him.

Larry told Mrs. Broweleit that he had been struggling with depression but was okay. She gave him another glass of water and told him about the healing power of God. When Larry assured her that he was a Christian, she explained that although being a Christian was great, he needed the *power of God* in his life to *heal* him. She sent Larry home with the book, *The Blood and the Glory**, and a box full of sermon tapes from *that very same* church.

We finally decided to attend *that* church on Sunday morning. This pleased Travis, who had just received his driver's permit. We said he could drive, and he was excited to drive forty miles. Halfway through our journey, the unmistakable lights of the state patrol flashed behind us.

Travis carefully pulled the car to the side of the road. As far as we knew, he had obeyed every traffic law. When State Patrolman Joe Maj asked for Travis's license and saw the name on the permit, he glanced in at Larry and recognized him. The officer was a satellite customer!

When Patrolman Maj asked where we were going, we told him we were going to *that* church. He also attended *that* church and told us the service had started at 10:00 instead of the usual 11:00. He encouraged us to continue on our way, thinking that although we'd miss praise and worship, we could enjoy the preaching.

Officer Maj had stopped us only to tell us that our headlight was out. I was relieved that we had missed praise and worship and I wouldn't have to do the Hokey-Pokey; Larry was relieved that we could still attend church; and Travis was even more relieved that he hadn't received a traffic citation.

When we walked into the sanctuary of the church, a warm fog of God's presence embraced us. We slipped into seats in the back. During the service Larry's depression lifted as he felt the same blanket of peace he had felt in the parking lot months before.

At the close of the service a church member, Steve Wilson, approached Larry and introduced himself. After visiting for a few minutes Steve asked Larry if he was dealing with depression. Larry swallowed hard, wondering if it showed that much. When Larry acknowledged his depression, Steve admitted that he had battled depression, but God had healed him. Larry thanked Steve for sharing. We made our way to the exit, shook the pastor's hand, and went on our way.

Monday morning brought another week of horrible existence for us. Although we had been hearing words of hope, we didn't have the ability, knowledge, or strength to bring it to fruition in our lives.

In Larry's warped state of mind, he thought our family would be better off without him. He did little more than lie curled up in a ball. He cried a lot and couldn't be comforted. He felt his life insurance would be enough to get us out of debt so Travis and I could start over. Sitting in his office, Larry started thinking about ending his life.

When life became most unbearable, Larry was at my flower shop curled up on the floor in the back room while I went about the day's business. Larry had decided he couldn't live any longer and was making a plan to end his life that evening. At the same time he wished he could talk to Steve Willson just one more time.

Suddenly Steve walked through the door of the flower shop. He warmly greeted me, shook my hand, and asked if I knew where he could find Larry. I led Steve to the back room. Steve reached down like Jesus might have, picked Larry up, and hugged him. He asked Larry how he was doing and told him to come for a ride. They drove for almost an hour while Steve ministered to Larry.

Steve brought Larry back to the shop and told him to stay there while he drove to his home. He then drove the fifteen miles home to get another box of sermon tapes and books. He made Larry promise to listen to the tapes continuously and to read the books. He explained the concept of a "renewed mind" and how the Word of God heals those who hear it. Steve said the key to his recovery from depression was listening to at least two tapes a day and attending church every time the doors were open.

Finally, we had hope. The books and tapes became key in our lives. And we decided that driving forty miles to church should become a priority also. We began that drive on a Wednesday night. The service was different than we had ever experienced. Almost three hundred people attended, sitting around tables led by table leaders.

Our table leaders, Bill and Carol, were a delightful, smiley couple. When Bill asked for praise reports or prayer requests, Larry said he had been dealing with depression for a long time and needed to be healed. Bill wrote it down, and without skipping a beat moved on to the next person.

We joined hands after everyone had voiced their praise or prayer need, then Bill prayed a simple prayer of faith and thanked God for healing Larry. Bill reminded God that the prayer of faith shall save the sick and that with Jesus' stripes Larry was already healed.

That was it. No fuss, no fire, no shaking, no shouting. Just the confident speaking forth of the Word of God. But that moment was the end of Larry's depression! Although it was not the end of our problems, they seemed more manageable now that we realized we were connected to Someone bigger and more powerful than we had ever experienced before.

Bill's prayer at the Wednesday night Bible study table became our first Word anchor. If symptoms of depression began to return, Larry prayed the prayer from James 5:15 and Isaiah 53:5. Praying that prayer enabled him to think straight and reason logically again.

We faithfully followed Steve's formula of listening to two tapes a day and attending church whenever the doors were open. One day we realized that although we were driving 240 additional miles a week to attend church, we always had enough money for gasoline. This was the first miracle of provision God performed for us. We hadn't learned about tithing; we hadn't fasted and prayed; we hadn't even asked God for anything. Yet He did it for us anyway!

Although we were now walking down the right road, we still had $250,000 in debt with interest compounding at a fantastic rate. Because fear was our main battleground, we overcame it by listening to God's Word on tapes or in church services.

Right and Wrong Thinking by Kenneth E. Hagin became a staple in our Word diet. When other tape series were loaned to us, we listened to them repeatedly because they gave us hope. Before long hope eradicated fear. With renewed hope, we knew we could overcome the ugly monster that had invaded our lives.

With the introduction of the small satellite dishes to the market, Larry's business softened. He rolled up his entrepreneurial sleeves and stepped out into a new business called "The Concrete Doctor." He repaired damaged concrete and sealed the bases of grain bins for local farmers who had purchased satellite systems from him earlier and farm machinery before that. Because Larry had always been an honorable businessperson, the honorable seeds he had sown brought a harvest of fruit as God gave him ideas and favor to service the same people.

Though we were beginning to earn a living once again, we had much to learn about receiving from God. One incident became the turning point of God's blessing in our lives. Larry's big pick-up truck loved to chew up its tires. New tires were expensive, and we had no way to purchase them even though they were a necessity. Larry's solution was to rummage through used tire piles at area businesses to pick out any that were better than his tires.

Steve noticed the worn tires on his truck and asked Larry if he could buy him a new set of tires. Larry, knowing the cost of such a gift, said he couldn't possibly accept it. He thanked Steve for his generosity, but told him he simply couldn't allow him to buy the tires.

Larry later related Steve's kind offer to Brian Main, a friend in another town, who became indignant when he heard the story. He explained that Larry's refusal to accept Steve's gift had robbed Steve of a blessing. He told Larry he should have received the gift with thanksgiving as a provision from the hand of God. That philosophy was foreign to us.

One Saturday morning, on our weekend to help clean the church, we drove the pick-up instead of our car. While cruising along several miles from our home, we heard an incredible explosion-like noise. One of the worn tires had blown up with such force that it dented the wheel well of the truck.

As Larry tried to regain control of the vehicle, a pick-up truck drove past us. After Larry brought the truck to a stop by the side of the road, we noticed that someone had pulled up behind us. It was Steve. I didn't ask why he was driving on State Route 23 that particular morning. Steve heard the explosion when he passed us and had come back to see if he could help. He asked, "Now, Larry, can I buy you those tires?"

Larry laid his pride down beside the exploded tire and quietly answered, "Yes."

That small act of submission and humility was the turning point in our finances. From that moment on, jobs poured in. The knowledge and ability to complete them were at Larry's fingertips. We received divine favor with bankers, who extended payment deadlines and rewrote bank notes.

We began to give. Even when we didn't have money to give, we gave anyway. God never failed to replace it in time to meet our needs. We received bigger and better work orders. Orders came to Larry that were meant for other contractors. One of our largest orders was granted to us because a customer thought another contractor was on vacation, and they needed the work done right away. He wasn't on vacation, but instead there had been an office mix-up.

Larry placed a fair bid on another large job. The man receiving the bid increased it by $20,000 and granted us the contract! Another customer gave Larry a $1500 tip because he had been so patient with her complaints and had redone a job to her satisfaction.

God's hand of blessing brought miracle after miracle. When Travis completed his junior year of college at Oral Roberts University, he was debt free. He had not needed any loans, grants, or anonymous checks sent in the mail. When the money needed to be sent, it was in the bank account. We were faithful to tithe and give to the work of the ministry, and God was faithful "to supply all of our needs according to His riches in glory by Christ Jesus" (Philippians 4:19).

God's love is beyond comprehension. We were spoiled, rebellious backsliders who got so far into debt—as our pastor has said—even a bull-dozer couldn't dig us out! Yet, our lives were healed and restored because God loves us and had a wonderful plan for our lives.

Our journey was frightening at times. We started down a rocky path as broken, desperate, hopeless people; and by putting one foot in front of the other to follow the little light in front of us, we found God's victory. God's Word was a lamp to our feet and a light to our path. (Psalm 119:105.)

We are grateful for our heavenly Father's unconditional love, patience, longsuffering, and guidance. We thank God for our pastor, who faithfully preached and taught the living Word of God. Our hearts are filled with thanksgiving and love for the fifteen couples from *that* church that ministered to us even before we attended their church. A God-given bond remains to this day.

Today we walk in financial freedom. Not only are our bills paid, but we're debt free. Money no longer controls us, and our priorities are straight. We faithfully tithe, give to the work of the ministry, and give as the Holy Spirit directs us. We seek *first* the kingdom of God and His righteousness, as instructed in Matthew 6:33, and find that, true to God's promise, *all* other things are added unto us. In just a few days, we get to bless the IRS! And after walking through a financial crisis, it's a privilege to write that check.

Our previous pastor called us "Faith Freaks," but we see ourselves as three people who received God's grace and mercy. Psalm 40:2-3 describes it perfectly: "He brought me up also out of an horrible pit, out of the miry clay, and set my feet upon a rock, and established my goings. And he hath put a new song in my mouth, even praise unto our God: many shall see it, and fear, and shall trust in the Lord."

Now that we have finished our little detour in life, we continue our life journey following after the plans and purposes for which God made us. Isaiah 43:19 describes our future: "Behold I am doing a new thing! Now it springs forth; do you not perceive and know it and will you not give heed to it? I will even make a way in the wilderness and rivers in the desert." We are on our way, and by God's grace and continued faithfulness we will run the race and finish our course.

In over thirty-three years of marriage Larry and Carol Harrison have experienced firsthand God's miraculous restoration of finances and health. Larry owns a concrete repair business and Carol writes and publishes a newsletter, **Faith, Flowers and Friendship.** *They have one married son. Larry and Carol attend First Church of the Open Bible in Spokane, Washington, and live in St. John, Washington.*

* Billye Brim, *The Blood and the Glory* (Tulsa: Harrison House Publishers, © 1995). Available from www.harrisonhouse.com.

6

ONE TINY SEED
by D. F. Higbee

*For assuredly I say to you, if you have faith as a mustard seed,
you will say to this mountain, 'Move from here to there,' and it will
move and nothing will be impossible for you.*

MATTHEW 17:20 NKJV

*L*ife's circumstances can seem as tall as Mount Everest. Life-threatening illnesses, financial ruin, and relationship collapses all can present themselves as insurmountable obstacles in our lives. But Jesus promised that if we could just manage to have a tiny seed of faith, we could overcome those problems and freedom would be ours. For the people in this story, that one tiny seed of faith changed their lives forever.

Early in October 1997 thousands of people flocked to a park in New Delhi, India, where healing services were set to begin. Our small ministry team of Tom Greenfield, Chuck Lindquist, Pastor Ron Doyl, Pastor Donna Sanders, Tammy Reams, Lorelei Salvatore, and myself—all from Spokane, Washington—had travelled to India under the leadership of Pastor Lonny Bingle to join with the local pastoral team for the crusades.

The crowds pressed so tightly around the stage area that Pastor Lonny asked members of the local pastoral team—Pastor James Sebastian, who translated during the services, Pastor Vimal Sen, and Pastor Raoul—to create a zone so people could file through the prayer line in an orderly fashion. As they roped off the designated spot, the crowd surged against the ropes. I had a keen view of the forceful crowd from where I was playing keyboard on stage.

In the midst of what seemed like chaos, a woman pastor who spoke little English reached into the crowd and lifted a young boy of about seven years old into the center of the healing line, bypassing the eager crowd. As she set him down, it became obvious that he had suffered the ravages of polio. His frail legs barely held him up as he leaned on two twisted tree branches used as crutches. He was an "untouchable," an outcast. He had no future, no hope, and nothing to live for. But he had one tiny seed.

Pastor Lonny and his team reached out and laid their hands on the young boy's head and prayed. The people behind them seemed to surge forward, and the young boy disappeared into the frenzied crowd. As the service finished, the team found one small crutch leaning up against the stage. They wondered what that could mean.

The next evening the pastoral staff again had to gain control of the eager crowd. A tall, nicely dressed Indian man led his son by the hand to the ministry team in the healing line. To no avail he had spent most of his money on medical doctors to help his little boy, who was completely cross-eyed, to see.

The father was a local policeman, sent by the New Delhi government to watch the Americans for any violations of the law. He had come the first night to arrest the ministry team in case of problems, but instead he had witnessed an amazing move of God's healing power. So with one tiny seed of hope, he brought his son back the second night for prayer.

As Pastor Lonny and his ministry team laid hands on the little boy, we saw his eyes move to their correct positions. In one miraculous moment, the little boy saw clearly for the first time in his life! His father began weeping with joy, ran to the stage with his son, grabbed the microphone, and testified of how this God, this Jesus, was the true and only Living God. With one tiny seed, new lives were given to the Lord, new friends were made, and futures were changed.

A woman pushed her son forward into the line. He was bent over, his eyes darted from side to side, and his head wobbled in jerky movements. His arms were covered with scars and knife cuts where he had used a sharp object to tear at his own flesh. His mother told the ministry team that he lived in the local cemetery and could not function in normal society because of his mental condition.

Pastor Lonny touched him on the head and commanded him, in the name of Jesus, to be healed and free of the torment. Immediately the boy fell to the ground—writhing. After they prayed again, the team helped him stand up. And then suddenly, with his back straight and his eyes normal, he looked around and asked calmly where he was. As his right mind returned, he reached for his mother. She leaped for joy and ran to the stage to tell of God's love for her son. He followed her with a docile nature she had not seen since he was a baby. One tiny seed—God's mountain-moving power.

As more people pressed into the line, the woman pastor reached out into the crowd and picked up the same young crippled boy who had come the night before. This time he stood on one crutch, leaning carefully on it lest he fall. Pastor Lonny again touched the boy on the head and prayed as the line moved forward. The woman pastor picked him up and set him outside the roped area. Again, the crowd seemed to swallow him up as he disappeared from view.

The evening drew to a close, and the crowd dispersed into the night. The team had prayed for more than fifteen hundred people. The excitement of miracles and healings left an almost electric charge in the atmosphere. Many had come to see what this Jesus could do, and no one left disappointed. As the team cleared off the stage, we noticed something extraordinary: two crutches leaned against the stage where one had been. Both had the same crude material wound around the twisted branches, both had been under the arms of the young boy with polio-ravaged legs.

In the blink of an eye, we recalled—one tiny seed.

Dorothy Faye Higbee is pastor of Raven Ministries, a home church based in Post Falls, Idaho. She is also currently a local leader of A Company of Women Ministry in Post Falls, and has been involved in leadership for numerous other ministries since meeting the Lord in 1978. She has served as a drama coach and a worship leader. In 2004 she retired after thirty-one years in law enforcement. Faye has been married to Myron Dennis Higbee for more than fourteen years, and the couple has two deeply loved children and one grandchild.

7

JOYRIDING: A TRANSPORTATION TALE IN THREE ACTS

by Laurie Klein

He holds victory in store for the upright, he is a shield to those whose walk is blameless, for he guards the course of the just and protects the way of his faithful ones.

PROVERBS 2:7,8

ACT I

"*S*houldn't we slow down?" I asked. Our ancient car shimmied, its vibrations traveling along my shins, into my sitz bones, up my spine. The speedometer jittered at 60 miles per hour as we crested Barrow Pass near Mt. Hood and began our descent. Before us, two lanes snaked through strands of hemlock, spruce, and larch, the pavement scored and rutted. In the backseat Rachel's fussing segued to a full-blown wail. Reaching back, I searched her car seat for the teething biscuit, tied on with Christmas ribbon, then slid the gummy wad between our daughter's lips. She bit down, her eyes glassy with tears.

"Too fast, Will," I said. "We're scaring her."

"She's not the only one," he said, white-knuckling the wheel. "Stupid brakes won't grab."

Our '63 Chevy picked up speed as we rounded the first curve. Momentum thrust me against my husband, the seatbelt biting into my chest. We careened along the guardrail, Will pumping the brakes.

"It won't steer!" he gasped.

In the greenish glow of the dashboard, the needle nudged 65. The car shook. He flicked on the flashers and downshifted. The engine didn't respond. He yanked the emergency brake, and the air sizzled with burnt rubber. The second turn heaved me against the passenger window. "Jesus!" I cried. And then we were praying aloud, entreating God to stop our car.

Earlier that day we had packed our station wagon with two guitars, suitcase, baby equipment, and P.A. En route to lead worship at a church in Portland, we'd been eager to share new music we'd written. Now the speedometer nudged 70 then surged higher. Still sucking her biscuit, Rachel whimpered. What we needed was a runaway truck ramp, but beyond the shoulder the mountainside plunged through tumbled scree to the valley.

"Hang on," Will said, jaw clenched. His beard jutted forward as he cranked the steering wheel in frustration. The car responded belatedly, sluggishly, and we straddled the opposite lane.

I wanted to close my eyes but couldn't. Fixated on that unreeling stretch of macadam, I was morbidly curious. What if we met an oncoming car? We were both twenty-four, and Rachel was less than a year. Was this it?

Call it denial, call it faith; but everything around me wavered as if I'd strapped on a scuba mask and flippers, and dived underwater. Details seemed magnified. I noticed those wiry hairs that sprung from Will's knuckles, the dark pores like a sprinkle of pepper across the back of his hands. I was mesmerized by the padded steering wheel, its lawn-green leather evenly lashed with white stitches. Unexplainable calm welled within then eddied around me and buoyed my spirit. I thought about heaven and how—very soon—we'd meet Jesus. Yet I was intensely alert, quivering, like razor wire in strong wind. I couldn't speak, didn't pray. It was God's move.

"Hey," Will cried.

The road ahead was leveling out. A shallow incline materialized, and the orange speedometer wand slid back to 60.

Will grinned, his moustache lifting, angling up at the corners. "A rise," he said. "Pretty small, but it might be enough."

Lord, stop the car, stop the car, stop the car. We braked with our bodies, backs plastered against vinyl, and hope sparked between us as the incline siphoned off speed: 50, 40, 35. An airplane pulls and pushes a person's torso this way as it lands, simultaneously tugging the shoulders, shoving the lumbar vertebrae backward. The steering was slightly more responsive, and Will inched the car toward the shoulder. Gravel pinged against hubcaps, the guardrail loomed. At least there were no other cars around. Deceleration would continue unless the road nosedived again before we could stop.

That small hill was like a sheet being shaken over a bed, undulating in slow motion, then settling. Our speedometer plateaued at 30, dipped, then dipped again. The rise was longer, higher than we'd thought. Imagine an angel grasping the road at the far end, shaking it out until our car slowed to a crawl and—finally—paused with a judder. We rolled backward a ways, and Will managed to steer us flush with the guardrail. A few cars shot by, and the chassis rocked.

In the subsequent hush we stared at each other, shaken, speechless. Rachel spit out her cookie and cooed. Numbly we unbuckled our seatbelts, all snap and whiz as they sucked back into their metal housing. And then such joy! Relief was a tide we could have surfed, followed by giddy laughter, and the seasick aftermath of ebbing adrenaline.

We freed Rachel from her seat and stumbled out of the car. Will whistled in disbelief. The entire front axle had let go. No wonder he couldn't downshift, and no wonder he could barely steer. The two front fenders alone had held the axle and wheels in place—and maybe an angel. We wouldn't make it to Portland that day to lead worship, but halfway down Barrow Pass we leaned together like saplings, worshipping God in that evergreen-scented mountain air.

ACT II

Because God had spared our lives, we thought He must have big plans for our ministry. Maybe we'd tour like the 2nd Chapter of Acts and Phil Keaggy. We had the car towed and repaired but mistrusted it now. Daily we prayed, believing God would provide a reliable car—and more songs and gigs.

But what to do with this Chevy wagon the color of lima beans? The car was a classic. Someone must want it. The tall, affable deacon who had sold it to us had rebuilt its engine and had also burnished the rounded front grille and back fins to a sheen. He'd mounted a glassy green knob on the steering wheel, striped curtains at the side and back windows. He'd even jury-rigged air conditioning in the form of a fist-sized electric fan, installed near the ceiling in back. With one flick of a toggle up front, the blades whirred. He had sold it to us months ago, albeit wistfully. He loved it too, but he didn't want it back.

If we used it as a trade-in it might provide six hundred dollars toward another car, cash enough for a clunker back in the '70s. Will was a pastor, newly ordained; I was a stay-at-home mom, singer and songwriter, gardener, canner of produce, and baker of bread. Our permed hair was long, and Will's brown beard tickled his collarbone. He wore a leather vest and flannel shirts; I favored loose embroidered gauze and scarves twisted around my head. Of the three of us, Rachel was the clotheshorse, decked out in the pastel booty of church baby showers and the added bounty of being the first grandchild on both sides.

Raised as middle-class Lutherans, our desire for a good car—or was it a sense of entitlement?—seemed inevitable. But we were granola folk at heart, dewy with the charismatic awakening then sweeping the West. The abstract Deity of Sunday school and Luther League days had revealed Himself as Companion and Father, and now the saving Worker of Roadside Wonders too. He was the Three-in-One we consulted about everything, be it what to serve the new neighbor for supper or buying a car.

We traded the psycho Chevy for a cadet blue Volkswagon Bug. Its rusted-out peek-a-boo flooring—which revealed pavement skimming beneath—didn't bother us, nor did torn upholstery the color of week-old oatmeal, nor the lack of radio, heater, insulation, and headliner. We ignored the tacky moonscape splashed across the dashboard in flaking acrylics. The Bug had a rebuilt engine, sturdy axles, and new brakes. Best of all, we could afford it.

We were thrilled, even though the sound of its closing doors resembled the garbage can lid routinely slammed by *Sesame Street*'s Oscar the Grouch. Because of the steel ceiling engine noise was deafening, but we bombed around town those first few weeks belting out "Easter Song" by

Annie Herring. The Bug suited our ragtag wardrobes and flower child sensibilities. We had praise on our lips and no clue as to whom the Lord of Transportation would soon awaken, on our account, in the wee hours. We slept soundly through the night, especially on Sundays.

ACT III

Mondays were sacred, a respite amid the ever-pressing demands of ministry: our day off. We guarded them fiercely. After several weeks of driving the Bug, just as we finished supper, a yellow car pulled into our driveway, engine humming.

"Must be Dave," Will said, pointing. We pushed aside the remainders of broccoli soup and grilled cheese—my weekly budget stretcher—to find Pastor Dave in sweats on our front stoop, twitchy as a leprechaun.

"We gotta talk," he said.

Shutting the door behind him, we expressed surprise. It was his day off too. Dave smoothed back his thinning hair, extra long on top for coverage, clucked Rachel under the chin and said, "Couldn't wait."

Rachel burrowed into my shoulder, and Dave plopped into our massive oak rocker, his agile fingers drumming its down-turned arms. "You need to hear a story," he said. "Sit down."

I swung Rachel into my lap, and we settled onto our Goodwill couch, rental green except where the foam peeked through.

"Last night the Lord woke up two people, one at a time. Never mind who—they don't want you to know. The point is, He spoke to each of them separately. Then they fell back asleep. This morning they compared notes over breakfast." He pulled a package out of his bomber jacket. "They asked me to give you this."

Will held up a box the length of his index finger, elegantly wrapped and tied with ribbon. Rachel reached for it, fingers waving like a sea anemone. This wasn't a birthday or holiday or anniversary, and we looked at each other with lifted brows.

Dave stood then, practically jogging in place. I'd never seen him like this.

"Open it," he urged.

Will tore off the wrappings, opened the box, and something dropped into his palm with a clink: two keys. "What do these go to?" he asked.

Dave threw open the front door and pointed outside. In the drive, behind our disreputable Bug, a car the color of ripe bananas gleamed beneath our landlord's yard light.

"Wow, man, you're loaning us your car?"

Dave rolled his eyes. "You're not getting this, are you? Those keys go to that car, yes, but it's not mine."

It had been a long weekend at church with extra services. We were wiped out. Will and I stood and exchanged dumb glances.

Dave assumed his AM radio voice. "Folks, it's a four-door hatchback goldenrod-yellow 1976 Vega with less than 8,000 miles on it. And, as of this moment, it's yours."

Will's brow wrinkled. "What's the catch?" Dave was known for practical jokes.

"No questions asked. The givers wish to remain anonymous."

I switched Rachel to the other hip and, like a magician whisking a tablecloth, she pulled off my scarf, its silky fringes tickling her face, making her chortle. "Peek-a-boo," I said absently, then turned to Dave. "You're saying two people we probably don't even know are giving us a car. A new car. To keep."

"Yup." Dave beamed. "Sell that decrepit V-dub. From now on, you've got bonafide wheels."

We trooped outside and circled the Vega, shock giving way to grins and exclamations. We peered through tinted windows, admired the aerial, showed Rachel her face in the chrome bumper. "A-boo!" she squealed, covering her face.

"Okay kids, test-drive time. Wife's waiting for me out front."

We called good-bye, Rachel waving my paisley scarf as if flagging a race. Will hauled out her car seat and strapped her in, traded the scarf for the teething biscuit. I slid into the flawless black leather bucket seat, crossing my legs in their knee-split jeans, seams widened with wedges of curtain fabric. Will turned the key, and the engine hummed. I flicked on the radio, saw the cassette player too, and shrieked. We could listen to Phil Keaggy tapes and re-play our favorite Sunday sermons.

Off we drove, savoring the pungent new car smell, pristine interior, and adjustable seats. Our raveling sweaters were woefully out of place amid such luxury, and we were too broke to afford new duds, but when we pulled onto the freeway to see what the Vega could do, it didn't matter. Nothing mattered. We were high on God's lavish provision, joint owners of a flying four-door golden chariot.

Even though Vegas became legendary lemons in the automobile industry, ours would serve us faithfully for twelve years with nothing more troublesome than a clutch replacement. Along the way, we'd rise above poverty too, as God gifted us with songs that would eventually travel across the world. Not long after the Barrow Pass rescue I wrote "I Love You, Lord," a praise chorus still being recorded and used widely thirty years later.

Of course the road has been far from smooth since that initial Monday evening when Pastor Dave delivered the Vega. There have been numerous breakdowns. But Will and I, who survived the self-destructing Chevy, who embraced the Oscar the Grouch can on wheels, have traveled together these many miles, for the most part joyriding.

Laurie Klein, award-winning writer of poetry, prose, and songs, including the chorus "I Love You, Lord," has published in literary journals, anthologies, periodicals, songbooks, and recordings. She is consulting editor at Rock & Sling: A Journal of Literature, Art, and Faith. Her forthcoming chapbook of poems, winner of the 2004 Owl Creek Chapbook Competition, is "Bodies of Water, Bodies of Flesh."

8

TAMI, COME FORTH!
by Tami Hedrick

He cried with a loud voice, "Lazarus, come forth!" And he who had died came out bound hand and foot with graveclothes, and his face was wrapped with a cloth. Jesus said to them, "Loose him, and let him go."

JOHN 11:43,44 NKJV

In February 1994 our seven-year-old son Justin woke me up at 4:20 A.M. Peaking out from under the covers, I said, "Shhh, Justin. Go back to sleep."

"Mommy, wake up!" he said. "God just woke me up and told me that we're going to have a baby boy in the tenth month."

I glanced at my husband, Steve, remembering that we had recently discussed the possibility of having another child. "How could you tell our kids that?" I asked Steve.

"I didn't!" he said.

"Mommy," Justin interrupted. "I told you…*God* woke me up and told me that we're going to have a baby boy in the tenth month."

"How did God tell you?"

"He just woke me up and told me in my heart," Justin answered.

"Okay," I said, and tucked the conversation away for the moment. Later I learned that I was one week pregnant when Justin spoke of a pregnancy. Ultrasounds confirmed that I was carrying a boy that was due in October.

Although everything had been perfect throughout this pregnancy, October came and went with no little boy. When I visited the doctor I learned that I had entered the tenth gestational month of pregnancy. Because I was overdue, my doctor scheduled me for induced labor.

Steve and I headed for St. Joseph's Hospital in Chewelah, Washington, on the scheduled morning of November 2. Although I had been excited about having this baby, a suffocating fear hit me as I stepped out of the car at the hospital. "I don't want to do this!" I said as I got back in the car. "I'm going home. I don't want to have a baby."

Steve got back in the car with me. "Let's pray about it," he said. Steve prayed a powerful prayer, asking God to go before us to prepare the way for the day. He asked God to prepare the doctors, nurses, medicines, and everything needed for the baby's delivery.

God heard our prayer.

After Steve prayed, we got out of the car and entered the hospital. Dr. Johnstone induced labor, and because everything seemed to be progressing smoothly, she went home and told the staff to call her when it got close to delivery time.

One of the nurses checked me about ten minutes before it was time to deliver the baby, then left again to call Dr. Johnstone. As she left the room, the baby's heartbeat crashed. The normal heartbeat for a baby is 160-180 beats per minute. The baby's heartbeat dropped to 40 beats per minute, then flatlined. My baby was dead.

Suddenly I started gasping for air. I couldn't catch my breath and felt as if I was suffocating. The nurses ran back into the room but couldn't figure out what was wrong with me. They thought if the baby had pinched the umbilical cord, it might have caused his heart to stop. Yet, even that shouldn't have affected me.

Dr. Johnstone arrived as I had a seizure and lost consciousness. The medical team tried to revive me for about twenty minutes. The baby had no heartbeat while they worked on me. The medical team knew they had to get the baby out, so they performed an emergency Caesarean. The doctor started working on our new son, Matthew, thinking they had already lost me.

After trying to revive Matthew for about twenty minutes, they were about to give up. They realized that when something tore in my uterus, both my uterus and Matthew's lungs and stomach had filled with my blood. Suddenly somebody who had been working on me noticed that I was still alive and put me on life support.

I had been blessed with a godly woman doctor who operated in faith and humbly followed God's direction. She suspected this was a case of amniotic fluidembalism, which occurs in approximately one out of eight hundred million pregnancies and has a survival rate of .03 percent. The only known survivor at that time had been a vegetable for ten years and was completely brain dead.

Dr. Johnstone called Deaconess Hospital in Spokane, Washington, hoping they would take me, but they couldn't accept my case. With both Matthew and me on full life support, the medical team had little hope for either of us. After the hospital called my mom, she and my dad, along with my sisters and brothers, came to the hospital immediately. Mom called her prayer warrior friends and asked them to start praying.

I went into DISS, the last stage before death. At this point the blood vessels can no longer hold blood and the blood thins. It begins coming out the skin pores, ears, nose, and eyes. Because I was bleeding from everywhere in my body, they began blood transfusions immediately.

After ten to fifteen minutes one of the nurses ran into the waiting room, threw her arms around my mom, and started sobbing. "Pray like you've never prayed before," she cried. "We're out of blood and don't have any more in Chewelah. Since the hospital didn't have time to match my blood, they had used different blood types and used up Chewelah's entire blood supply. My dad offered to donate his blood, but they said he wouldn't be able to provide enough to make a difference.

All they could do is wait and pray. The nearest blood supply was in Colville, Washington, about twenty minutes away. Officials shut down all roads between Colville and Chewelah, so the sheriff's department could transport the blood to Chewelah as quickly as possible.

As the blood was being ordered, Dr. Johnstone talked to my family. "You really need to pray because it's out of our hands now," she said. "It's in God's hands."

The doctors called our pastor, Dal Shjerve, into the operating room, the first time they had ever allowed a nonsurgical person in the operating room. Dal Shjerve says that as he entered that room, my entire body was gray except for my fingers, toes, and lips, which were black because I was bleeding to death.

Dr. Johnstone asked Pastor Shjerve to pray. He couldn't reach my body so he put his hands on the doctor's back and began to pray. Everyone in the room joined him in prayer. There was nothing they could do medically because I had bled to death. I had no heartbeat, no pulse, no blood pressure, and no blood in my body.

As Pastor continued praying, a nurse standing down by my feet screamed, "Oh my God! Her feet are turning pink!" The medical team saw a line of color rise in my body. When it reached my forehead, my heart started beating. My heart beat for twenty minutes with no blood in my body. When the Colville blood supply arrived, it was still frozen, so they had to thaw it slowly to avoid damaging it. As soon as it was in an icy, slushy consistency, Dr. Johnstone started forcing it into the IV and into the vein.

Because I had lost all blood, all of my blood vessels had collapsed. They found only one site in my right arm where they were able to keep the needle inserted. One of the nurses, a Seventh Day Adventist, told me that she held the needle in that vein for three hours, like holding a knife in a warm patty of butter. If she moved at all and lost it, they would have no other place for blood to enter into my body.

After three hours of transfusions in Chewelah, it became obvious they couldn't save me there. A Spokane hospital sent Heartflight, a medical helicopter service, to transport me. Dr. Johnstone met with my family and asked them to come in to say good-bye and to encourage me. Later she told me that she didn't think they'd see me alive again.

When my family came into the room, they had to wade through blood to get to my side because so much blood had gone into my body and right back out. After they had said their good-byes, the baby and I were flown on separate helicopters to a certain hospital in Spokane, Washington. During the flight the helicopter received a phone call informing them that plans had changed. I was now going to Deaconess Hospital.

Those calls could not be traced, and today there is no recording of them. No one knows where they originated from. We found out later that the receiving person at the hospital I was originally headed to was a practicing witch. She would have been the one to receive me that night. But because Christians were praying God intervened and sent me to Deaconess.

Only two units of blood remained when I was flown out from Chewelah. The helicopter's medical personnel didn't feel it was enough to get me to Spokane. When I arrived in Spokane, Deaconess and flight personnel said I was basically dead on arrival. Medical records from the flight confirm that during the entire flight I had no pulse, no blood pressure, and no heartbeat.

Endeavoring to pick up the sound of my heartbeat, helicopter medics used a Doppler on me, which is used to listen to babies' heartbeats. Because of its sound sensitivity, it can pick up the soft sound of a ten-week-old fetus's heartbeat. They inserted the Doppler into my heart but were unable to detect a single heartbeat.

When I arrived at Deaconess teams of specialists, all headed by Christians, were waiting for me. Several of the doctors were not supposed to be in town that weekend, but plans or vacations had been cancelled, making them available to work on my case.

My brother-in-law, Jay Hedrick, was at Deaconess Hospital when I arrived. Jay called Doreen Leake, his mother-in-law on the West Coast, and asked her to pray. She said they had already been praying. God arranged for prayer requests to go out, and within two hours people in every state were praying for us.

After being rushed into ICU, all they could do for me was continue blood transfusions because no medication would help. Although it's fine for babies in the womb to drink, swallow, and swim in amniotic fluid, if it enters the bloodstream—as is the case with amniotic fluidembolism—it becomes dangerous because it has a chemical almost identical to strychnine. When farmers use strychnine to kill rodents, it causes their lungs to rupture and they drown in their own blood.

It was explained to me later that when the amniotic fluid entered my bloodstream and was pumped into my lungs and throughout my body, every cell ruptured within the cellular wall and exploded. Every cell was destroyed, including all brain cells.

Transfusions continued throughout the night. The doctors left my side only long enough to call their churches and to start prayer chains in Spokane and the northeast Washington state area.

Matthew was admitted to the intensive care unit for babies. Live babies are rated from 1-10 on the Apgar scoring system. He was given 0, which means dead. For three days they tried to get my husband, Steve, to take baby Matthew off life support and let him die because he was a mere shell. On the third day the doctor said, "Your son is a vegetable. We told you to let him go, but you didn't. He's had so many brain seizures." They showed Steve the CAT scan, which confirmed the brain was completely gone. "Now we've accidentally overdosed him, trying to control the seizures."

Neonatal doctors said, "Your son is an example of when doctors go too far and try to play God."

"I don't believe God is going to do a half of a miracle," Steve said. "He's going to finish what He started. If you're killing him with the medicine, then take him off the medicine! Either let God heal him or take him home." Although they didn't like it, they did it.

After twenty-four hours the medical staff continued to pour blood into me, ten units at a time. A woman holds between five and seven units of blood. Yet my body had swollen to three times its normal size and after eighteen hours of transfusions my blood vessels started to disintegrate and split apart. They compared my blood vessels to an old garden hose that had split and could no longer contain fluid.

The medical specialists managing my case told my family that they would either have to take me in for emergency surgery, which would likely kill me, or they could give me another half hour, and I would be dead because of the blood vessels splitting apart.

My dad, Len McIrvin, asked the doctors how they could ask the family to decide—knowing surgery would kill me and waiting would also mean certain death. The doctors told him they wanted to *try* the surgery, so they made the final decision.

Before surgery began the doctors called my family in again to say good-bye. This was my family's lowest point because they knew both the baby and I could die at any moment. They also knew that I had been given 156 units of blood, a national record for the amount of blood to enter a person at one time.

As I was wheeled into surgery my family and Steve's family cried out to God. My dad suddenly spoke with boldness, "She's going to make it! I feel the presence of God. The Holy Spirit is here!" As the Holy Spirit enveloped every person in that room, they started to praise and worship God.

When the doctor returned from surgery and came into the room, he was shocked to see the family praising God. "She made it through surgery," he said.

"Yes, we know," they responded cheerfully.

The doctor explained that though it was medically impossible for me to have survived surgery, I had survived. Then the medical specialist called another meeting to tell our families that I was not out of the woods. They said even if I survived the next two weeks in intensive care, life would be very, very difficult. I would need a tracheotomy because a respirator can only be down the throat for two weeks. My lungs had hardened to a cement-like consistency, which meant a mandatory transplant because lungs do not recover from that. My heart, liver, and lungs had been destroyed from the amniotic fluid. The doctor compared them to an apple being made into applesauce, and applesauce can't be made into an apple again.

The hospital did a nationwide search for a liver and lungs. My sisters, Debbi Wishon and Julie Pierse, talked to doctors about donating kidneys. I was scheduled for double leg amputations because my legs had been without blood for over twenty-four hours.

Doctors said that if I survived, I could expect six months in the hospital recovering from the transplants and amputations. I would experience severe infections throughout my body because in Chewelah there had been no time for medical personnel to scrub (normal medical protocol requires washing of hands and arms with disinfectant soap for five minutes before any surgical procedure). If I survived the bleak report they had just outlined, ultimately I would still be a vegetable in a nursing home for the rest of my life. When brain cells are destroyed by drugs, alcohol, or injury, they don't regenerate.

After hearing their grave report, Steve said, "Then why did you keep trying?"

"We don't know why," they said. "We don't have an answer. We just kept trying."

I had been unconscious through most of this, so it wasn't until later that I realized what an important report the morning of the fourth day would bring. Sometime earlier Steve had professed that God wasn't going to do half of a miracle, and that morning doctors came in to the waiting room where my family stayed during this whole ordeal to confirm him right. "Not only did your son survive the night, which is unexplainable," they said, "but he has enough brain activity now to breathe and function on his own."

On the fifth day they moved me from ICU to the critical care unit. In fact, doctors were able to take me off the respirator/ventilator as my lungs had miraculously been restored. This was impossible in the natural; there was no medical explanation.

The hospital had set up several phone lines into the waiting room for my family. Many churches called in to ask, "What can we pray for now?" The night Matthew was expected to die, they had stayed up all night, meeting in churches, parking lots, and other places to battle for his life in prayer.

On the eighth day they brought Matthew to see me. I have no memory of it, but my husband was excited when they brought our baby boy out of the NICU. After I held Matthew for a short time, doctors took him back and called another meeting.

Top specialists were called for consultation and study because my case was so rare. When they met with Steve, the doctors were blunt. "You're in denial," they said. "You need to start facing reality. Your son is a vegetable. He has a zero percent chance of a normal life. You'll never take him home. We're looking for a special needs home for him right now."

"You had the chance to take him off life support and let him die when we asked you to," they continued. "Now the best prognosis we can give you is that someday he'll be a sixty-year-old man lying in a nursing home, cooing at nurses with a newborn mentality. That's all he'll ever be."

Four days later the doctors that had given Matthew no hope for recovery examined him again and rated him a perfect 10 Apgar score. They didn't understand how it could be possible but told Steve, "Take him home to live a normal life!"

Doctors examined me the same day Matthew received a clean bill of health. "We don't understand it, but she can go home!" They said, "When a patient is being wheeled around the hospital because she's too bored to stay in her room, it's time to go home!"

Every doctor and nurse who had worked on me came to see me and say good-bye. Some didn't believe in God. "I don't know what to say," they would say. "I've seen the hand of God in your life. Everything we did medically, we did with the best that medicine had to offer. But not one of those things should have worked. Yet they did and there's no medical explanation."

My medical records indicate kidney failure spontaneously resolving with no medical explanation available. When I came home, doctors told me that I'd never walk again, as I was paralyzed from the waist down. They said that lack of oxygen caused brain damage and killed the nerves of my spine. "You'll never walk," they said.

I said, "But watch!" and I took two tiny steps.

"You can't do that. Sit down!" they said. "You can't walk!"

The truth is, God walked with me through every step of my recovery, and two years later I could fully walk again.

I received a phone call from one of the medical people involved in the decision-making at St. Joseph's Hospital about a year after being released from the hospital. The lady broke down crying, saying that she had wanted to call for over a year but didn't have the nerve.

"That night, November 2, was my first night back at work since I had tried to kill myself in August," she said. "I was going to try again, but that night I saw God in that room over and over. I knew He was real and knew He had a plan for my life." She surrendered her life to the Lord Jesus and became a Christian that night. God had touched both of us.

About a month after coming home from the hospital, I called my mom and told her about a memory I had about my near death experience. She wept.

For the first three days, she said, I would become conscious and panicked because I wanted to say something. I couldn't because the respirator tube was down my throat. She said during moments when I came out of the coma, she would tell me to communicate by writing in her hand. I wrote, JESUS—PRAY—SATAN IS TRYING TO KILL ME. I wrote it over and over and would also spell it in sign language.

I do remember hanging between life and death. I saw Satan laughing at me. *Laughing and laughing.* I wasn't afraid I was going to hell, but I was horrified to see the devil and hear him laugh. In his hand, he held a bow and arrow. I knew the arrow was death and that if he shot me, I would die. He continued to laugh. When he pulled the bow back and released the arrow, I started running. The arrow followed me as I ran through deserts and jungle areas, falling, getting up, and falling again. When I couldn't run anymore, I turned around and stood still.

As the arrow was about to enter my chest, Jesus stepped in front of me and took the arrow for me. As He fell down and was dying, He said, "I died so that you could live."

Jesus died for all of us so we could live. The same loving eyes that looked up at me when Jesus said, "I died so that you could live" are looking at you as well. His sacrifice was for every one of us.

Nothing is too hard for God. He healed a brain-damaged baby who was a vegetable. He restored my brain when they said I had no brain left. He restored my legs, my heart, and my lungs when doctors had no explanation. *Nothing* is ever too big for God!

Tami and Steve Hedrick live in Valley, Washington, with their three children, Justin, Brittanie, and Matthew. They are intimately involved with their church and community. They work extensively with youth in the area, including incarcerated youth. Their home is always filled with extra teens, and love, laughter, and occasional craziness! Tami and Steve operate their financial company from their home, where they keep up with the demands of their ranching lifestyle and the busyness of life with teenagers. Tami travels frequently sharing God's miraculous power in her life and the hope that is complete in Jesus.

9

A MANGO FOR JESSY

by Samjee Kallimel

If you are insulted because of the name of Christ, you are blessed, for the Spirit of glory and of God rests on you. If you suffer, it should not be as a murderer or thief or any other kind of criminal, or even as a meddler. However, if you suffer as a Christian, do not be ashamed, but praise God that you bear that name.

1 PETER 4:14-17

On January 1, 1987, I wanted to wish a New Year greeting by giving a gift to my neighbors and to the very important people in Jammu Kashmir, India. After packing New Testaments, Christian tracts, and gospel packets in nice-looking gift papers, I took my two older daughters with me to distribute our gifts in Katra, a Hindu Pilgrim center in Jammu Kashmir.

As we wished New Year greetings to everyone, we told them we also wanted to give them a New Year gift. Even though everyone said they gladly accepted our gift, many were not happy with the Christian literature we gave them. If we had given our gift on any day other than the New Year, it would not have been received.

After greeting many and distributing gifts, we finally reached the Post Master, a man who had been friendly toward us in the past. "Happy New Year, sir," I said.

"Same to you," he said smiling.

"My daughter Jessy brought a New Year gift for you," I told the Post Master.

He gladly accepted the packet from Jessy, who was nine years old at the time. "Can I open it now?" he asked.

"Yes," I told him.

After opening our gift, the Post Master's face reddened with anger. He started speaking vulgar and filthy language, obviously disgusted with the

Christian materials we had given him. Still hostile after expressing his disapproval, he spat in Jessy's face.

Jessy cried out. I wiped the spit from her face with my hand towel, then quickly took her home and asked my wife to give her a bath.

This incident greatly saddened me as a father and as a Christian, but I believe it paved the way for God to bless Jessy. About two years later, she was attending a Christian residential school in Kashmir to study and to receive her education. While she was home visiting for her annual vacation, I took her back to my mission field, where we minister to the leper colonies. Before the end of her vacation she reminded me that she loved mangoes and asked me repeatedly to buy her a mango before she returned to school.

I had no money, not even enough to buy a mango. I was much worried about the school fees and hostel fees for my two daughters, and knew I could not spend anything on a mango. Because Jessy was only about ten years old, I knew she couldn't understand my financial crisis or stress. So for ten days she continued insisting that I buy a mango for her.

On Sunday, the last day of her holidays, Jessy came to me and said, "Pappa, tomorrow I am going back to my school. Before I go, I need mangoes!"

My heart broke. I told Jessy once again that because I needed to have money to put her back in the school, I didn't have money for mangoes.

"Pappa, always you say that our Jesus hears our prayer and answers all of our prayers. You say that nothing is impossible." Determined, Jessy continued, "Jesus answers prayers. Now I am going to pray for mangoes. Tomorrow, before I go back to school, I need mangoes." After hearing Jessy's determination to ask God for a mango, I was speechless and couldn't open my mouth. I could only smile at her and nod my head in agreement.

Jessy went to the prayer hall and closed the door. After singing several songs, she prayed to her heavenly Father and asked Him for mangos. Some time later she came out, lifted my face towards her, and said, "Pappa, I prayed, and I believe that my Jesus will give me mangoes." Looking into Jessy's red face, I could see the marks where tears had streamed down her cheeks. I, being her father, was shaken by her emotion and prayed in my heart that God would honor her request.

A couple of hours later, Christian believers started arriving for Sunday worship and prayer. Elisha, one of our believers, arrived carrying a large basket. He said, "Pastor (Padri Sab), I brought something for your second daughter Jessy. Where is she?"

I called for Jessy, and when she came I said, "Look at Elisha, Jessy. He brought something for you."

Jessy peered into the oversized basket then started shouting with joy. "Pappa! It's mangoes. Mangoes! Mangoes!" she burst out with joy. We all watched in awe at the wondrous miracle God had done for Jessy. The basket was filled with more than five killograms (about twelve pounds) of plump, ripe mangoes.

We all enjoyed eating mangoes that day. On Monday, the next day, Jessy travelled in a bus headed back to her school in Kashmir, savoring her luscious mangoes with a heart of gratitude.

Jessy had asked me for one mango, but God gave her an abundance of mangoes. I, her earthly father, couldn't buy even one mango for Jessy. But her heavenly Father did a miracle and brought more than we could ask or imagine.

After being in residential school for two years, God made a way for Jessy's admission to the best school at Santhosha Vidhyalaya in Tamil Nadu, South India. While Jessy was studying in her high school she became the state athlete in sports. Because she excelled and was honored in the local school, in district level and state level, every year I received scholarship money from the Tamil Nadu government to pay for her schooling. It was a great relief for me to pay her school fees. Because of the talents God gave Jessy, I was also honored by the school principal and other teachers. Jessy completed her college education in Nagpur, India.

In 2004, just before coming to the United States for Jessy's arranged wedding, I asked her if she realized how God had honored her by bringing her to the United States to get married. This was her first trip to the United States, and she didn't understand my question. I continued, "Do you remember when the Post Master spat in your face after you gave him a gospel packet and New Testament?"

When she said she didn't remember, I reminded her of God's miracle mango provision. "When the Post Master spat at your face," I told Jessy, "our God recorded honor to you in heaven."

Samjee Kallimel, a full-time minister of the gospel for over twenty-five years, teaches love and salvation through Christ to leper colonies in the mountains of Haldwani, Rajpura, and Uttaranchal, India. He has three daughters: Jessy lives in California with her husband; Joyce and her husband are missionaries in an interior tribal village in Madhya Pradesh, India; and Sheba lives with Samjee in Nagpur, India, where she is studying biotechnology. Samjee's beloved wife, MaryKutty, who blessed countless lives with her love, hospitality, and giving heart, went home to be with her Lord in 2003 after a courageous battle with cancer. Samjee says the secret to his ministry was MaryKutty's prayer and dedication. In March 2005 God joined Samjee to Mary Devasia in marriage and together they continue the work of the ministry.

10

GOD GIVES!

by Raven Nelson

And they overcame him by the blood of the Lamb, and by the word of their testimony; and they loved not their lives unto the death.

REVELATION 12:11 KJV

I am a full blood Native American. At age three the powers that be took me from my family and placed me in what was called a Christian home. Between the ages of three and nine I was taken to a hospital many times because of physical and mental mistreatment at the hands of these people. Consequently, my view of Christianity turned dark and slanted. I didn't trust anything carrying a Christian label.

As an adult I began a career in bail enforcement, which is essentially working as a bounty hunter. This can be dangerous, as gangs retaliate and things happen. On February 28, 1996, I had a near death experience in the emergency room at St. Joseph's Hospital in Vancouver, Washington. My heart stopped twice, and I needed a blood transfusion. While my body lay on the gurney, my spirit floated up in the room where I could observe the medical staff working on me.

Because I had no blood pressure and a faint pulse, they started compressions on my chest and used electric defibrillation paddles in an attempt to start my heart. The hospital had no AB negative blood available for a transfusion. The emergency room doctor, also AB negative, had a supply of his blood at the hospital in case of emergency and told the team to use his blood for my transfusion.

While my spirit floated above, I saw what appeared to be a tall man standing to my right. He wore a white robe with a gold belt tied at the waist, had flowing white hair, and appeared to have fire in His eyes.

The Man lovingly reached out, held my hand, and said, "I died for you. Won't you give Me a chance?" His love penetrated my heart. My spirit returned to my body, and the emergency room team started my heart. Four days later I walked out of the hospital.

After the emergency room experience, I felt a more personal realization of God's love. I started searching for the loving Man I had encountered in the hospital, wanting to learn more about Him and to have a more personal relationship with Him.

When I approached some Christians ministering in the streets, I met a gentle giant named Lobo. He and another brother we called "Brother Al" prayed that I would come to the realization of who God is.

God heard their prayers. I began to read God's Word and entered a personal relationship with the Lord. I read in John 14:12 that we would do even greater things than Jesus did. I read in Mark 16:15-18 that signs and wonders would follow after those who believe.

I ventured from church to church looking for the signs and wonders I had read about in the Bible. Even though I had experienced a personal encounter with the Lord in the emergency room, I needed healing for the aches and pains resulting from damage done to my body earlier in my life. I had breaks in my back and neck from bullet wounds, fights, and beatings on the street. Lifting more than ten pounds was painful. I could not sit or stand for long periods of time because of my heart condition, diagnosed as arrhythmia. I was unable to walk long distances.

To ease the pain of my infirmities, I became like a walking pharmacy. My prescribed medications included 40 mg. of morphine three times a day, Roxicodone as needed, Verelan for my damaged heart, two sleep medications including Ambien (as the pain was constant), Prilosec, Cyclobenzaprine as a muscle relaxer, and Stadol spray for weekly migraines.

I took pills to get up in the morning and other pills to make it through the day. I also used a Tens Unit for my back to relax constantly knotted muscles. My vast array of medication was a drug addict's dream—except for the pain that accompanied it. At one doctor's appointment I received eleven steroid shots up and down my back when I should have received only four at the most. The presiding doctor was amazed that I was even able to walk into the office, considering the pain I was suffering.

Not only was my life negatively impacted with chronic pain, but my wife, Vi, suffered along with me. God blessed me with such a good helper and helpmate. I thank God for Vi, for her understanding and her love. I never experienced good days—only days with less pain and days with more pain. I wondered how I could possibly survive another winter. So did Vi.

Vi stood firm on God's Holy Word day-by-day and sometimes hour-by-hour. Those days, she says now, were the days of desperate prayer. Through personal experience, Vi knows that living with someone suffering with chronic pain is in itself very painful. Clinging to Jesus who is deeper and higher than all of our pain, insufficiencies, misgivings, and disappointments enabled her to persevere. While she stood in faith for my healing, she prayed over my medications each day, knowing that in God's timing I would be healed spirit, soul, and body.

Although I carried a lot of baggage, I continued searching God's Word. It says, "Faith comes by hearing, and hearing by the Word of God" (Romans 10:17). As I read, I understood that I needed faith to be healed.

In 2001 some friends gave me a video of David Hogan, a missionary to the jungles of Mexico. I heard about the miraculous: people healed, blind eyes given sight, damaged hearts made whole, lepers cleansed, the dead raised. I took note of this man and his ministry.

On September 13, 2003, I met Brother Hogan. After searching the Internet for his itinerary, I learned that he was coming to Living Waters Ranch in Challis, Idaho, which was seven hundred miles one way. Because of my desperation and chronic pain, the long distance didn't matter to me. I purposed in my heart to find out whether or not God was moving through this man as I had seen and heard on the video I had watched.

After traveling to Challis, I saw the man I had seen on the video, his wife, and his kids. When I first approached him, it wasn't exactly a glorious meeting. I was in pain and wanted to *know* that I was going to be healed. I challenged him, telling him I wanted to see a demonstration of what I had seen on the videos. I wanted to know that miracles didn't just happen in the deep jungles of Mexico but in America too. I didn't want to see a man of God—I wanted to see *the God* of the man.

Brother David was undaunted when I approached him. "I'll see you in the prayer line," he said. Vi and I promptly took our seats.

I vaguely remember the meeting. However, I recall a great anticipation in my heart that healing really would happen in that place. I couldn't wait for the prayer line to get started. I got into the line with Vi. Still in pain, I waited as Brother David started moving around and praying for people. As he prayed, I saw some falling under the power of the Holy Spirit, unable to stand in the presence of God. Although I had witnessed this in the past, I had never sensed the power of God in a measure as I did at this meeting. I felt so stirred to get over to Brother Hogan, so I grabbed Vi's hand and started to lead her toward him.

He turned. Our eyes locked. When he started walking toward me, I sensed a thrill in my heart knowing that *my time had come* to find and see. By the time he got to me, I could see that He was operating through a divine power and presence of God. It wasn't him any longer. He asked, "What's wrong with you?"

I started telling him about the breaks in my back and neck. Before I got a chance to rattle off my other health maladies of my heart, headaches, and other wounds, he said, "Enough!" He blew, "Whewww!" He didn't touch me—he just blew—as if invoking the Holy Wind of Heaven. As he blew I saw something that looked like crystal clear water coming out of his mouth. My first thought was, *I don't believe!* But by that time the presence of God was all over me. His presence felt like a complete peace and wonder that I had never experienced before.

I suddenly realized that I was lying on the floor. I felt a hand propping my head up and realized that Brother David was telling me about healing, courage, the mercy of God, and the love of heaven. He told me to accept what I was receiving. So I did!

I got up later—I don't know *how much* later—and all pain was gone! Pain that I had carried for years was instantly gone! Although I was still stiff, I felt no pain. I told Vi what had happened and about Brother David holding my head and talking with me.

Vi said, "No, he just blew, then kept on walking by." But in the spiritual realm, I saw and heard him speak courage, strength, healing, and the love of God! What a blessed moment! I had come to the meeting looking for the God of the Word, for signs and wonders following after those who believe, and got what I came for! I met a faithful servant who believes the Word of God and is a conduit that God's power flows through.

Throughout the meeting and when I returned home, I felt stiff but still had no pain. That night I went to bed taking no medication—no sleep aides, no heart meds, and no muscle relaxants. I woke in the morning pain free and with minor stiffness.

Vi and I attended another meeting, soaked in more of God's Word, and met new friends and brothers. When I shared my healing testimony with Brother David, he said, "This happens all the time!" I love the fact that when you're in the good graces of heaven, things happen! GOD GIVES! And there *were not simply a few* healings that evening. One woman walked out of her wheelchair and left it behind. Her empty wheelchair sat alongside three sets of crutches and a cane that were no longer needed.

Throughout the meeting, I believe I was too overjoyed to really hear anything that was being said, so *overwhelmed* with the feeling of "Wow! I'm healed! My pain is gone! What I had been looking for has come!"

Toward the end of that meeting Brother David said, "We're having a meeting in Seattle, Washington, September 18-20. Please come." So Vi and I were privileged to partake in a blessed time in Seattle. I was given the opportunity to share my healing testimony publicly for the first time.

When I visited my doctor in Colville, Washington, on October 10, 2003, about a month after my healing, he saw a different person than he'd been treating for the last few years. I could bend down, twist, hop, and jump.

After listening to my heart he said that if he hadn't been taking care of me, he wouldn't have believed that my heart was beating so strong and steady. Previously my heart consistently beat out of rhythm. Before God healed me I visited the doctor monthly, and when new nurses listened to my heart they thought I was going into cardiac arrest. Once they called in a crash cart, but my doctor came in and laughed, "Oh, that's okay. It's just Mr. Nelson!"

I shared my faith with my doctor, telling him that I quit taking all medications cold turkey and experienced no withdrawal symptoms whatsoever. He said, "You couldn't have just quit like that with no withdrawal! You're a marvel!"

"God did the work," I said. God did a *thorough* work.

For weeks after my meeting in Challis, I ran and jumped for joy when I got up in the morning, completely free from pain and stiffness and able to think straight. I felt like the man in Acts 3:1-10, who had been crippled from birth. After he was healed in the name of Jesus, he jumped to his feet and began to walk then went into the temple courts, walking and leaping and praising God.

My doctor said, "You should open a pain clinic to help others get people off narcotics, if you could kick it that easy." But I told him it was the Lord that did ALL for me.

I met God in Challis in a way I had never met Him before. My once-damaged heart now burns for Jesus. The wounded heart that once needed medication now is fueled with God's Word. God gives me understanding in a head that previously only knew pain.

He has given me the *Good News* of salvation and that He is my healer. He is my Shepherd with a rod and a staff that comforts me. Jesus took stripes on His back for my healing, shed His blood for my righteousness, and sent the Holy Ghost power to flow through me just like Brother Hogan. He works through *every* believer.

Raven, a full blood Native American from the Thlingit tribe, and his wife, Vi, have been married for more than nine years. They give individuals and couples Christian counsel and testify of the wonderful things God has done in their lives. Raven ministers the Word as God gives opportunity. Along with his brother, Ron Hutchcraft, he works closely with On Eagle's Wings to see lives of Natives restored to wholeness in Jesus Christ. Raven leads prayer meetings and Bible studies, and Vi has led a prayer meeting and Bible study for women for three years from different denominations and backgrounds. Together Raven and Vi are blessed with seven children and ten grandchildren.

11

BROTHER NOLAND

by Pastor Russ Doyl

Therefore confess your sins to each other and pray for each other so that you may be healed. The prayer of a righteous man is powerful and effective.

JAMES 5:16

*B*rother Noland, a powerful man of God and of faith, blessed me every time I saw him. As the assistant minister of visitation at First Church of the Open Bible in Spokane, I was assigned to visit him regularly. He was also a dear friend. I felt he often ministered to me more than I ministered to him.

I loved to sit and talk to him about his days of serving the Lord. I remember him telling me the story over and over again about hearing the audible voice of the Lord in his kitchen one day. After boiling some water for tea, Brother Noland left the teakettle on the stove with no water in it—with the burner on. When he walked away from the stove he heard the Lord say, "Turn your stove off."

When I first started visiting Brother Noland, his wife was in a nursing home. I picked him up at his retirement home once a week and dropped him off at the nursing home to visit his wife. Brother Noland brought special treats to feed his wife during their visits. Sometimes he even crushed an orange and fed it to her. I visited other shut-ins while he visited with her.

In 1993 my pastor, Norm LeLaCheur, told me that Brother Noland had been hospitalized at Sacred Heart Medical Center in Spokane, Washington, and was asking for me. After a bad cold had progressed into pneumonia in both lungs, Brother Noland had been admitted to the hospital the day before my visit. The hospital took X-rays of his lungs after admitting him.

Brother Noland, in his eighties at the time, had always believed in the healing ministry God gave me and had great faith to believe that if I came to pray for him, then everything would be all right. When I walked into his hospital room that day his face lit up, and he motioned for me to come over to his bed. I saw evidence of how sickness and disease can destroy someone's life. He had always been full of energy and life, but was now on oxygen and barely able to take his next breath. Seeing what sickness could to do a healthy man shocked me.

Brother Noland smiled then coughed because he was having trouble breathing. It seemed as if he was relieved that someone was there to pray for him because he was too weak to pray for himself.

Sitting next to his hospital bed, I could hear the fluid gurgling in his lungs as he struggled to take a breath so he could talk to me. "You pray for me now," he whispered, "and when I'm able I'll pray for you later."

Leaning over him I placed both of my hands on his chest. While praying I felt God's power flow down my arms, into my hands, and into Brother Noland's lungs. As I finished praying a nurse entered the room. "We're going to take him down to X-ray again," she said. "You'll have to leave now." As I left Brother Noland's room I told him I would continue to pray for him and would come by to see him later.

Later I learned that when the X-rays were taken and the film developed, the X-ray technician couldn't see any sign of the pneumonia. "Mr. Noland," he said, "there must be something wrong. We need to take another set of X-rays." After the second set was completed, Brother Noland was taken back to his room.

Brother Noland told me that when the doctor came to see him, he showed him two sets of X-rays. The first set, taken when he was admitted to the hospital, showed both lungs filled with fluid. But the second set of X-rays, taken immediately after I prayed for him, showed both lungs completely free of fluid! The doctor showed him the second X-rays and said, "I've never seen a more perfect set of lungs." He released Brother Noland from the hospital the very next day!

Many times after his recovery from pneumonia Brother Noland prayed for me. In fact, he prayed for me every time I visited him. I remember accompanying Jack Collett, another minister of visitation, to see Brother Noland during another hospitalization. At the end of our visit, he said, "Come over here boys, so I can pray for you."

After Jack and I knelt in front of his wheelchair, he laid hands on us and asked the Lord to bless us. As he prayed the power of God hit both of us so hard that we almost fell over. After we left Brother Noland's hospital room Jack looked at me and said, "Did you feel that?"

God used the miracle He performed in Brother Noland's life many times to teach me about praying for the sick. When I've prayed for other people, the Lord reminded me how He healed Brother Noland. "I used you to heal Brother Noland," He'd whisper, "and I'm going to use you to heal this person too." The Lord used the experience with Brother Noland to help build my faith for the many others I have prayed for. Knowing him continues to make a great impact in my life today.

Pastor Russ was born and raised in Spokane, Washington. Russ and his wife, Cindy, have been married since 1983 and have a daughter and a son. After Bible College, Russ served as Visitation Pastor, Interim Pastor, Associate Pastor, and currently serves as Senior Pastor of Destiny Church. In 1989 he started traveling the country as an evangelist. He ministers in gifts of healings, prophecy, and general encouragement. He also exhorts members of the body of Christ to be all God has called them to be. Pastor Russ is dedicated to doing the works of Jesus found in Matthew 9:35– teaching, preaching, and healing every sickness and disease among the people.

12

NO PAIN, NO CANE!

by Patricia Oberstar

And the power of the Lord was present for him to heal the sick.

LUKE 5:17,18

*B*rought up in a loving family, I attended a traditional church where every Sunday I learned about God, giving money, and confessing my sins. I didn't, however, learn about the Holy Spirit and Jesus, the Son of God, who died on the Cross and rose again for me personally. Many years passed before I heard about the saving grace of Jesus Christ or how to get to heaven.

In my single years I started longing for more spiritually, but I didn't know *what* I was searching for. God faithfully demonstrated His love to me, protected me, and put Christians in my path—but they kept silent about the spiritual truths I needed.

I thought I was a good person because God had given me a natural gift of love for people. *So* I wondered, *Wouldn't that get me to heaven?* I didn't know Jesus had said, "I am the way, the truth and the life. No man comes to the Father except through me" (John 14:6).

In April 1980, when I was forty-five years old, God opened my eyes and prepared my heart for Him. The first miracle in my life was about to happen. While shopping at a Christian Bible store in search of a gift for a friend, God led me to pick up a booklet on the bottom tier of a bookshelf. I didn't purpose to pick it up, and didn't realize what I was doing.

When I returned home I went to my bedroom and read Bill Bright's booklet, *Four Spiritual Laws*. I learned that all people are sinners and the penalty of sin is eternal death or separation from God, but the gift of God is eternal life through Jesus Christ. I read that the only way to get to heaven is through Jesus. Immediately I repented of my sins and invited Jesus into my heart as Lord and Savior. At the time I didn't fully comprehend what I had done.

About five months later my neighbor invited me to Bible Study Fellowship. There I learned about salvation and received understanding of the great price Jesus had paid for the forgiveness of my sin. This study built my faith, humbled me, revealed God's love, and helped me understand that we are saved by grace as a gift of God. I realized I couldn't earn this gift of salvation by doing good works. I came to the powerful realization that I had received the greatest miracle of all—forgiveness of sin and eternal life through Jesus.

Twenty-five years later, in April 2004, the stage was set for me to receive yet another miracle from Almighty God. I was suffering from severe pain in my left knee and had been using a cane for over a year to help me walk. The pain was so great that walking down stairs, getting in a car, or even bending became increasingly difficult.

Seeking medical attention, I first saw Dr. Robert Laprade at University Medical Center in Minneapolis. An X-ray of my left knee showed osteoarthritis. The doctor said the cartilage was worn and that I had many spurs, which are bony outgrowths. Looking for a second opinion, I saw Dr. James Larson, an orthopedic surgeon at Orthopedic Consultants in Minneapolis. He came to the same conclusion: I needed a left knee replacement.

I dreaded the thought of having knee surgery as I had heard about the pain and long recovery time from others who had gone through knee replacement. Although I knew that all people face trials, I wanted God to heal me. I remembered that Jesus had said, "You have not because you ask not" (James 4:2). So I prayed, "Lord, if it would please You and glorify You, would You please heal my knee?"

Dr. Larson's office gave me a thick book to read about preparing for and recovering after surgery. So I gathered the tools I would need: a chair for the bathtub, crutches, and a walker. I also prepared in prayer, choosing to rely on God to see me through this season of trial. I embraced Him as Jehovah Rapha, my healer.

I was scheduled for surgery at Abbott Northwestern Hospital in Minneapolis, the second week of September 2004—but God had different plans for me. A Benny Hinn healing crusade was scheduled for the first week of September at the Target Center in Minneapolis, which holds about eighteen thousand people. Many from our church, Emmanuel Christian Center, planned to attend the crusade.

That Sunday after our church service, my husband, Richard, and I arrived at the crusade. We could only find seats high in the balcony because the building was so crowded. When Richard asked an usher if we could get down to the stage for prayer, the man said it would be difficult because there were no railings for us to hang on to. Then the usher added, "When the anointing comes, you'll get it right in your chair."

During the crusade God healed many people on the main floor of various illnesses. One by one they stepped up to the platform for prayer and to share their testimonies. Then near the end of the crusade Benny Hinn received a word of knowledge from the Lord. "Someone up there is scheduled for surgery next week," he said pointing up to our section. "Cancel your surgery! You're healed!" Then he added, "You don't need to feel anything to be healed." And I didn't feel a thing.

Lord, is this for me? I asked in my heart, knowing my surgery was scheduled for the following Tuesday. I looked around our section and saw nobody cheering or appearing to be excited. *Is it me, Lord?* I prayed again.

By the time Richard and I arrived home, I had my answer. I ran up and down our stairs—no cane, no pain—just the joy of knowing that the Lord had healed my knee.

The day after the crusade, several people from Emmanuel Christian Center who had also attended the crusade called to see if I was the one they witnessed Benny Hinn pointing to and telling to cancel surgery. Hearing confirmation that God had healed my knee, they rejoiced with me. My sister-in-law, Barbara Grahek, and a friend, Lynn Dearey, who attended the crusade, and many other friends and relatives who heard of my miracle were overjoyed. Then, when I called to cancel my surgery at Abbott Northwestern Hospital, I had the opportunity to share my testimony of healing with medical people involved in my case.

More than two years later I'm still thanking and praising the Lord that I can walk with no pain. I give God all the glory and praise and thanks. He's a great God and healer and deserves all our love, praise, and worship.

God is *still* healing today! Praise His holy name.

Pat and her husband, Richard, have been married for over thirty-seven years and have two daughters, Diana and Jeanne. Dick and Pat attend Emmanuel Christian Church in Minneapolis, where Pat is co-leader of a Prodigal Group, funeral food preparation, Bible studies, and serves as a Sunday greeter. They live in New Brighton, Minnesota.

13

IN AN INSTANT: A NEW MAN
by David Gurno

So if the Son sets you free, you will be free indeed.

JOHN 8:36

"*C*lang!" slammed the door of my new home, a room in the state hospital. A guard shuffled down the hall with the key in his pocket. Still drunk despite the three-hour trip from Minneapolis, I looked around. A small bed and a toilet were the only furnishings.

When I glanced up at the ceiling, several large birds appeared to come flying down out of it. They took bites out of my face. Throwing up my arms as a shield, I looked down at the floor. Snakes and other creeping, vile-looking vermin seemed to be crawling up out of the drain.

Right then I knew there were only two choices: I would either lose my mind or die. If there was a hell, I must have stepped into it.

As an eleven-year-old boy, I never imagined the grief that would follow my first sip of alcohol. I just wanted to fit in with the other Chippewa on the Red Lake Reservation in Northern Minnesota. All the adults I saw liked to drink. So did my peers and ten of my twelve brothers and sisters. That day I drank until I passed out, and I continued to do that nearly every day of the next thirty-eight years.

Dropping out of school after eighth grade, I started hanging out in a town near the reservation. My escapades led to thirty to forty nights in jail and five times as many trips to a detox center. At seventeen I migrated south to the Twin Cities, as Minneapolis and adjoining St. Paul are known. When I wasn't drinking, I panhandled or worked odd jobs as part of the daily labor pool. If I managed to work two days straight, I took off the next three to get drunk.

One winter I earned my high school equivalency diploma while staying in a treatment center. It wasn't worth much, considering my main ambition was to use my alcoholism to qualify for Social Security disability payments. I was nearing bottom, and it was two years before going to the state hospital.

Running low on cash and ways to get it, several drinking buddies and I resorted to using Lysol to get high. Puncturing a couple holes in the top of the can to let out the aerosol, we would drain the fluid into an empty milk jug. Filling the jug with water, we passed it around.

Well-known in the inner city neighborhood where I hung out, I was usually left alone by the police. But several months before going to the state hospital, they started picking me up regularly. Finally a county social worker came to see me in detox. "David, you're costing us too much money," she said of my treatment and hospital merry-go-round. "The next time this happens you're going to the state hospital. They have a lock-up treatment facility, and that's where you're going."

"That'll never happen to me," I replied.

Now I stood in this tiny room in the state hospital and wondered how I could escape these insane hallucinations. Suddenly my mind cleared. I remembered the man who had appeared at my bedside for four months every time I had awakened from a stupor in detox or the hospital. He would say, "Dave, I know Someone who can help you," said this stranger, who I am now convinced was an angel. "His name is Jesus."

"No, I don't want to hear that," I would moan. "I'm an Indian." But now I was desperate. I wanted to believe that Jesus could set me free, make me whole again, and give me a new life. If anyone needed a new life it was me!

Kneeling, I said, "Jesus, if You can really do what this man told me You can, and You're really real, I need You to help me. I need You to take this desire of alcohol away from me because it's driving me crazy."

Nothing obvious happened, but I crawled up onto that bed and slept soundly for the first time in more than two years. When I woke up, I felt different. I didn't have the shakes. For the first time in longer than I could remember, I didn't feel sick. I felt strong again. Then I realized what had happened. Jesus had answered my prayer! He had come into my life. I knew He was the Son of God. And at that moment He became my Lord.

Soon after this another inmate gave me a Bible. I wanted to read it, but I needed help. So I prayed again, "Jesus, if You want me to learn about this Book, You're going to have to teach me."

Not only did God show me how to read the Bible, He helped me understand it. For the ninety-three days I spent in the state hospital, I read it whenever not in a group meeting or other required activity.

Afterwards I returned to Minneapolis and moved into a halfway house. I started going to church and found steady employment. I also looked up my old drinking buddies. They were amazed to see me sober, working, and happy.

"Dave, where did you learn about the Bible?" many asked.

After I explained, eight hard-core drinkers made the same decision to follow Christ. Five of them have since gone to heaven. I see the other three occasionally. All of them are still in great shape.

I was so grateful to God for what He had done, but He wasn't finished blessing me. The year after my trip to the state hospital, I was walking past the American Indian Center one morning on the way to work. A staff member was outside picking up litter. Just then, God told her, "Go and share your testimony with that man." De-Bora walked up to me and repeated those instructions. Then she told me about a life that sounded just like mine.

A mix of the Sioux, Arikora, and Hidasta tribes, she was born in North Dakota. After abusing drugs and alcohol for years, in 1983 she killed the man who raped her sister. Although sent to prison for life, after deciding to follow Christ she had been paroled early.

As I listened to her story, tears filled my eyes. Afterwards, I asked if I could give her a hug. When I did, I think I fell instantly in love! Getting her phone number, I called and we began attending church and Bible studies together. Soon we entered premarital counseling. Four months after we met we were married.

Together we travel nearly every weekend, telling others the true story of how God changed our lives. We are especially concerned with persuading Native Americans that Jesus is Lord of all. He isn't some "white man's religion." He is the answer to the curses that have plagued our people for far too long. I know because He rescued my life when it was going nowhere. He filled me with His Holy Spirit and gave me a wife to stand beside me. He is the way to happiness on earth and to heaven after this life ends.

David was born and raised on the Red Lake Indian Reservation in Northern Minnesota. He is the fourth youngest of thirteen children. A member of the Minneapolis Chapter of Full Gospel Business Men's Fellowship (FGBMF), David Gurno has worked steadily in recent years as a security guard. He and his wife, De-Bora, celebrated their seventh anniversary in August of 2005. They attend the Potter's House church in Minneapolis, Minnesota.

* This story appeared in the September 2005 issue of *Answer,* a publication of Full Gospel Businessmen Fellowship.

14

REBORN FREE
by De-Bora Gurno

A new heart will I give you and a new spirit will I put without and I will take away the stony heart out of your flesh and give you a heart of flesh.

EZEKIEL 36:26

*M*y father molested me when I was only three years old, so I moved from foster home to foster home in North and South Dakota from age four to sixteen. A male relative sexually abused me from ages nine to eleven while living in Deadwood, South Dakota. And by age twelve I started prostituting myself, searching for love through sex because it was the only kind of love I had ever known. Although this lifestyle created self-condemnation, shame, and guilt, I assumed that everyone lived like I did and thought it was normal.

In 1978 I was arrested for drunkenness in Fargo, North Dakota, and spent the weekend in jail. While there, a woman from Gideons International ministered love to me and told me about Jesus. I accepted Jesus into my heart, but because I lacked Christian discipleship I returned to worldly ways to serve earthly lusts.

After abusing drugs and alcohol for many years, on May 31, 1983, in Grand Forks, North Dakota, I was charged with first-degree murder for killing the man who raped my sister. "You'll be sentenced to life in prison with no chance of parole," my court-appointed attorney told me.

While waiting for my sentencing date, my attorney told me he would ask for a reduced sentence of forty-five years. We argued about a possible plea-bargain. "Just let me go and do my time," I said. Yet my lawyer persisted.

On October 4, 1983, I agreed to the plea bargain and was sentenced to forty-five years. It would be thirty years before I could be eligible for parole and ten years before I could appear before the pardon board. The Sheriff's

Department from Grand Forks drove me to Bismarck, North Dakota, State Penitentiary Men's Prison. I became their eighth female prisoner–and had the longest sentence of them all.

On arrival I was placed in isolation, where a spirit of suicide tormented me. Medical staff gave me lithium to help me sleep and to control my behavior. Desperate to find peace of mind, I asked one of the Native Indian men to help me. He gave me six black tobacco ties to hang on the post of my bed, which were supposed to ward off evil. But the tormenting only grew worse. I asked a priest to bless my cell, but the darkness and demons continued to torture me daily. Nothing freed me from my spiritual prison.

One month after my arrival in Bismarck, I wrote to the governor of North Dakota, asking to be executed for the crime I had committed. He wrote back: "DENIED."

A federal marshal visited me during my incarceration. His office had been looking for me for ten years, he said. They charged me with stealing and cashing government checks, and officials scheduled me for another relocation to Pleasanton California Federal Prison. The new charges added four years to my sentence.

After being air lifted from Bismarck to Pleasanton, California, I was placed on suicide watch because I wanted to die. On October 23, 1986, I was sent to M.C.C. San Diego, California Federal Prison, a temporary federal holding place, for nine months. While incarcerated, two potent medications were administered to me twice daily for depression. Instead of swallowing the pills, I hid them under my tongue, spit them out, and saved them. When I had stashed a half bread bag full of pills, I swallowed them all at once and committed the crime of suicide.

I arrived at Harborview Hospital dead on arrival. While hanging between life and death, I saw a glimpse of hell and heard both evil and heavenly voices. My soul felt like a battlefield where two entities fought for possession.

The doctors tried everything to revive me, with no success. As my spirit floated above the scene on the table below, I saw medical staff cover my body with a sheet. I screamed and cried, but no one could hear me. An officer later told me that while I was dead on the table, she kept telling me that I would see my children again one day and that I needed to live. But I couldn't respond.

In a distance I heard a comforting voice. "I love you," He said. Although I had hungered for these words all my life, I had never heard them before. Hearing of His love, I felt my soul fling back into my body. The One who loved me brought me back to life.

"Why did you let me live?" I asked the doctor.

"It's not up to me," he said.

A couple of days later I was taken back to prison and placed in "the hole," which is like a small bathroom with a bed, as punishment for misusing my medication. While I waited in isolation to be shipped out once again, I heard that same loving voice. "De-Bora," He whispered. "Don't you think it's time for you to give your life to Me completely?"

Falling to my knees, I asked God to forgive me for everything I had done to hurt Him and others. I rose from my knees feeling the love, peace, joy, and forgiveness I had always longed for. First John 1:9 says, "If you confess your sins, He is faithful and just to forgive you your sins and cleanse you from all unrighteousness." I was forgiven.

A man in the next cell heard me crying out to Jesus. He told me later that when he saw a bright light shining through the tiny crack in the wall, he also accepted Jesus Christ as his Lord and Savior. Also, when God freed me He gave me boldness to speak His Word. After my conversion two federal officers, a husband and wife from the San Diego prison, also gave their lives to the Lord.

My relocation was delayed, so I returned to general prison population and started GED classes. As I sat on the bench waiting for class, my teacher approached me, looked at me, and said, "De-Bora, what happened? You're glowing!"

"I accepted Jesus into my heart!" I answered with a big smile.

Although I was transferred to five different prisons after my conversion, little did anyone know that God was sending me on a mission for

Him. At every prison I was placed in the hole and shared with others what God had done for me.

One evening in 1988, in Alderson, West Virginia, I asked God in anger, "Why am I *still* here?" He woke me up at midnight to answer my question. With open eyes I saw a vision above the sink in my cell of Jesus getting nailed to the Cross, yet not complaining. I fell to my knees and asked God to forgive me for hurting Him.

In 1991 God gave me favor when I received a thirteen-year cut in my sentence, even though I'd been denied many times before because of the seriousness of my crime. After serving sixteen years in various prisons I was sent to the Minimum Security Women's Correctional Facility in Shakopee, Minnesota, where I attended a Christian service being held in the gymnasium. "Miracles will happen here," Bishop Alexander said. "People will be released who never thought they would get out."

I claimed my freedom in Jesus' name. Revelation 3:8 says, "I know your deeds. See, I have set before you an open door that no man can shut. I know you have little strength, yet you have kept my word and have not denied my name."

After standing in faith for fifteen months for my miracle, on January 6, 1998, I was granted parole! My original date for parole was 2028, but *nothing is impossible for God* (Luke 1:37).

When I learned I would not be released until April 1, 1998, I asked God, "Why then?"

"I want you to tell the warden about me," He whispered. Two days before my release, I shared my faith with the warden as the Lord directed, telling him what Jesus had done for me by giving me a second chance to live for Him.

While in prison God helped me heal the wounds from my past by forgiving those who had hurt me. He wanted me to forgive others as He had forgiven me. So on February 10, 2003, I expressed forgiveness to the relative who had molested me as a young girl. When his wife died, I called to express my sympathy for his wife's death. After telling him how much his sexual abuse had affected my life, I also told him I forgave him.

After listening to me, he said he regretted what he had done and was sorry. He explained that at the time he had been out of his mind with alcoholism. He said he was now a believer in Jesus Christ.

In May 1998, while I was working as a maintenance worker for the American Indian Center in Minneapolis, the Spirit of God led me to witness to David and told me he was my husband-to-be.

I said, "No, Lord! I want to serve You alone." When I hesitated the Lord reminded me of a prayer I had prayed ten years earlier, asking Him to find me a godly man. I remembered Psalm 37:4, "Delight thyself in the Lord and He will give you the desires of your heart." Obeying God, I shared my testimony with David, and we were married on August 7, 1998.

When we searched for a church God led us to Broadway Tent Crusade under the guidance of Pastor Frank Correa. God convicted David to tithe, and as he obeyed we have been truly blessed. Deuteronomy says, "Thou shalt remember the Lord your God for it is He who gives you the power to get wealth."

In my past I had given birth to five children, but because of my lifestyle I gave them up for adoption and never expected to see them again. When my mom died in 1995, the Lord brought my oldest girl to visit me in prison. I felt scared, not wanting her to reject me for what I had done, and she didn't. Then God opened more doors for me to meet my youngest son and daughter in September 1998. They were happy to see me and to meet David. My two oldest sons were three weeks old and one year old when I gave them away, but that same month I received a call from both of them, now twenty-seven and twenty-five. We have all reconciled.

We pray that every person who reads our story would know Jesus as Lord and Savior as we have. Confess your sins and repent and believe that God has forgiven you. Find a church where God's Word is preached in truth and love. It isn't God's will that any should perish, but that all would come to the saving grace and knowledge of Him.

De-Bora, a Sioux Indian, was born in North Dakota. She and her husband, David, a Chippewa Indian, were ordained pastors September 24, 2005. They celebrated their seventh anniversary August 7, 2005. De-Bora and David live in Minneapolis, Minnesota.

15

JAKE AND THERESA'S STORY

by Jake and Theresa Raven

*Believe me when I say that I am in the Father and the Father is
in me; or at least believe on the evidence of the miracles themselves.*

JOHN 14:11

THERESA:

*L*ate November 2001 my husband, Jake, and I accepted an invitation
from Pastor Ron Legary to serve the community dinner being held at
Grand Forks Christian Center in Grand Forks, British Columbia. Some
time later we were invited as personal guests to attend Pastor Ron's ordi-
nation, and later Jake visited Grand Forks Christian Center in an official
capacity as mayor.

In December 2002 Jake and I accepted another invitation to serve the
congregation's Christmas dinner being held at the church. We thought it
sounded like a fun activity, not realizing that the Lord was working in our
lives. After serving the dinner, we left immediately to attend another
Christmas dinner with city officials.

On Wednesday, January 7, 2002, when Bruce Allen and Andre Ashby
were scheduled to speak at Grand Forks Christian Center, Pastor Ron
Legary invited us to attend the meetings. Because we liked Pastor Ron, we
thought, *Well, we'll just go down and listen.*

Jake and I didn't have a Christian upbringing. Although I was born and
raised Catholic, I had walked away from God long before this time. Jake
had never known God and wasn't walking with Him at all. After listening
to Andre and Bruce's messages, we returned home. I got little sleep that
night. It seemed as if God kept stirring my heart throughout the night.
Every time I woke up God was on my mind, and I sensed His presence in
the room.

The Bruce Allen and Andre Ashby meetings continued on Friday, but Jake couldn't attend because of another commitment. "Are you going to go?" Jake asked.

"If I can talk Ann into coming, then I'll go," I said. "But I'm not going by myself."

After telling our daughter Ann about the meetings, she said, "Sure, I'll go with you if you'd like." That night the same thing happened when I returned home from the meeting and got into bed. God stirred me throughout the night. And after Jake and I attended the meeting on Saturday, He continued to stir my heart after we got home and went to bed.

On Sunday morning when I got dressed and ready for church Jake said, "Where are you going?"

"You started this," I told him. "So I'm going to finish it."

At church that morning Cassandra and Cindy, two young women students from Heart for the Nations Bible College in Spokane, Washington, shared during the service. Cassandra preached a message on treasure boxes. As she talked about storing precious gifts in these little tokens, it was as if God opened my heart and my treasure box. I opened my heart that morning and received Jesus as my personal Savior.

Returning home, I knew I had to tell Jake that I had accepted Jesus, but since Jake was an unbeliever it was a very hard thing. Yet, I knew I *had* to make a public statement to let him know of my newfound faith. On Monday morning I stepped into his woodworking shop and said, "Jake, I have something to tell you." Then I explained to him that I had received Jesus as my personal Lord and Savior.

"Well," Jake said, "I'm not going to keep you in bondage, but don't expect me to come to church with you."

"That's fine," I said. And we let it go at that.

The next Sunday morning when I saw Jake getting dressed, I said, "What are you doing?"

"I'm coming to church with you," he said. "But don't expect me to come every Sunday."

In the beginning of March 2002 I attended a Wednesday morning prayer meeting, something I participated in since accepting Christ two months earlier. At the time I had a rash on my abdomen that I couldn't get rid of. After seeking medical attention, doctors took biopsies. When biopsy results came back negative, they were unable to determine the cause of the rash.

I thought, *I'll just go up for prayer and see if they can pray for me.* As a new Christian, I knew little about healing. To me, healing was a brand-new thing, just like everything else in the church. When I walked to the front to have the group pray for me, I didn't specify what type of healing I needed; but after receiving prayer the rash disappeared slowly and never returned. That was only the beginning!

At the time I had also been suffering from severe arthritis in my hands and had received cortisone shots in my thumbs every six weeks to relieve the pain. I had been taking Arthrotech and Plaquenil medication for about five years. To help ease the pain in my hands I also used to sit down with my hands in a wax bath for fifteen minutes every night to coat my hands with wax. I'd then wrap my hands in plastic for a while to keep the wax from getting cold too quickly.

Because Jake and I run a small greenhouse in Grand Forks called *Raven's Garden Center,* I use my hands much of the time. While transplanting petunias, marigolds, and tomato plants, my hands would swell and the joints would stiffen. The only relief I could find was sitting with my hands in a hot wax bath.

After receiving prayer that Wednesday I returned home and sat in my chair to start the hand exercises I did regularly to keep my hands from getting completely stiff. I suddenly could touch the front of my fingers right down to the knuckles of the hand—something I hadn't been able to do for three years! I didn't realize it at first, but God had healed me during prayer that morning.

As I continued my exercises, I thought, *My gosh! I haven't been able to do this for a long time!* Still not realizing the miracle that had happened that morning, I did more exercises. I marveled again, *Gosh, I haven't done this for a while!*

Jake had been at a meeting that evening so I was anxious to tell him about my hands. When he returned home, I said, "Jake! Look what I can do!"

"Oh my gosh!" Jake exclaimed. "You haven't been able to do that for three or four years!"

I then realized what had happened. "Jake, my hands are healed!" I explained. "I went up for prayer this morning, and the Lord healed my hands!" Then I added, "I'm going to call Leona, the pastor's wife, because she was at prayer this morning too. I want to tell her the good news."

"No, you're *not* going to call her," Jake said. "I'm going to talk to Pastor Ron in the morning about this, and I don't want him swayed either way."

Jake visited Pastor Ron the following morning to talk about the miracle in my hands. Jake couldn't believe or understand this miracle because he had never witnessed anything like it before.

JAKE:

I spent several days in Pastor Ron's office, talking about Theresa's miracle healing. I hadn't grown up in a Christian home yet was taught Christian manners, so I had a difficult time coming to terms with her healing. Theresa's healing went against anything I believed in at that time, which I told Pastor Ron. My mind was in turmoil that week.

After much discussion Pastor Ron finally said, "Jake, you either believe or you don't believe, but the evidence is in Theresa's hands." With those words I came to the conclusion that there *is* a God, an *awesome* God that can heal, a God the human mind really cannot comprehend. My questions to Ron were based on common sense and human reasoning, not on God's way of doing things.

I decided to attend church the following Sunday with Theresa. Throughout the service I felt very uneasy and kind of restless. It is hard to describe, but I felt as if I was being pulled one way and then the other. It was like hearing a voice yet not hearing or understanding the sound.

Pastor Ron did an altar call after the service, but I did not want to go up to the altar at that time. Then after the service Pastor Ron called me into the prayer room. When Theresa saw me in the prayer room, she joined us.

After talking further with Pastor Ron, I accepted Jesus as my personal Lord and Savior. Since that day our life has been like a roller coaster—up and down. Actually, there have been no downs! We go up to a level, remain there for a while, and then we seem to go to a higher level.

THERESA:

Since the Lord healed my hands, I haven't needed one shot of cortisone and haven't had one hot wax bath. Praise the Lord!

A few weeks after Jake accepted the Lord, our daughter Ann accepted Jesus as her Lord and Savior. All three of us were baptized on Easter Sunday 2003. God has completely transformed our lives and given us such peace that surpasses understanding.

God continued doing miracles in my life. I was scheduled for knee replacement surgery September 4, 2003, due to deterioration from severe arthritis. Because of calcium build-up in my knee, at times I could not put any weight on it, which made it very painful to walk. A couple of weeks before the hospital called for the operation, I realized I could bend my knee and it didn't bother me anymore. I cancelled the surgery and have been fine ever since!

I also had suffered from an irregular heartbeat and had been on a medication called APO Propafenone (generic version of Rythmol) for about six years. After being on monitors in the hospital a couple of times, doctors said that if things didn't improve and if the irregularity didn't stop, I would need a pacemaker.

On October 19, 2003, Bruce Allen and his father, Ed Allen, visited Grand Forks Christian Center to teach. When Ed gave an altar call after his message, I responded and asked him to pray for the healing of my heart condition. When Ed laid hands on me and prayed, I sensed the Lord healing my heart instantly.

The Holy Spirit gave me a strong conviction to stop taking my heart medication that night. After Ed prayed my heart felt different, beating with a strong, regular beat. I was in such awe that God would heal me—again.

A couple of weeks after Ed Allen prayed for me, I saw my doctor and told him that I had stopped taking the APO Propafenone. He said, "Why did you take yourself off the medication?"

When I told him that God had healed my heart, he just shrugged his shoulders. So I let it go at that.

Although the Lord performed many miraculous physical healings in me, the most important healing the Lord did was the spiritual healing when He called me back to Him and I dedicated my life to Him. Although I had known *of* Him, I never really *knew Him* through a personal relationship. The longer I've been committed to Christ, the more I want to walk with Him daily. I hunger for Him and His Word and desire for that intimate relationship to continue to grow as He draws me closer to Him. My heart's desire is for our other five children to come to the Lord and *know* Him also.

Jake and I have enjoyed serving God through several ministry trips under our pastor's wing. They have included places like Mexico, Seattle, Cranbrook, Richmond, Chillewack, and Libby, Montana. God has blessed us with our beloved pastor, Ron Legary, who is also our mentor and my spiritual father. God has blessed us so abundantly, and He keeps blessing us and blessing us.

JAKE:

In August 2003 I woke up with a strong desire in my heart to start a TV program. When I told Theresa about it she said, "Pray about it to make sure it is the Lord and not your own fleshly idea." So I prayed and prayed.

When I felt peace in my heart about doing the program, I talked to the owner of the cable company. I didn't have to do a sales job at all. After I finished talking he said, "Go for it, Jake! Just talk with the boys who look after the community channel who are volunteers."

It is wondrous to see how the Lord works! By February 2005 we had already aired four shows. The area we live in is called "The Boundary" because we are on the US border, so I thought we ought to call the show *Live in the Boundary* or something like that.

The volunteers at Sunshine Communication Cable Division's channel 10, the community channel that airs the show, felt we must call it *The Jake Raven Show,* and at the time I thought, *That's kind of blowing your own horn!* But because both guys are retired professionals from radio and TV broadcasting, I realized they knew best and went along with it.

I thank God every day for this program because it has opened a much wider field of operations to influence for the Lord. We are not bound to our local area but can include any subject we feel would be of interest to our viewers.

We continue to work on more programs with God's direction. And the whole thing seems like no work at all. I tell somebody about the show, and it just comes together!

Although this is a general interest program, we want to slowly introduce religious issues. We're currently working on a show with a missionary in Africa where we will talk about life in Africa—and of course can include a little Word of the Lord.

God is guiding our lives, even if at times we don't realize it until later. Since we gave our lives to the Lord, He has enriched our lives beyond our imagination. All I can say is, "Praise the Lord!"

Jake and Theresa have been happily married for over forty-four years and live in Grand Forks, British Columbia, Canada. They have six children, seven grandchildren, and one great grandchild. They have travelled on ministry trips with Pastor Ron Legary, serving various churches needing help. Jake and Theresa are involved in intercessory prayer and love to serve the body of Christ through their God-given gifts of hospitality and compassion.

16

HAVE NO FEAR!

by Therese Marszalek

If you forgive anyone, I also forgive him. And what I have forgiven—if there was anything to forgive—I have forgiven in the sight of Christ for your sake, in order that Satan might not outwit us. For we are not unaware of his schemes.

2 CORINTHIANS 2:10,11

On May 28, 2002, while at House of the Lord in Tum Tum, Washington, I received a prophetic word from Victor Oniugbo, Archbishop from Enugu, Africa: "I see you in a van. Your ministry is reaching in that van. Get ready for that window. Stand on your feet and take this anointing. Who told you you'd be stopped? No one will stop you. The anointing is on you so strong in your life: teaching and prophetic. Be ready for seminars…for conferences. Your anointing will be unique. God will show you ahead of time what you will speak. This light will no more be under the bushel. Take the anointing; let it come upon you. Supernatural clarity and direction. On December 7 your ministry begins."

I wonder what's going to happen on December 7, I thought in the days after receiving this word. Although I didn't understand, I prayed, "Be it unto me according to Your Word."

Hearing about future seminars and conferences pushed me out of my comfort zone. As far back as I could remember I had been terrified of public speaking. I didn't merely sense butterflies fluttering in my stomach as many feel when they step up to the microphone; I felt a debilitating terror.

In spite of my fear, God put me in situations where I had to speak in front of people. My twelve-year career at Honeywell required me to give presentations regularly, often to Fortune 500 company executives. At church pastors asked me to teach Bible classes. In high school fellow students and teachers often nominated me to lead various groups.

Yet, whenever I stood up to speak in front of a group, big or small, fear gripped me. My mouth became like cotton. My knees and hands shook like an earthquake, and my voice crackled. My stomach knotted and ached for weeks before scheduled events. Even introducing myself in a small group setting brought tremors.

I remember a women's Bible study I attended while living in Seattle, Washington. The speaker delivered her message, then we broke into groups of twelve for prayer. After we got settled in the room, the leader said, "Let's join hands. We'll go around the room and pray."

PRAY?! I thought with great trepidation. I had never prayed out loud in my entire life! Being raised in the Catholic church, I had not been taught to pray out loud. We had only learned the "Hail Mary," the "Our Father," and the blessing over our food: "Bless us, O Lord, and these Thy gifts which we are about to receive from Thy bounty through Christ our Lord, Amen."

As the women prayed one by one, sweat dripped from my brow. *What will I say when my turn comes?* I fretted. Wishing I could yank my clammy hands from the ladies on each side of me, I wanted to bolt. When my turn came, I sputtered out a short, weak prayer with great fear and trembling.

It seemed odd to me that the audiences I spoke in front of had no idea what I faced. "Great presentation," I'd hear from peers and business associates. "Awesome message," church class attendees would say. What they saw on the outside vastly differed from the turmoil and quaking on the inside. They didn't realize how much I *suffered*. But God did.

When I gave my life to the Lord in 1979, I had promised, "Lord, I'll do anything You ask me to do," and I meant it. So, when God continued to open doors for me to speak, I obeyed. But fear continued to plague me. I hated the torment, but I didn't know how to get free from it.

In 2002, I became desperate. "Lord, You know I'll do anything You ask me to do," I prayed, but I'm tired of being scared. I don't want this fear anymore." Dropping to my knees I cried, "God, deliver me from fear! I want to be free!"

December 5-7, 2002, I attended a Family Foundations International Ancient Paths Seminar held at Word of Life Community Church in Newman Lake, Idaho. Along with the other attendees, I listened to a video-taped message from Craig Hill, the founder of the Christian organization.

I recall nothing of Craig Hill's message on the evening of December 6. As Mr. Hill ministered via video, the Holy Spirit ministered to me, reminding me of an experience I had at age fifteen. I had never spoken about it and hadn't even thought about it for almost thirty years.

In ninth grade at South Junior High in Hopkins, Minnesota, my social studies teacher gave the class a challenging assignment: an oral report. The Catholic grade school I attended had never required me to give an oral report. Now in public school, I faced my first opportunity to step in front of the class.

For the next week I studied and prepared. I practiced my report in front of the mirror until I felt ready. On my scheduled report day I headed to the front of the class when the teacher called my name. When I finished my report, I wasted no time returning to my seat. My relief was short-lived. "Therese," the teacher said, "come back up to the front."

I didn't want to obey his request, but because I had been taught to respect those in authority I slid out of my seat and headed to the front of the room. I faced the teacher, waiting for his next command.

"Turn around and face the class," he instructed.

Although I wanted to face the class about as much as I wanted the dentist to drill my teeth, I obeyed. Turning toward my classmates, I felt their piercing stare.

"I want you to lift both of your hands straight above your head and leave them there," he said.

I turned to face him. "Why?"

"*I said* lift your arms straight above your head and leave them there!" he repeated firmly.

My face reddened. That fall day I had worn a light gray turtleneck made of a nylon fabric. Because I had been so nervous while delivering my report I had perspired profusely.

Inching my hands above my head, I exposed two gigantic circles of underarm perspiration. My peers continued to stare at me with a haunting silence. In the deafening silence, my arms became heavy. After what seemed like an eternity, the teacher said, "Okay, you can be seated now." Then he continued with the class as if nothing had happened.

I slithered into my seat, humiliated, embarrassed, and ashamed. I wanted to shrivel up and fade into the woodwork. From that day forward, whenever I stood in front of people, the spirit of fear, intimidation, shame, and humiliation tormented me just as it had that day in junior high.

When the Ancient Paths Seminar video message ended, we broke into small groups for ministry time. After sharing my school experience with fellow believers, the facilitators prayed for me.

At that moment in prayer I forgave my ninth grade social studies teacher and released my shame, embarrassment, and humiliation at the feet of Jesus. I repented for any unforgiveness I may have carried, put my trust in God—and He set me free instantly.

"You'll *never* again experience this fear. You'll *never* again experience the humiliation and intimidation," the facilitator prayed. "In Jesus' name, you are free." And I was free indeed. The Most High God lifted a burden I had carried for over thirty years.

Since December 6, 2002, my day of deliverance from fear, I launch onto platforms with confidence, knowing the Lord is with me. He imparts to me the boldness of a lion to share His Word. Fear has *never* tormented me again.

Satan, the enemy of God, was focused on destroying God's plan for my life. Part of God's divine purpose for me is to speak in front of groups to bring hope and healing through Jesus Christ. My ninth grade experience was a scheme of the enemy to abort God's plan. God does not want us to be ignorant of the enemy's schemes and enables us to overcome them.

While driving my minivan from Spokane, Washington, to Post Falls, Idaho, to minister, God reminded me that He had freed me from the spirit of fear on December 6 to fulfill His prophetic Word brought through Archbishop Victor Oniugbo. Just as God said through the prophet, December 7, 2002, ministry began and has continued just as He said.

In addition to enjoying the privilege of authoring Extraordinary Miracles in the Lives of Ordinary People, *Therese is author of* Breaking Out *(Publish America),* Take Her Off the Pedestal *(pending), and co-author of* Miracles Still Happen *(Harrison House). Therese serves as a columnist and freelance writer for publications across the country. She is an inspirational speaker, passionately ministering hope and healing through Jesus Christ. Therese and her husband, Tom, live in Spokane, Washington with their two children, Emily and Joseph. Their son James is proudly serving his country in the US Army.*

17

MARIO

by Tom Blossom

And these signs will follow those who believe: in my name... they will lay hands on the sick, and they will recover.

MARK 16:17,18 NKJV

I met Mario while serving a seven-year prison sentence at the Airway Heights Correctional Facility in Spokane, Washington. Although I had the opportunity to be released after five years, I told the Lord that I wanted to be released on *His* time frame. I asked Him to make His plan clear to me, and since He hadn't given me a plan I was perfectly content to stay. A correctional officer once said, "You don't even see the fences, do you, Tom? You're more free than I am, aren't you?"

"My life is in God's hands," I told him. "Wherever He puts me, I'm free indeed."

Seeking a respite from the sweltering heat on a summer afternoon in June of 1997, three of my Christian brothers and I were playing cards in the prison day room. Unexpectedly, one of our group was "called out." When an inmate is called out, it means he has been prescheduled for an approved medical appointment, work assignment, or other reason.

"We can finish this later," I said.

"Need another player?" came a voice from behind me. Turning around to see who was speaking, I saw Mario for the first time. "That is, if I can sit in," he said. "Name's Mario."

"Yeah," said one of the men. "We'll play another game."

"Sure. Why not?" I said, welcoming Mario to the table.

Introductions were made and the cards dealt. While we continued playing, Mario shared part of his life story. He had just come from the medium security camp, an area for prisoners in the pre-release phase of their incarceration. Mario needed an operation because his lungs were slowly filling with fluid.

"Without this operation," he told us, "I'll drown...sitting right here."

We played cards until close to dinnertime, then the game broke up. With the looks of a member of a Mexican Mafia gang, I found Mario an interesting character. I was certain that his past must be quite a story—a colorful story!

I ran into Mario again on the smoking pad after dinner. "Hey, Amigo," he said, smiling.

Standing on the smoking pad, we shared our stories while enjoying the night air. At age fourteen Mario had come to America with his girlfriend in a car he had stolen. "Some time ago," he said. Mario was now fifty-three.

"I killed a man too," he continued. "Was self-defense, you know."

How many times, I thought to myself, *have I heard stories of a drug deal gone bad?*

"I've done fourteen years of a twenty-one year sentence," he said. "I get one-third off for good behavior. That means I'm almost done. I'm supposed to be released on December 11, but I got nowhere to go, no one to go to. And on top of that...I'm dying." The sadness of his dark brown eyes pierced my heart.

Stamping out his cigarette, he added, "Ain't life a bitch?" Our conversation ended abruptly. On the duty roster for breakfast, it was past my bedtime. Four o'clock in the morning came very early some days.

Back in my cell, I prayed before lying down. The Lord spoke to my spirit. *I want you to pray with Mario and lay hands on him that I might heal him.* I had not shared anything about the Lord with Mario, nor had I engaged him in any conversation about spiritual matters. Frankly, I thought perhaps I had misunderstood what I thought I had just heard.

After completing my work schedule the next day, I visited the day room to play cards. Again Mario came by and we played cards together until supper.

I attended a chapel service that evening, and shortly after retired to my cell. When I began to pray, again I sensed the Lord speaking to my spirit,

"I want you to pray with Mario and lay hands on him that I might heal him." Finishing my prayers, I lay down to sleep.

While leaving the kitchen the next afternoon, I noticed Mario sitting alone at a table. He smiled and waved. After acknowledging him, I walked back to my cell. As I closed the door, I again sensed God speaking to my spirit, "Pray with Mario." I walked back to Mario's table and sat down beside him.

"Mario," I said. "I know we've not talked of such things, but will you pray with me?"

The Mexican looked at me askance. "Pray with you?" he asked.

"Yes. You see, the Lord has asked that I lay hands on you so that He might heal your lungs. Do you mind?"

"Let me get this straight, amigo. You want me to pray with you. You gonna lay hands on me, and the good Lord, He's gonna heal my lungs?" Mario said. "Is that what you say?"

"Yes, Mario, He'll heal your lungs," I said with a faint doubt of my own.

"Sure, man. I'll pray with you. You go ahead. And, what you say, lay hands on me? Then the good Lord will heal my lungs."

It wasn't a long prayer, and as I finished praying Mario repeated, "Amen."

Angels didn't appear and lightning didn't flash. I looked at Mario and said, "It'll be okay."

In the following days Mario seemed upbeat, at least. Soon he was assigned to the kitchen and began working with us there. He started attending chapel with me as well. As our time together increased, so did a developing friendship.

Nearly a month passed from the time I had prayed with Mario and laid hands on him. Then one day he was called out for his medical. He had been excused from work the next morning, so I did not see him until late in the afternoon. When he spotted me, he called me over to the table where he was sitting. I could hear the excitement in his voice.

"Tommy," he beamed, "they couldn't find *anything* wrong with my lungs. Nothing, man. They even want to know why I'm there."

"Nothing?" I asked with amazement.

"That's right, man. *Nothing*. It's like there was never anything wrong with my lungs." Mario couldn't contain his enthusiasm.

"Praise God!" was all I could say.

"But, you know, man," he said in a serious low tone, "that night—you know, the night we prayed together and you laid hands on me?"

"Yes?"

"Well," he continued. "I never told you. But when you prayed, I felt something run through my body—like electricity. You know, a funny feeling. I thought I was sitting wrong or something."

Because the remarkable medical test results indicated that nothing appeared to be wrong with Mario's lungs any longer, Mario was called out for a second medical appointment. This time a CAT scan confirmed what God had already done. Mario said the CAT scan was perfectly normal, and his lungs were perfectly healthy.

Together Mario and I praised God for His wonderful promise of healing. We continued to share a deepening friendship. We spent our time working together, attending chapel, and playing cards.

The evening breezes were cooling out on the smoking pad, and the leaves were falling from the trees. Now October, an anxious Mario looked forward to his release. He came to me one evening requesting that we pray together for his release.

"Tommy," he said, "you know that I can be released on December 11."

"Yes, I know that."

"There's this problem, though," Mario continued. "You know I'm here on a violent crime charge. What that means is, I can't be released without an address. And I got nobody."

It was true. Mario had no money, no family, and no address that he could provide to enable him to be released.

"What I'm going to ask the Lord for," I told Mario, "is that you have a release address, a job, clothes, and the necessary funds for you to get out. I just can't mandate to God a time limit."

"Would you pray for me to have a good Christian wife too?" he begged.

"You don't ask for much, do you?" I laughed.

We spent much of that evening, and many others, praying for Mario.

There are no Christmas stockings "hung by the chimney with care" in prison. Had there been, Mario still would not have gotten his release. Nor did he receive it as a New Year's resolution. Valentine's Day did not see a new Christian wife or a release from prison. Both March 11 and April 11 came and went without his release. Finally, April 29, 1998, Mario received a release address.

The address was submitted to the prison system for approval. After that, all other answers to our prayers for Mario's release date came as well. Having spent more than fourteen years in prison, Mario's scheduled release was finally scheduled for May 11, 1998. The night of May 10, we spent praying for Mario, then we sent him on his way.

I received a letter from Mario two months after his release. He included a telephone number, so I called at the first opportunity. Hearing Mario's report, I wept.

"The Lord gave me a job," he told me. "I have my own apartment too. I go to church every Sunday just to thank Him. And…there's a real pretty lady there who smiles at me every time I'm there."

It was almost Christmas, December 23, to be exact, when I spoke to Mario again. He had been promoted to assistant food manager for a Safeway store. His pretty lady had become his wife only six days earlier.

Mario's final words to me were, "God has answered every prayer we prayed."

"Would you expect anything less of a Father who loves His children?" I asked.

When I talked to Mario in 2000 he was the assistant manager for a Safeway store in Wenatchee, Washington, and was enjoying God's blessings.

At over seventy, Tom's greatest pleasure comes from watching God renew the lives of homeless men. Having been incarcerated for seven years, he also watched God do the same within the confines of prison. Tom has been shot at, beaten, incarcerated twice, through six typhoons, earthquakes, tornados, hurricanes, and should have died five times due to health issues, yet he considers these light afflictions. Currently he lives in Spokane, Washington, where he ministers at the Union Gospel Mission and wherever God opens doors.

18

WITHOUT A DOUBT
by Art Pope

I tell you the truth, if anyone says to this mountain, 'Go, throw yourself into the sea,' and does not doubt in his heart but believes that what he says will happen, it will be done for him. Therefore I tell you, whatever you ask for in prayer, believe that you have received it, and it will be yours.

MARK 11:23,24

*F*resh out of high school in Petaluma, California, I started working in drywall construction, mainly in the finishing area. In 1974, at age thirty-five, I started experiencing problems with my right knee. Whenever I stepped down or up the steps of an entrance to a house while working construction, sharp pain shot through it. It felt as if a knife were stabbing from the inside out of my knee joint. The excruciating pain caused me to keel over and fall down. When I fell, I'd bend my knee slowly a few times, get back up, and proceed with my work.

The condition of my knee steadily worsened for more than six months. Also during this time in 1974 my wife, Olita, myself, and our five children relocated to Cloverdale, California, at Christmastime. My parents were pastoring a little church in Cloverdale named Church of God of Prophecy. They held prayer meetings at the parsonage in the garage on Wednesday nights.

The day before one Wednesday evening meeting, I was on a construction job site in Ukiah, California, with my father, Arthur C. Pope. He was also in the trade at the time. While on the job I stepped out and fell again. When the agonizing pain became unbearable, my father drove me to Cloverdale, where our family doctor examined my leg and took X-rays.

"Your knee is completely deteriorated," he said, while reviewing the X-ray. "You've abused it over the years with all of the side motion to run the equipment that you're working in the trade."

Then more bad news came. "It's going to be necessary to rebuild your knee with pins." The doctor explained that they don't perform this type of surgery in Cloverdale, but he would call a specialist in Ukiah and set up an appointment for me. He said, "You'll have to be off work from five to six months after surgery."

"There's no way with five children that I can afford to be off for five or six months," I told my father. "I have to return to work. I'll just have to work with a cast."

When I saw the surgeon, he said my kneecap was like fragments of an eggshell. The pain intensified when I bent the knee a certain way that allowed a fragment to turn at a right angle and hit a nerve. The cartilage and ligaments on the kneecap were damaged also. Surgery, he said, was expected to correct these issues.

That evening, only a few hours after my meeting with the doctor, I attended a prayer meeting in my father's garage. Because I had to work and carry on even though I was in pain, I wore an Ace bandage to get as much knee support as possible. Over the Ace bandage, I wore another elastic-type bandage in a padded, fitted form.

Because of the problems I was having with my leg, I couldn't bend my knee without feeling great discomfort. Keeping my leg straightened seemed least painful. When the pain continued increasing during the prayer meeting, I left the meeting and went into the living room so I could straighten my leg out on the couch to get some relief.

After I had stretched out on the couch for a few minutes, the prayer service ended. My father came into the living room with some of the church congregation who knew I had been suffering. "Would you like prayer for your leg?" he asked.

"Yes," I said, welcoming the prayer.

As they began to pray, I remembered when I had hurt my leg in a snow accident about eight years earlier. Going down a hill in a homemade toboggan, I hit a snow-covered tree stump, which sent me spinning in the air. When my leg landed in the snow, it got stuck in the snow while the rest of my body kept spinning. This resulted in painful torn ligaments.

After the toboggan accident I attended a Saturday evening revival meeting and received prayer. The pain completely left, and I returned home. The next morning I woke up and said, "I wonder what my leg is going to feel like now. I wonder if God healed me." I doubted my healing, and when I put my foot down and stood up, the pain stung so badly that I fell to the floor and couldn't get up. That day my leg was put in a cast.

Now I was about to ask God for healing again, and I knew better than to doubt. In my heart, I said, "Lord I want Your will."

The group prayed a short, simple prayer, and I felt a tingling sensation in my knee. I *knew* in my heart that something special was happening. I *knew* the Lord was working and knew a miracle was taking place. I stood up, bent my right leg two or three times with the bandages still on. I felt *no pain.* I took the bandages off and bent my leg freely two or three times. I still felt no pain. I told the saints, "I thank God that He healed me."

I got up and walked out where I could try walking up and down steps. After going up and down the steps with ease, I still felt no pain. "I've been healed!" I testified to the group. But it seemed as if they didn't have the faith to accept the miracle and were surprised when God healed me.

Later I thought how important it is to pray with belief. I knew we *wanted* to believe but wondered if we really *did* believe. Seeing the surprise at God's miracle, I realized I was seeing doubt.

The next morning before I got out of bed, I remembered again the first time the Lord had healed me and how I had doubted my healing.

My wife, Olita, said, "How's your leg?"

I said, "Olita, I *know* I have a new knee, so I *know* everything is fine." I knew, with no doubt, that God had healed me.

The next day back at the job site I would have the opportunity to prove it. A supply truck had arrived to deliver sheet rock to the house we worked on, but the truck couldn't make the steep, dirt incline to the house. So along with my coworkers I carried twelve-foot sheets in double packages of sheet rock up the hill and long driveway to the house—about one hundred feet.

We also had to carry the sheet rock into the house, requiring us to step up some temporary stairs of approximately thirty-six inches. By the time we had stacked about 150 double-package sheets in the house, journeyed back and forth up the steep hill, and climbed up and down the stairs, there was no question that I was healed. I felt absolutely no pain.

I never made another appointment to see the surgeon and never had knee surgery. In the months that followed my healing and to this day, I've *never* experienced pain in my right knee again. God gave me a new knee, and it's still new today!

For years after being healed by the hand of God, I had asked myself, "Why did the Lord give me a new knee? Why did He heal me?" I felt so undeserving of such a miracle. I never talked to anyone else about my feelings. Although I didn't understand why God healed me, I knew it was for His glory. Then about fifteen years after God healed my knee, our youngest son, Kimble, was pastoring a Church of God of Prophecy in Bakersfield, California. Because Olita and I were traveling through Bakersfield at the time, we had the opportunity to attend the Sunday morning service.

During his message Kimble said, "No one can ever convince me that God is not real because I saw Him heal my father." I knew then that part of the reason God healed me years earlier was to make Himself real to my son.

Art was born in Santa Rosa, California, and moved to various locations where his father accepted pastoral assignments. Although Art accepted Christ as a child, it wasn't until middle age that his faith became an abiding personal relationship with God through the Lord Jesus Christ. He and his wife, Olita, have been married for over forty-five years. They travel to oversee retirement facilities for a retirement management facility company. Art and Olita have three grown sons and two daughters.

19

MIRACLE TIMES TWO
by Carla Estes

Before I formed you in the womb I knew you, before you were born I set you apart; I appointed you as a prophet to the nations.

JEREMIAH 1:5

*O*n Monday, August 18, 2003, I waddled my way up to my obstetrician's fourth floor office with my husband, Kurt, for a routine appointment. Pregnant with twin girls, I was thirty-two weeks along, huge, miserably hot, and much too tired. Although the twin pregnancy had progressed well with relatively no complications, that day everything would change.

After running routine tests—blood pressure, urine sample, and weight gain— Dr. Julia Richards discovered that my blood pressure had risen and protein was present in my urine. Both were signs of a dangerous condition called pregnancy induced hypertension (PIH). Because the only cure for this condition was to deliver my babies, my doctor hospitalized me at Capital Medical Center in Olympia, Washington, that very same day. Kurt returned home to care for our five-year-old daughter, Emma Christine, and nineteen-month-old son, Benjamin Reilly.

That night the nursing staff gave me a shot to help the lungs of our unborn girls develop. Knowing delivery would come soon I felt a bit nervous, but I had read about having twins and knew they often arrived early and did fine.

My doctor had already decided that a Caesarean section would be the best option because I had delivered Benjamin by C-section. After calling home to tell my family to await the Caesarean date and time, I enjoyed my quiet rest at the hospital.

It was a great comfort when my pastor, Richard Peterson of Calvary Lutheran in Aberdeen, Washington, called to pray with me. Pastor Richard had been my pastor since I was six years old, had confirmed me, had married Kurt and me, and had baptized our children. Now he was interceding for our soon-to-be-born daughters. I asked God to cause the delivery to take place at exactly the right moment.

On Wednesday, August 20, the medical staff said I would be moved to Tacoma General Hospital where they were better equipped to handle complicated premature deliveries. After arriving that evening, I met the doctor on call. He said he preferred that Dr. Dashow—referred to as the best high-risk obstetrician—take charge of my case. Dr. Dashow was expected in the morning.

Seconds later I overheard the on-call doctor talking to the nurse. "I won't touch her with a ten-foot pole," he said. Hearing his words, panic overtook me.

The evening of August 20, the longest night of my life, I lay awake all night wondering what was to come. I knew something was wrong yet no one would say *what* was wrong. I started developing flu-like symptoms and a sore throat.

Because I couldn't sleep I surfed TV stations. Flipping through the channels, I kept coming back to the worship channel, feeling like I needed to be there to focus on God. I found comfort into the wee hours of the night, hearing the soothing music and watching nature scenes while Bible verses flashed on the screen. As Kurt slept peacefully on the chair next to me, I prayed for our girls and their safe arrival.

The sun rose early, a welcomed sign. I expected our girls to be born by scheduled C-section early in the day by the best of the best obstetricians. When Dr. Dashow came in around 9:00, he silently sat at the foot of my bed reading my chart and jotting notes down. The silence was deafening, and I felt like I couldn't breathe.

When Dr. Dashow finally closed my chart, he looked up at Kurt and me. "Things couldn't be much worse," he said bluntly. "It's the most severe case of PIH I've ever seen." He explained that my liver and kidneys were failing. I also experienced eyesight disturbances and was severely overweight. I had been gaining up to twelve pounds per day from water retention.

This condition caused two major complications in my case. First, because I had become so swollen, they couldn't insert an IV port anywhere. Looking down at my legs, now the same size from top to bottom, I couldn't see even one vein. The same issue was occurring in my arms. Secondly, scar tissue from my previous C-section had become severely swollen and formed a hard mass from water retention, something Dr. Dashow had never seen before. It felt like I had a twenty-pound bag of flour tied under my belly. He said I would die from infection if he tried to cut through the mass. Both complications ruled out a normal C-section delivery.

Dr. Dashow presented us with two options. First, he could perform a C-section using no pain medication except local anesthesia, cutting high on my uterus to avoid the mass. Pain medication could not be given because I couldn't get an IV, and I couldn't have anesthesia because I was sick. I felt choosing this option would result in me literally dying from the pain but would enable me to deliver two babies alive.

The second option was to allow me to go into natural labor and deliver vaginally. However, this option was risky too. Because my body wouldn't fully go into labor at this early date, my uterus would rupture, and I wouldn't be able to push the babies out through the hard tissue mass. Also, something might happen that would cause the second twin to be delivered incorrectly after the first. I felt choosing this option would result in a ruptured uterus and a real chance that I could die, not to mention that they may not be able to get both babies out alive. I could not make this decision, as all options ended in either my children or me dying.

My parents, Randy and Carol, and my sister Bonnie were brought in to hear the news. As tears rolled down our faces I told Dr. Dashow, "We'll do whatever you feel is best."

Dr. Dashow suggested that I try delivering vaginally. After leading my family to the waiting room, he encouraged them to pray. They contacted Calvary Lutheran's prayer chain who contacted many others to pray.

Alone in the delivery room Kurt and I cried and said our good-byes. I gave him messages for our two young children, Emma and Benjamin, and we held hands in silence. At that moment God graced me with an incredible peace, which enabled me to move forward with the labor process.

Every time I closed my eyes it seemed as if God gave me glimpses of my life in an elaborate slideshow, moments I will always treasure. I felt calm, with no fear of death. This divine peace enabled me to relax and let my body take over to handle the contractions rather than tensing up against them.

While I progressed slowly, Dr. Dashow was patient with my progress and allowed the natural process to take its time. After seventeen hours of labor the nurse checked me one last time and found I was still only at nine centimeters, as I had been for three hours. Dr. Dashow felt we needed to fall back on the C-section option, but before proceeding he decided to check me himself.

I believe Dr. Dashaw heard a whisper from God at that moment. He told me to go ahead and push, hoping I might be able to push "Baby A" through nine centimeters. When I pushed, she came right down. "She's doing it!" Dr. Dashow exclaimed. "Let's move her to the operating room and see what happens."

Being slowly wheeled down to the operating room, the pain became intense and although I felt the urge to push, I couldn't push. Her head was causing great pressure. On his way to the operating room, Dr. Dashow stopped at the waiting room to tell my family that he knew he could get Baby A out but wasn't sure about Baby B or me.

In the operating room I suffered extreme pain yet was determined to deliver our girls. The small room was filled with people: two teams of neonatal intensive care unit (NICU) nurses and doctors, one for each eight-week premature baby and a team to care for me.

After I pushed twice, out came our Chloe Rose. As they held her up I felt so blessed to see her. Dr. Dashow looked at me and said, "Okay, Carla, it's do or die time." Although my cervix had retracted to eight centimeters, he wasn't stopping. God had gotten us this far, and he believed He would take us all the way.

"Okay!" I said.

I pushed, but Dr. Dashow said it wasn't good enough.

Kurt held my hand. "Come on, Carla," he pleaded. "Please!" Hearing Kurt's words, I opened my eyes to meet his because I could feel our Ainsley Jane slip into the world.

My body became limp when I heard a nurse from behind my head ask if my uterus had ruptured. For the next thirty minutes I endured a thorough examination revealing no rupture—a genuine miracle. Dr. Dashow hugged me and said he couldn't believe it worked. "You're my hero," he said. But we both knew that God was our only Hero.

Although our miracle baby story could end here, the miracle continued. The girls were doing well, yet being eight weeks premature, a lengthy hospital stay was expected. The nurses encouraged us, hinting that we may only need to stay a couple of weeks. Overall, Chloe and Ainsley looked great, weighing a healthy five pounds three ounces and five pounds one ounce.

In the NICU the nurses said our daughters needed only one more test: a cranial ultrasound. I felt unsettled about this test and realized later it was a heavenly whisper reminding me to pray. Before the cranial ultrasound results were read the girls were released from the NICU and moved to the intermediate care nursery (ICN), a huge step in their recovery. Although their progress seemed to be going well, I still felt unsettled in my heart.

The ultrasound showed some abnormalities in both girls regarding the horn and ventricles of the brain, not necessarily abnormal with premature babies. But the next day while holding Chloe I noticed her eyes fluttering. I brought it to the attention of her nurse who said it was probably just Chloe's "little thing." By the next day Chloe's eye flutters turned into full-blown seizures. They called in a pediatric neurologist who ran additional tests.

After Dr. Swati Vora told us that Ainsley was fine, she delivered the devastating news that Chloe had an extremely rare brain disorder called hemimegalencephaly, a condition where the left side of her brain was formed incorrectly and larger than the right side.

Stunned at the blow, I hungered for the overwhelming sense of peace I had experienced during their delivery. That peace did not come. The news only got worse. One NICU doctor said Chloe would never hold her head up and would probably never smile.

I needed something else to focus on other than the negative medical reports, so I did the only thing I knew to do: be Chloe and Ainsley's mom. I made it my mission to start the grueling process of breastfeeding premature twins. When I wasn't breastfeeding or talking, I soaked deep in prayer.

They started Chloe on a drug called Phenobarbital, which did not control her seizures. Before we knew it she was on three medications to control seizures, and when the medications didn't work I prayed, "Please God, just stop the seizures!"

To my surprise I sensed God's answer, "Not yet. In My time." I didn't question God.

"Okay," I told God, "then give me strength to get through this."

We brought our babies home at five weeks old. Chloe was on round-the-clock medications but still seizing several times a day and in need of a home health nurse three times per week. I pumped breast milk every two hours to keep up my supply. We scheduled several appointments with specialists two hours away from our home and made numerous emergency room visits. When people ask how we survived this chaotic time, it seems obvious to me that God answered my prayer request for strength.

When Chloe was two months old her neurologist suggested an extreme drug therapy that could only be administered once in a lifetime. I gave Chloe daily steroid injections of ACTH for six weeks, a treatment known to eliminate infantile spasms, the type of seizures now dominating our days.

Although the first three weeks on the steroid freed Chloe from seizures, her blood pressure skyrocketed. Her home health nurse, Mary Sheldon, a treasured gift from God, caught the problem and sent us to Mary Bridge Children's Hospital. Chloe's blood pressure was 200/100, in an adult the equivalent to 300/200. We thank God for using Mary, our favorite nurse in the world, to intervene in this life-threatening situation.

Amazed that Chloe didn't suffer a stroke with such high blood pressure, the doctors told us to thank our lucky stars. We knew Whom to thank.

When the blood pressure was under control and we tapered her steroid dose, Chloe's seizures returned. After the treatment didn't work, our neurologist referred us for neurosurgery, specifically a hemispherectomy, the only treatment for hemimegalencephaly.

While I felt frustrated and emotionally drained God breathed another divine message. I sensed in my heart that after doctors learned key information from Chloe's medical condition, she would be fine. I clung to that thought as if it were a life preserver and shared it with my family to give them hope as well.

Immediately after receiving the referral from the neurologist we took Ainsley to a cardiologist appointment. A nurse we had never seen on previous trips to this cardiologist and never saw again asked where we planned to have Chloe's surgery. We told her we had assumed the surgery would be performed at Children's Hospital in Seattle.

"Children's Hospital may be a fine choice," she said, "but you should research surgeons and hospitals first, then interview and visit the top ones to find the absolute best." Her advice was invaluable beyond measure and changed our course of action and possibly our lives.

We headed home to begin our research. The surgery itself would entail disconnecting the left hemisphere of Chloe's brain from the brain stem and right hemisphere, surely a risky surgery. Blood loss during the procedure was the biggest risk. If the surgeon wasn't meticulous or touched the other hemisphere, Chloe could have a stroke, making it almost impossible to lead a normal life.

Choosing a surgeon was the second hardest decision of our lives. We interviewed two surgeons and prayerfully decided on Dr. Mathern at UCLA (University of California, Los Angeles). Our insurance at the time would not cover the total cost of the out-of-state surgery and hotel stay. Once again, God intervened and through my mom's group and church, the folks living in our community raised close to $40,000 to help us pay medical expenses.

Chloe, then five months old, was scheduled for surgery Friday, February 13, 2004. Interestingly enough, the month before surgery Chloe had fewer seizures than usual, making us question whether we made the right decision in having surgery this early in her life.

Kurt, the girls, and I travelled to Los Angeles a week before surgery to donate blood for Chloe's transfusion during surgery. We cherished every moment with our twin girls as the day of surgery drew closer. Although an emotion-filled week, still there were few seizures.

The night before surgery I stayed with Chloe while Kurt took Ainsley back to our hotel. Shortly after midnight Chloe suffered a severe seizure, then another one again at 2 A.M. It seemed as if God let me know we were making the right decision to proceed with surgery. As horrifying as the seizures were that night, it gave me the reassurance I needed.

I spent the rest of the early morning watching, holding, touching, and singing to Chloe. I told her how much we loved her, how God loved her, and assured her that I would always be her mommy. At 6 A.M. the medical staff got us ready to take Chloe to the operating room. Led by a stranger, I carried her sweet, naked little body down what seemed like miles of hallway to the operating room. Tears flowed but I didn't make a sound. These were moments I never want to experience again but will always revere.

Chloe and I sat in a corner as hospital staff arrived and set up for surgery. Memorizing Chloe's face, tears streamed down my cheeks. I felt angry for a moment, wanting the world to stop so I could run out of the hospital with my baby. Then I prayed that the medical staff would work miracles for Chloe.

After an unusually tall man took Chloe from me, I gave her one more kiss on her forehead, then walked out the door. While we sat in the waiting room, the nurse delivering periodic messages about surgery status chatted with us. It arose in conversation that Chloe and Ainsley were identical twins. The nurse thought for a moment, then said, "You mean you had identical twins and only one twin has this disorder?"

Although Ainsley did not have the MRI to confirm that she did not have hemimegalencephaly, she showed no symptoms. This could be ground-breaking information, the nurse said, as it was unknown whether hemimega-lencephaly is acquired during pregnancy or is a genetic condition. If we allowed Ainsley to have the MRI to confirm that she did not have this disorder, it would prove that hemimegalencephaly is not genetic but acquired during pregnancy. This key medical information could give researchers a direction to study.

After agreeing to the test we learned that Ainsley did not have hemimegalencephaly. This was a huge discovery in neuroscience at UCLA and confirmation of the message God had given me earlier.

Eighteen hours later Chloe laid in the ICU recovering. When we saw her that night she looked perfectly normal and angelic. Today Chloe continues to be seizure free. It has been more than two and a half years since the surgery. She is a living miracle for our community that was united in caring for her and praying for her. Chloe has accomplished significantly more than doctors originally thought she would—and we continue to expect miracles!

Carla was born in Portland, Oregon, and moved to Hoquiam, Washington, at age six. She received her master's degree in teaching from Saint Martins College in Lacy, Washington. Carla and Kurt, the love of her life, were married on St. Patrick's Day in 2001. Carla has been a teacher in the past and is now a full-time mom. Kurt is a wildland firefighter. They live in Aberdeen, Washington, with their four children.

20

TRUTH THROUGH ADVERSITY
by Arnie Suntag

That the trial of your faith, being much more precious than of gold that perisheth, though it be tried with fire, might be found unto praise and honour and glory at the appearing of Jesus Christ.

1 PETER 1:7 KJV

*M*any of us have come to recognize that life is not without trials. As Christians we often wonder why we ever have to experience a bad day. We go to church, read our Bibles, and serve as witnesses to others by professing our faith in Jesus Christ. But the trials still come.

We often find ourselves suffering with family discord, job stress, financial burdens, and, most frequently, problems with our health. Perhaps we are missing something. Perhaps some element of our faith escapes us. We *seem* to do all the *right* things as Christians, yet we often wind up teetering on the brink of discouragement and despair. How can we explain this apparent paradox?

The answer may be as humbling as the lesson Elijah learned after he hid in the cave from Jezebel. (1 Kings 19:9.) The Lord was not in the great wind. He was not in the earthquake. Nor was He in the fire. He was merely a *still, small voice*. The question we need to ponder is whether we are paying attention to the still, small voice or focusing all of our energies on the highly visible and ceremonial ways of professing our faith. In other words, do we have a heartfelt relationship with Jesus Christ, or are we merely mouthing the words? "These people draw near to Me with their mouth, and honor Me with their lips, but their heart is far from Me" (Mathew 15:8).

For me, the truth could not be more straightforward. For many years I professed to be a Christian, but I did not really *know* Jesus Christ. I attended church, read my Bible, and even witnessed to others. But in reality I was nothing more than what I call a "cardboard Christian."

As described in the Parable of the Sower (Mark 4:1-20), I was like the stony ground or ground filled with thorns. I professed to be faithful, but when trials came I often found myself bewildered and without hope. I learned—through great adversity and the boundless grace of a forgiving and merciful God—the meaning of true faith.

Faith is not about when to stand up or sit down in a pew, which songs to sing during a worship service, or how many verses of the Bible to read before bedtime. It is not about making gratuitous sacrifices or about ceremony or ritual. It is simply trusting and believing in God from the heart. "And you will seek Me and find Me, when you search for Me with all your heart" (Jeremiah 29:13). It was not until I faced the greatest trials of a lifetime that I came to understand this plain and simple truth.

By the year 2000 I had reached the pinnacle of my career. As a corporate executive I had achieved a comfortable six-figure income and expected to retire in two years with a couple of million dollars in the bank. I had a beautiful home in the forests of northern Arizona and expected to buy another one in Hawaii. I attended church when it was convenient, occasionally read my Bible, and proudly referred to myself as a Christian. But I did not know the Lord. I was about to get a wake-up call.

In October 2000 I was diagnosed with cancer that had spread throughout my body. The doctors asserted that I had only a short time to live, so I began to rewrite my will and make plans for an impending early death. I did not say much about it to anyone, but stubbornly continued in my corporate role determined not to die.

In order to confirm their prognosis, doctors ordered a liver biopsy. Everyone insisted that I submit to this test, but I refused and urged them to find another less invasive method. An MRI was ordered, and it revealed that the lesions on my liver were actually hemangioma, or blood-filled sacs, from an accident earlier in my life. Had the doctors been permitted to perform the needle biopsy, I would have bled to death.

Although this discovery rendered the earlier prognosis a bit too aggressive, it confirmed that I had a tumor of the left adrenal gland. It was later discovered that I also had a brain tumor. I gradually became disabled and stepped back from some of my routine executive responsibilities.

Ironically, however, I did not recognize that the Lord had kept me from an almost certain death on an operating table. I also did not know that my trials had only just begun.

As the year 2001 dragged on, I gradually became more disabled and my company began to feel the pinch of a recession. My disability benefits were stalled due to administrative red tape and I was no longer drawing a regular income. My dream of early retirement dwindled, as lines of credit burgeoned and debts mounted.

Determined not to lose my bid for financial freedom, I continued to negotiate major deals for my company even under the duress of severe illness. The most important opportunity to achieve my goal was embodied in a meeting scheduled for 9 A.M. on September 11 in the World Trade Center. Oddly enough, I did not initially know that the meeting had been scheduled for that particular date and time. I had asked my staff to arrange the meeting for either September 10 or 11 because I planned to leave New York on September 12. I was very enthusiastic about attending the meeting because of its potential benefits. But just a few days beforehand, I felt urged to cancel it—something I had never done in my entire career. Much to the amazement of my entire staff and all who knew me, I did exactly that. I asked them to cancel the meeting for me and flew back to Arizona to be with family.

As I watched the carnage on television in abject horror from my home in the forest, I did not fully recognize what had actually happened. It was not until the CEO and founder of my company called to express his amazement about my safety that the full reality of the situation became evident. He thought I was in the scheduled meeting and could not imagine how I managed to escape, given the fact that the meeting was right in the middle of the first impact zone.

"God must have really been looking after you," he said. Ironically, he is a professed atheist. Yet here I was, a professed Christian, not fully recognizing what the Lord had done to preserve my life.

Adding to the irony is the fact that, having grown up in New York where I watched the Twin Towers being built, I had never been in them. This meeting would have been my first visit. My brother-in-law, who was at the scene, ran as the first tower collapsed. Many people we knew died. My life was spared. Yet, the recognition of God's presence in my life still escaped me.

During 2002 my health and finances continued to deteriorate. Urged by the doctors to take some time to find relief from the stresses I had faced, I arranged a trip to Mainland China using the voluminous frequent flier miles and other non-cash perks I had accumulated from my years of corporate travel. During my extended tour, in a very remote part of the country where few people spoke English, I developed a serious respiratory problem and found myself in a medical facility poorly equipped to manage the severity of the illness.

Gasping for air and barely able to walk, I arranged emergency transport back to the United States and somehow managed to travel across Mainland China to Hong Kong to connect with my flight home. After I arrived back in the U.S. for treatment, my condition spontaneously began to stabilize and it appeared that I was out of danger.

The X-rays taken in China were compared to previous films on file. They revealed that the lung involvement was far worse than the time I had suffered with a severe case of pneumonia that left me hospitalized for two weeks in Phoenix in 1997. The doctors shook their heads and remarked that it was an absolute miracle I was able to make the long and arduous journey home.

I learned from my primary care physician, after reviewing X-rays nearly a year later, that I had been exposed to SARS. Certain abnormalities in my left lung led to the discovery. The real miracle of my journey back from China is that an accident in 1987 left me without a spleen, thereby compromising my immune system. Surviving an exposure to SARS under the circumstances, particularly after traveling thousands of miles to get home, defies medical precedent. Although I was thankful to overcome this ordeal, I still did not understand how miraculously the Lord was working in my life!

During the remainder of 2002, after arriving home from China and recovering from SARS, my overall condition continued to worsen. I developed advanced spinal stenosis and rotator cuff damage causing fatigue, an inability to concentrate, and severe pain and lack of mobility in my right arm. Each day I became more disabled.

After receiving very little income for nearly two years, my home stood in danger of foreclosure. Then, without warning, the largest forest fires in Arizona history broke out, threatening my home and the surrounding area. All alone at my home in the Tonto National Forest, I struggled to get important possessions packed up and ready to be moved to a storage unit as the national guard rolled into the area. Scarcely able to move at times because of the pain, frequently confused and walking into walls because of the brain tumor, I could barely choke back the tears while I toiled to save what little I had left in the world.

As I prepared to leave my home the nationally publicized fires that had burned nearly a half million acres of pristine forest were brought under control. The huge inferno came within mere miles of my home. But my home still stood, unscathed. I breathed an enormous sigh of relief, but by now my ability to cope had almost completely left me. I could not say that I knew the Lord, and I surely did not understand why I was suffering such great trials.

Finally the day of reckoning arrived. Taking an inventory of my life, I recognized that I had lost my career, my financial security, and my health. I was alone in a great big home in the forest, in severe pain, and could no longer think clearly. I did not know where the Lord was in the midst of all the turmoil.

My heart ached. I looked up at the rafters in my high living room ceiling, wondering how to make a good slipknot. I was determined to end it all. I walked outside to take one last look at the beautiful mountains and trees that the hand of the Almighty God had created. I simply could not go on.

As I gazed at the amazing scenery around me, a neighbor I had not seen in some time approached me and, with the most earnest and heartfelt expression, said, "I'm so sorry to hear about all the things you've been through. My heart goes out to you."

Moved by his expression of sympathy, I paused for a moment to ask how his family was doing. As tears welled up in his eyes, he said, "My daughter was murdered." He went on to tell me perhaps the most gruesome story I have ever heard in my life. Spontaneously, I began to minister to him. It was nothing short of a miracle. Here I was with my faith waning, reaching out to a brother in need and extolling the benefits of knowing Jesus Christ.

Having helped him to find comfort in God's presence, I returned to my living room and dropped on my knees to pray. With the deepest earnestness in my heart I tearfully blurted out, "Lord, thank You for giving me back my hope. Thank You for showing me that my life has a purpose."

From that moment on my life was transformed. I began fasting, praying, and intensely studying my Bible. I attended a Bible school sponsored by one of the local churches and became involved in ministry. Still facing challenges, I asked the Lord for desperately needed direction in my life.

While I realized that I had lost virtually all I had in this world, I also knew that I had gained everything. Despite the enormity of the challenges facing me, I felt happier than I had ever been.

I still had practical everyday matters to deal with. I was seriously ill. I had no income. I was alone. Then one day, after fasting for days and praying earnestly for a greater closeness with Jesus Christ, something incredible happened. As I sat on the edge of my bed praying, an overwhelming flash of bright light surrounded me, an experience I can scarcely describe. In a matter of moments I felt as though an enormous stone had been lifted from my shoulders. I suddenly knew that everything would be fine, but I did not know how. I have often thought of this extraordinary event as somehow akin to Paul's experience on the road to Damascus. (Acts 9:1-8.)

In the days afterward I was inspired to write a theological work on the last days. Barely able to care for myself, I worked on the book day and night knowing the Lord wanted me to finish it. Each day that I immersed myself in writing and prayer, I faced challenges. Small fires broke out around my home and smoke billowed into the windows, oftentimes making it impossible to work. On one occasion, a bat somehow got into my home and tried to attack me while I worked.

About one month into my monumental effort, I mysteriously developed an inguinal hernia, causing great pain and discomfort. When I sought a surgical opinion, I was told that the relatively simple surgery to repair the hernia could not be performed because of an inherent risk associated with the adrenal tumor. Because of concern that I could suffer a hypertensive crisis while under anesthesia and die, doctors urged me to consider a complex surgical procedure that would remove my adrenal gland prior to performing the hernia surgery.

The doctors insisted that each day I waited, I placed my life at risk. Convinced that the Lord wanted me to complete the book, I continued undaunted for nearly five months, trusting that I would survive. During that time, the challenges I had previously faced each day remarkably ceased. Much to the amazement of those who knew me at the time, my electricity and telephone service remained intact and my home was not taken from me, despite the fact that I was unable to pay any of my bills. To this day, I cannot fully explain the incredible circumstances and events I witnessed during the writing of this theological work.

Toward the end of 2003 I completed the book and my life began to change radically. Funds that had been owed to me by the company I had worked for began to pour in, enabling me to start paying my bills again.

The Lord brought Susan, a special and most wonderful woman into my life—one who loves Jesus Christ as I do. We were married and began building a ministry together. Through changes in our lifestyle and our diets, guided by Scripture and prayer, the effects of the devastating medical problems I struggled with began to reverse. The tumors began to shrink. I began to speak at churches around the country about my incredible experiences in the Lord. But I still had a long way to go.

After considering various medical needs, we came to the conclusion that Hawaii would be the best place to live because of the moisture, sun, and availability of fresh produce. Lacking the financial wherewithal to make such a move, we placed the matter completely in the Lord's hands.

On a visit to Hawaii in October 2004 we happened upon a small rural community deep in the rainforest. Susan, a special education teacher, noticed a small school as we drove through the area. Even though it was late on a Friday afternoon, we felt impressed to walk around the campus.

Not expecting anyone to be there, we entered the administration area just out of curiosity.

As we walked toward the principal's office, we were amazed at what we found. The principal and assistant principal were seated together in the office *praying* for a special education teacher! We were all stunned by what could only be described as divine providence. Susan was offered a position, which opened the door to making a move that would otherwise have seemed impossible.

We still faced the challenge of finances and finding a place to live. Upon learning that affordable housing of any kind is difficult to find in Hawaii, we engaged in what can only be described as a complete leap of faith. The area in which we would be living had virtually no available housing. We shipped our van with the belief that we may wind up having to live in it.

Amazingly, the very day we arrived on the island two rentals opened up and we were guided to a place right on the ocean. When friends in the area have asked us how we managed to find such a place, our answer has always been that it was the Lord's hand. For those who know the area, it is a miracle that we found a place at all, much less the special place to which the Lord surely brought us.

In the past two years Susan and I have witnessed miracles in our lives of unprecedented magnitude. The greatest blessing of all, however, has been the amount of healing we have experienced. I am now substantially recovered from illnesses that, according to the doctors, should have taken my life two years ago. Our days are filled with the joy of Jesus Christ as we preach the Word wherever we go. Through our ministry we provide outreach services to the homeless and to victims of domestic violence. We are reaching many with the truth of Jesus Christ through studies and evangelism efforts. We may not own much in the way of material possessions, but we are genuinely satisfied and deeply enriched by all the Lord has graciously given us.

Though it was not an easy road to get to where we are today, we will always be thankful that the Lord allowed us the privilege of learning to rely exclusively on Him. I will never regret the trials I faced in my life, knowing now that they happened for a reason and, as a result, I have matured in Christ. It is often difficult for us, as frail human beings, to understand why we must suffer adversity in our lives. If only we can learn to recognize that, no matter what happens in this world, "we know that *all* things work together for good to those who love God, to those who are the called according to his purpose" (Romans 8:28).

Many of us have had *valley experiences* in our lives, that is, trials as described vividly by the 23rd Psalm, "Yea, though I walk through the valley of the shadow of death, I shall fear no evil for thou art with me." Indeed, the Lord is always with us. But sometimes He allows adversity so we will discover how to rely completely on Him. Others may disappoint us at times, but He will never let us down.

Arnie Suntag is a former executive for a global software company who left the corporate world after twenty-eight years to preach the gospel. Based on his book, **The Rational Christian,** *he founded a ministry dedicated to offering seminars on the end times, promoting community Bible studies, and providing assistance to the homeless and victims of domestic violence. Arnie has shared his testimony and message of hope at churches nationwide and on television shows such as* **Praise the Lord** *(Trinity Broadcasting Network). He and his wife, Susan, live in a remote area of Hawaii where they write their theological works and music.*

21

⁓⁓⁓

HONORING MY MOTHER: SOMETIMES IT TAKES AN ARMY

by Jan Coates

*Honor your father and your mother, so that you may live long in
the land the Lord your God is giving you.*

EXODUS 20:12

*D*riving out on the narrow, dark parking garage ramp, my eyes
slowly adjusted from the unlighted garage to the stark white, snow-filled
street of downtown Kansas City. I drove up to the cashier's window and
handed the clerk my parking ticket and money.

"Ten points if you hit the bag lady," Mike, my boss, teased as he leaned
forward in the passenger seat.

Distracted by the inability to focus my eyes, I asked, "What bag lady?"

"That one. Look, Jan, right in front of you," Mike said.

The clerk handed me my change. Tired after long client meetings, I
ignored Mike, hit the gas pedal momentarily, and then came to an abrupt stop.

My stomach lurched. I couldn't take my eyes off the bag lady just three
feet from my car. She was bundled up and wore a heavy tattered coat, two
brightly colored hats, and a scarf draped around her neck and face. Each
hand was protected from the blizzard-like weather with mismatched
woolen mittens, and held tightly in each hand was an over-stuffed black
plastic trash bag.

Fortunately I hadn't hit her. I sat frozen to my seat. My trembling
hands gripped the steering wheel and perspiration beaded on my forehead.
Ducking my head, I thought, *Lord, please don't let her see me.* I recognized
the black trash bags; she took them with her everywhere. The coat was a
bit more worn than I remembered, and the odd mittens made an interesting addition to her wardrobe.

The moment I peered through the hats and scarf and saw her piercing blue eyes, I knew it was my mother.

Oh Lord, I cried out silently in my heart, *I almost ran over my mother. Why didn't I get out of the car to see if she was all right? Why did I continue to hide from her? Why couldn't I tell my boss who it was? What was different about her?*

For as long as I could remember, my mother suffered from paranoid schizophrenia, alcoholism, and prescription drug addiction. Mental institutions, tranquilizers, and shock treatments coupled with the perils of drug and alcohol abuse made her life—and mine—a living hell. She was raised in a Christian environment during the 1920s depression. She married at age sixteen and had her first child by seventeen, which triggered an early onset of her mental illness.

Based on past experiences, I lived in fear of what my mother might do. She was unpredictable and often violent. *Why didn't she smack my car with her fists and bags as I almost ran her over,* I wondered? Interestingly, she kept walking as if the mishap didn't happen—how unlike her.

I kept my mother's identity to myself and drove Mike to his car. Once alone in my car, I felt consumed with guilt and a sense of urgency to do something for my mother. I felt helpless, then James 1:28 came to mind with words of love to reach out and help the homeless and loveless in their plight. I then prayed, "Yes, Lord, I must care for my mother in her troubles." *I can't keep her from roaming the streets during a blizzard, but I can help her stay warm,* I thought to myself.

I stopped by a rural farm supply store located in the stockyard district and bought her warm snow boots and ski gloves. I drove to a nearby grocery store and purchased various food items. "Lord, don't let her throw these things in her plastic bags and carry them around. Help me help my mother," I prayed.

Knocking on her downtown apartment door, I said, "Mom, it's me, your daughter Jan. Open the door."

"Jan, come in," Mom said. "I was hoping you would come visit me."

I looked around her government-subsidized apartment, holding back the tears inside me. As a child I prayed for years for a sober mother, free from drugs. When I married and became a mother, I also prayed Mom would know a peace within that comes from knowing Jesus. But I guess, at some point, I gave up hope.

"Here, Mom. I brought you some goodies," I said. "You may have to move the beer out of the refrigerator, though, to make room for food."

"No beer, Jan. I'm not allowed to drink it anymore. It's bad for me," Mom said. "I threw out all the pills. They were making me sick."

"It's okay, Mom. You're over sixty years old. You don't have to tell me stories," I said.

"I'm not telling you stories," she said. "I have a job. I go to work. I go to Bible study. This summer I'm going to camp. Come with me tonight for dinner, you'll see."

I'll call her bluff, I thought, saying, "Okay, Mom. What time?"

"Oh, we're going to be late," she said, rushing around getting her winter gear together. "We need to leave now."

Mom made up some pretty big whoppers, and she was prone to sudden mood swings. I wasn't sure I believed a thing she said. I skeptically agreed to drive and accompany her.

Inside the car, I said, "Mom, tell me where to turn, okay?"

"Just keep going straight. Turn right at the next street, and park on the corner. Oh, that's it. We're here," she said, pointing to a weathered building.

"But Mom," I said, "this is The Salvation Army."

"Come on, I'll introduce you," she said. "I can't wait for all my friends to meet you. I've told them all about my daughter, the certified public accountant."

"Mom, you didn't? I work for a computer company," I said.

"Oh well," she said, "you know how I get things mixed up." She smiled, then gestured toward of group of people, some oddly dressed and others in military uniforms, standing around talking.

"Everyone, this is my daughter," she said. "She's an important executive at an accounting firm."

"So nice to meet you. Thank you for opening your doors to my mother," I said.

As I enjoyed dinner with Mom and her Salvation Army friends, I reflected on the reality of the situation unfolding before me—I gave up hope, but the Lord didn't.

I felt the unconditional love for Mom, others, and me as I sat next to the saints of The Salvation Army. Mom, sitting to my right, elbowed me to make sure I listened and watched. She smiled real big and hummed, "And when the saints go marching in." Right before my very eyes, I saw peace in my mother's heart for the first time, a peace that passes understanding—a peace I never felt she would know.

The events of the day began to make sense. No wonder she didn't hit my car with her fists when I almost ran her over. No wonder she had given up the alcohol and drugs. My mother had received a new life in Christ Jesus through the works of The Salvation Army.

It took the Army to do what dozens of doctors couldn't—heal and love my mother through the power of Christ Jesus. Thanks to The Salvation Army, Mom lived in peace the last ten years of her life. She loved being a soldier for Christ. She went to every Bible study, rang the bells at Christmas and other times, and learned to help and love others. The Army fed her nutritious food for her body and the Word of God to nourish her soul.

Thank you, Salvation Army, for providing new life to my mother, Soldier Bertha Gower, through Christ Jesus. I know for certain she's in heaven. I thank the Lord and the Army for the miraculous wonders in my mother's last years.

Sometimes it takes an Army, but honor my mother I do.

Jan Coates is the author of Set Free: God's Healing Power for Abuse Survivors, *(Bethany House, June 2005). She is currently working on several books to share God's healing with the broken and lost. Jan has worked in sales, marketing, and creative writing for more than twenty-five years. She is a speaker, has appeared on television and radio, and owned her own sales and marketing consulting business. As a teen full of shame and guilt from child abuse, she turned her back on her Christian faith. Then in 1982 a drunk driver killed her only child. Jan rededicated her life to Jesus on Easter Sunday 1983. Today Jan and her husband are the parents of two teenagers who were adopted as babies. She and her family live in College Station, Texas.*

* Various versions of "Sometimes It Takes an Army" have been published in *Faith & Friends,* November 2004, *The Salvation Army War Cry,* May 8, 2004, and www.christianity.ca/faith/adventures/2005/07.000.html.

22

GAY NO WAY

by Steve Bennett

Therefore, if anyone is in Christ, he is a new creation; the old has gone, the new has come!

2 CORINTHIANS 5:17

*F*or years I believed the lie that I was born gay. My gay friends and society told me that my homosexuality was unchangeable, just as one's height or skin color. I was told that because God made me this way, I just needed to accept the hand I was dealt. I tried to accept this message, yet deep inside my heart I knew something was wrong with me. *Desperately wrong.*

I had always felt different from the other boys. Other boys were athletic. I was more sensitive and interested in the arts. Other boys felt like a threat to me. They were masculine and I wasn't. I wished I had what they had and wanted it more than anything. They rejected me and made fun of me from the beginning. The hurtful name-calling, bullying, mocking, and teasing were unbearable.

I wanted to fit in and be "one of the guys" so I tried playing several sports, but it just wasn't me. I hung around with girls, as it felt safer. In my teen years I tried dating girls, yet it seemed my natural sexual desire was for other men. Although I never chose to feel this way, I couldn't seem to help it. I continued the charade until eventually I couldn't take it any longer.

Away from my home, family, and friends in the fall of 1981, as a freshman at a New York art school, I engaged in a homosexual encounter with another student. This launched me into a decision to be who I "really" was. Acting on the feelings I had carried throughout my childhood and teen years plummeted me into the deep, dark world of homosexuality.

In a matter of days I "came out" as a gay man. Within two months, depressed and confused, I dropped out of college and returned home to my family in Connecticut.

Now openly gay, I felt ready to conquer the world. The fear of my family and friends finding out about my homosexuality was over. They may not have been pleased with my sexual preference, but after all, this was my life—not theirs. I was sick of living my life for others. I decided that from now on, it was going to be all about me.

When I learned that many of my friends from the past had also "come out," we started frequenting the gay bars together. I lived for the nightlife. I drank heavily, started using cocaine, and became very promiscuous. I also developed bulimia.

When my drug addiction worsened, I became a cocaine dealer to support my habit. I lost my art business to drugs and lost my dignity to a perverse, decrepit lifestyle that I couldn't break free from. While active in the homosexual lifestyle for eleven years, I had more than one hundred homosexual partners—many of whom are dead today from AIDS.

I deteriorated morally, mentally, and physically. In the winter of 1987, after a three-day cocaine and alcohol binge, I became desperate for help. After staying up all night and running out of cocaine, I looked in the mirror and was shocked at my reflection. Cocaine abuse and years of bulimia left a six feet tall, 135-pound living skeleton staring back at me.

Sobbing, I ran to a payphone on the street corner to call for help. After admitting myself into a drug rehabilitation program, I began my recovery as an inpatient for three months at a nearby facility. God had heard my cry.

Within a few months I was alcohol and drug free. Now delivered from bulimia, I had gained about twenty-five pounds and felt great physically. However, my dark, secret past remained hidden inside of me. I didn't know what to do about my homosexuality. I knew homosexuality was wrong, yet I could only try to suppress it.

I wanted to share my life with someone more than anything. The one-night stands and short-lived gay flings were unsatisfying and left me only more depressed. I had a few relationships that I thought would last, but as is common with most gay relationships, they didn't.

At last in 1989 I met and fell in love with a man who was going to be my partner for life. We were together from the first night and lived our storybook gay romance for the next three years. I believed I had finally found true happiness with the man of my dreams. I thought I had it all: a homosexual lifestyle and love without drugs, alcohol, or bulimia; a great job; a beautiful home; and good homosexual friends. I even attended church faithfully every week.

One day everything changed with a knock on our apartment door. Cathy, a friend I hadn't seen in years, stood at my door with a Bible in hand. She told me she had become a Christian when she asked Jesus Christ into her heart. Cathy claimed she was born again and that Jesus had changed her life. Knowing I was gay, she asked if she could come in to talk to me about her new life in Christ and to discuss what God says about homosexuality. Reluctantly, I agreed.

For the next hour and a half, she showed me in the Bible how homosexuality was an abomination and grievous sin in God's eyes (Leviticus 18:22, Leviticus 20:13), how the homosexual would not inherit the kingdom of God because of their sin (1 Corinthians 6:9-10, Galatians 5:19-21), and how the person who chose homosexuality over redemption in Jesus Christ would suffer eternal damnation, separated from God forever (John 3:18-20, Romans 6:23, Hebrews 9:27, Revelation 20:13-14).

Cathy showed me that God did not make anyone gay and that clearly no one was born gay. Most amazingly, she showed me how homosexuals could change through a personal relationship with Jesus Christ—completely change!

Although angry with Cathy for seeming intolerant, hate-filled, and bigoted, deep in my heart I knew she cared about me and was speaking the truth in love. And I saw God's view of my homosexuality in the Bible—clearly printed in black and white. It was not Cathy's opinion, but God's Word. My anger was not directed at her, but at God.

When Cathy asked if I would pray with her to receive Jesus Christ, I declined. She gave me a Bible and left our home, leaving me numb, confused, mad, and very troubled.

For the next year and a half I read the Bible at night while my partner lay in bed next to me. The more I read God's Word, I saw my homosexuality as sin and myself as a sinner before a holy God. Anytime my partner and I shared intimacy, I found myself on the bathroom floor praying for forgiveness to a God I didn't even know. He was seeking my heart.

In 1991 I knew God was tugging on my heartstrings. I left my partner, my job, and my family and headed to a homosexual subculture in Provincetown, Massachusetts, to live for the summer. I wanted to see if I could reconcile the pull I felt between homosexuality and Christianity. I had to learn if I had to choose one over the other, or if, in God's eyes, I could practice both at the same time.

That summer God opened my eyes to the truth and to the perverseness of the homosexual lifestyle. I witnessed, in full swing, transsexuals, transvestites, sadomasochists, and men and women taking part in sexual acts one would never even imagine. After five months in Provincetown, I nevertheless returned home to my partner and asked him to forgive me for leaving him. I told him I was sorry and assured him I planned to put this Christian business aside.

Four months later, while wrapping Christmas presents, I came across a Christian station while flipping through radio channels. When I heard the lyrics "men marching for their right to sin," I knew the song was talking about me. Although I had put God on the back burner, He was still chasing after me. On New Year's Eve I attended a homosexual party with my partner. For the first time in my life, I felt dirty. I hated myself and hated my lifestyle. Yet, I still couldn't break free.

I called my friend Cathy and told her I was going to move back to Provincetown to give myself completely to the homosexual lifestyle. I felt as if I had lost my soul. Yet when I cried out for help by calling her, Jesus Christ stepped in to draw the line in the sand. Cathy read to me from the book of Romans in the Bible. "God will call you," she said. "But if He keeps calling you, and you hear yet harden your heart, it may come to a point where you will become a reprobate in His sight, and He will give you completely over to your sin and allow you to believe the lie. At that point, according to the Bible, you have basically sealed your destiny away from Him forever." (Romans 1:15-32.)

That possibility scared me so much that I asked her what I needed to do to avoid that demise. "You need to pray and ask Jesus to deliver you from homosexuality," Cathy said. "You need to ask Him to forgive you for your sins, and invite Him to come into your heart and live as Lord and Savior." Cathy said I needed to give Jesus control of my life.

As we prayed on the telephone, something powerful happened. I physically felt the peace of God come upon me. That day in January of 1992, when I asked Jesus to come into my heart, He set me free. According to the Bible I was born again and made a new creature in Christ. I repented of my sin and completely surrendered my life to the Lord.

Within days I made one of the hardest decisions I had ever made and left the man I deeply loved for another Man—Jesus Christ. A new chapter in my life began as a Christian, a child of the living God. Yet two months after accepting Jesus Christ as my Savior, I knew in my heart that I still had to deal with the root cause of my homosexuality in order to move forward in my life. For me, the root cause was a broken relationship with my father.

For years I desired my father's love more than anything. I knew that just as Jesus had forgiven me for all of my sins—past, present, and future—I had to extend forgiveness to my father. After confronting him, pouring out my heart, and really talking with him for the first time, our broken relationship found reconciliation. Extending forgiveness, the chains that had bound me for years were unshackled.

My father and I now enjoy a close relationship. I love Dad and know he loves me. For years I had searched in vain for the love of my father in the arms of other men. Today, the search is over because I have the real love of my father.

Within a year of giving my life to the Lord, I became engaged to Irene, a beautiful Christian woman. Irene knew me as a homosexual and had been praying for me for years. We were married on June 13, 1993, and continue to be happily married. God blessed us with two other miracles, my beautiful, five-year-old daughter, Chloe Catherine, and a three-year-old son, Blake Stephen, who was born on Chloe's birthday. Chloe's middle name is Catherine, in honor of my friend Cathy who refused to give up on me. God used Cathy, His vessel, to change my destiny forever.

My story is a nightmare turned fairy tale. I no longer struggle with homosexual thoughts, feelings, or actions. I am free because of Jesus Christ and His love for me. I am a heterosexual man through and through, the way God created me. Through Jesus Christ, I was able to walk away from and abandon a life of loneliness, sadness, pain, and sin.

Jesus is the answer for all of our needs.

With God, *nothing* is impossible. I believe in miracles because I've seen a soul set free. That lost soul was *me*.

Stephen Bennett is a Christian song writer and recording artist whose music can be heard nationally on Christian radio. Stephen, his family, and ministry team travel across the country sharing his music, message, and life-changing story. His story and music have touched the hearts of millions worldwide, offering a message of hope and love to those struggling with homosexuality as well as to their family and friends. Stephen, his wife, Irene, and their children, Blake and Chloe, live in Huntington, Connecticut.

23

POINT MAN DOWN
by Roger Helle

'For I know the plans I have for you' declares the Lord. 'Plans to prosper you and not to harm you. Plans to give you hope and a future. Then you will call upon me and come and pray to me, and I will listen to you. You will seek me and find me when you seek me with all your heart.'

JEREMIAH 29:11 NIV

I grew up with alcoholic parents in Toledo, Ohio. When I was four years old Dad walked out on Mom, leaving her to care for me, my identical twin brother, Ron, and my four-month-old baby brother. Mom, still an alcoholic, had no ADC (Aid to Dependent Children), no welfare, and no way to care for us.

One day while Ron and I played on the living room floor, Mom slipped into the back bedroom, packed a couple of suitcases, took my baby brother out of his crib, and walked out the door. Although neighbors were accustomed to seeing Mom and Dad leave us alone while they went out drinking, that night our parents didn't return and the neighbors called state officials.

Officials arrived at the house and transported us to a state orphanage before my grandparents could get there. Although I remember little about the orphanage, I knew I didn't like it. After living there for six months, our grandparents gained custody of Ron and me. At age four, nothing could have been neater to us than living with Grandma and Grandpa.

Eighteen months after we left the orphanage, two years after Mom walked out, one day Ron and I found Mom having coffee with Grandma in the kitchen when we returned from school. I was glad to see her again, and we went to live with her.

Mom started dating a gentleman and shortly after they married. But life was still tough. She was still an alcoholic, and my stepdad was a workaholic. Dad rose early in the morning and left to work in a factory before we got up for school. When Ron and I returned from school, we'd see him eat a quick bite, then leave again to work another job. I grew up with a dad I never knew. Mom didn't drink until Dad left for work at night. Then she'd sit in the kitchen and drink until after Ron and I went to bed.

Because Ron and I were identical twins, only God could tell us apart—and Mom when she wasn't drinking. Something about me or my personality, however, reminded Mom of my biological father.

One night at age seven, I walked through the kitchen while Mom sat at the table drinking. She looked up, pointed her finger at me, and said, "You know something, Rog, you're never going to amount to anything. You're going to be a bum just like your real dad."

Although I didn't remember much about my biological father, I remembered the drinking and the beatings. I didn't want to be like him. Even as a seven-year-old kid, I knew Mom didn't really mean what she said. I knew it was the alcohol talking. Yet, I heard those words week after week after month after year until I graduated from high school.

A couple of months before graduation, while my brother and I were downtown, I said, "Ron, let's join the Marine Corps." When Ron agreed, we headed to the Marine Corps recruiting office. There I saw my favorite poster with the guy in dress blues and a sign above that said: *The Marines are looking for a few good men.*

We joined the United States Marine Corps and left for boot camp immediately following high school graduation. Although a shock to my system, I had found what I was looking for. Mentally and physically the Marine Corps was the toughest thing I had ever done in my life.

After basic training every marine is first and foremost an infantryman. Regardless of his planned occupational skill, he first must go through infantry training. In 1965, while at infantry training, I volunteered for Vietnam. I didn't know at the time that everybody in the Marine Corps was going to Vietnam. At eighteen I thought I knew what combat was all about. Growing up, I had seen John Wayne in *The Sands of Iwo Jima* three times! I also watched Vic Morrow every Tuesday night on *Combat*.

In late November 1965 my battalion shipped out and arrived in Vietnam. When my battalion left, I knew the war would be over soon because the Marines had landed. I felt like we were prepared and well trained. *Nothing* could have prepared me for Vietnam. *Nothing* prepared me for the first baptism of fire in early January 1966 when my company of 219 marines walked into a 650-man Viet Cong ambush.

In one 45-minute firefight, my company of 219 was reduced to only 78 men who had not been killed or wounded. When the enemy caught us in the open field and opened fire, my platoon sergeant, a Korean veteran, was standing about five feet away from me. A 51-caliber machine gun round hit him in the top of his head and literally took the top of his head off. As I threw myself to the ground, out of the corner of my eye I saw another 51-caliber round hit my best friend Danny in the chest, killing him instantly.

As I lay on the ground in the field, I could hear men screaming all around me and then dying. I shot at an enemy I couldn't see. When they gave the command to assault the tree line, I ran toward a jungle that I knew I'd never make it to. But somehow when that 45-minute battle was over, I was still alive.

I was assigned burial detail. Even as a grown man I cannot describe what it was like for an eighteen-year-old kid to walk to where Danny fell and see him lying dead in grass knee high. His eyes and mouth were open; his face already gray in death. I had never seen anybody die. After putting Danny's body in a body bag and the helicopter lifted off the ground, something died inside of me.

When my unit was temporarily disbanded, I volunteered for a Marine Corps pacification program where they sent squads of Marines to live in villages away from the main bases. Vietnam was different than WWII and Korea with the exception of the island fighting in the pacific: It was guerrilla warfare. The psychology of guerrilla warfare is that the enemy waits to let you find him when it's to his advantage. We had to take guerrilla warfare to their backyard.

I became a point man, whose job is to take a patrol out, try to avoid ambushes and booby traps, find the enemy, kill him, and return the men back to safety. I became good at being a point man, walking point at every patrol—morning, afternoon, and night. I knew the area we lived in and the villages we patrolled like the back of my hand.

Early 1966, a new squad leader arrived in Vietnam on his first tour. That afternoon I briefed this new corporal, explaining our mission for that night. Instead of letting me walk point that night, the new corporal walked point—down a trail he had never been. He led a thirteen-man Marine patrol into a sixty-five-man Viet Cong ambush. When the firing ended, one eighteen-year-old kid escaped that ambush alive. And that one kid carried the guilt of surviving for twenty-three years. That one kid was me.

I served two back-to-back tours in Vietnam and was wounded twice. We had a morbid sense of humor in combat, kidding about the day we would return to the world we called America, the land of the big PX (Post Exchange). Although we kidded, I believed that day would never come for me. I believed it was just a matter of time—a matter of one patrol, one trip wire, or one undetected ambush—before I was killed.

At 2:00 A.M. in the spring of 1967, while on a fire support base just south of the DMZ, four hundred North Vietnamese sappers hit our perimeter. They were wired up and shot up with morphine to dull the impact of wounds they might receive, so for four hours we were engaged in hand-to-hand combat, back and forth across that little perimeter. At dawn the few NVA survivors of that battalion began to withdraw. Dead bodies of Marines and North Vietnamese soldiers were strewn across that little perimeter.

After that battle I was told to get my gear. I was put on a helicopter, sent to DaNang, and boarded a plane to Okinawa. Within forty-eight hours of being involved in hand-to-hand combat, fighting for my life, I was in my living room in Ohio, back home with family and friends who cared about me.

Most soldiers in Vietnam tried to avoid getting close to anyone because when friends died, it brought great grief and pain. Grieving could result in getting yourself or somebody else killed. So instead, we stuffed our feelings down inside. When I arrived home in 1967, feeling I was now safe, I wanted to talk about many things. But at that time America had changed from the country I had known when I enlisted in 1965.

For two years we watched Vietnam every night on television. Unfortunately, the media brought a distorted picture into our living rooms.

By 1967 most of America had become embarrassed by the war in Vietnam. The media gave great visibility to a very small minority. These groups were not only embarrassed about the war, they were outright angry.

My family said, "Rog, we're glad you're okay, we're glad you made it home, we're glad you're safe, but this Vietnam thing—it's a little awkward, a little embarrassing. Let's just not talk about it; let's just pretend like it didn't happen and get on with our lives." In 1967 I wanted to forget and wanted to get on with my life, but there was one problem. Every time I closed my eyes at night, I remembered Vietnam all over again.

I served as a drill instructor at Paris Island, South Carolina, for a year and a half, and then became a CID investigator (Criminal Investigator Division) at the Marine Corps Supply Center in Albany, Georgia. Then in 1970 I volunteered to return to Vietnam. For many years, people asked me why I volunteered to go back a third time. They'd say, "You've already been wounded twice."

I would just nervously laugh and say, "I'm a Marine and we just ain't too smart."

By 1970 America had changed so dramatically that I didn't recognize it. When I wore my uniform, some peace protester wanted to kill me for the cause of peace. Or when somebody I had just met found out that I had been in Vietnam, suddenly instead of my name being Roger, it was "baby killer" or "murderer." Yet, I knew I had not done anything wrong.

The U.S. was not my home anymore. I felt more needed and accepted twelve thousand miles from home in a malaria-ridden, stinking, leach-infested rice patty or mosquito-infested jungle than I did in my own country. Survivor's guilt also drove me back to Vietnam. As a young man, I felt guilty because I was alive when men better than me had not returned.

When I volunteered to return to Vietnam I became a platoon leader. On July 11, 1970, while walking point and leading my platoon on a search and destroy mission in the Republic of South Vietnam, a grenade exploded at my feet. I stood up, was shot twice and bayoneted in the stomach. It seemed like a nightmare that wasn't really happening.

I lay on the ground being burned by a white phosphorus grenade. The pain wracked my body like I had never experienced in my life. Looking into a clear blue sky and seeing the beautiful green trees of the Vietnam jungle, I wanted to close my eyes and have the nightmare finally over.

Suddenly, an eighteen-year-old PFC (Private First Class) and a twenty-one-year-old Navy Corpsman ran out across that field under enemy fire and pulled me to safety. I tried to get up, thinking that if I didn't get up now, I never would. I watched as my men rushed forward and threw their battle dressings to the feet of the Corpsman as they tried to stop the bleeding.

I remember the helicopter ride to the 95th Evacuation Hospital in DaNang, and I remember being prepared for surgery. The doctor put the mask over my face, saying, "Son, we're taking you down for surgery." I was in and out of consciousness for the next several days.

Six days after I was wounded, I woke up in intensive care. I had suffered seventy-two major shrapnel wounds, both legs were shattered in three places, my arms were broken in three places, and one bullet had shattered my right elbow, almost taking my arm off. Another bullet had entered my stomach, the bayonet had gone through my intestines, I had an internal infection that was slowly killing me, and they couldn't stop the bleeding. My face was mangled, my head was swollen and black and blue, and my eyes were black and blue.

While in ICU I saw my twin brother walk past my bed to where a doctor was standing. "Excuse me, I'm Sergeant Helle's brother," Ron said. "Could you tell me how my brother is doing?"

Putting down the chart he had been looking at, the doctor looked at Ron. "Son, your brother is going to die," he said. "There isn't anything else we can do for him."

"Could I please see him?" Ron asked. "They told me he was in here, but I can't find him."

Out of the corner of my eyes, I saw the doctor take Ron by the arm. A nurse came alongside and they walked him back to my bed and stopped. Seeing the mass of human rubble lying on the bed, Ron stared in silence.

When Ron finally recognized me, his face turned white and he started sobbing. He tried to take a step toward me, but his legs gave out and he fell against my bed. Burying his face in the side of my bed, he wept.

I looked down but couldn't talk or move. I couldn't even lift a finger to let him know that I knew he was there. At age twenty-two, three months from my twenty-third birthday, fear gripped my heart more than it ever had in three tours of combat. I closed my eyes and prayed in my heart, *God, if there really is a God, if You let me live, I'll do anything You want.* Then I drifted off to sleep.

About ten days later the doctor came in, took my brother aside, and said, "Ron, your brother is going to live. He's pretty messed up, but I think your presence here has helped."

A week later I was strong enough to survive the short Medevac flight from DaNang to Yokuska Naval Hospital in Japan. Five weeks and eight surgeries later I was put on a Medevac flight to Great Lakes Naval Hospital in Chicago. When I arrived the doctor said, "Son, you've got gangrene in your right leg. We're going to have to take it off." But the gangrene disappeared. Unable to explain this medical miracle, the doctor said this kind of gangrene doesn't ever go away. I didn't learn until years later that my grandmother had been praying for me.

They discovered bone infection in my lower arm and said they'd have to amputate the arm above the elbow to stop the infection. But when they took me down to surgery, the doctor said, "Roger, I was all prepared to amputate, but I felt compelled to cut it open first." After cutting into the arm, he couldn't find the infection.

Doctors told me I would likely be at the naval hospital for two years, maybe more, because I needed surgery, therapy, recovery, more surgery, therapy, and more recovery. They said I would have only 15 percent use of my right arm. They said I would have pins and plates in my legs and would have to wear leg braces. They said I had shrapnel in my eyes that would cause me to go blind. And they said that because of other injuries, I would never have children.

Yet, nine and a half months later, after twenty-seven operations and four plastic surgeries, I walked out of the hospital. I had 85 percent use of my right arm, no pins, no plates, no leg braces, and I wasn't blind. Since I wasn't married I wasn't concerned about having kids. So I walked out of the hospital thinking, *I did it. I made it!*

After being released from the hospital in 1971 I worked for a private detective agency and discovered that I could put on a suit and cover many wounds. I met Shirley and convinced her that I was normal. We were married September 9, 1972, two years after I was wounded. For the next two years I made her life hell, yet I was successful in my career.

I dreaded the time of day when I had no more crimes to solve, no more cases to work on, the bars were closed, and I had to go home. Eventually I had to go to bed, and when I went to bed I'd have to go to sleep. When I'd go to sleep I'd find myself standing in a field with a grenade lying at my feet. I'd struggle and fight. I'd try to run and kick, until finally the grenade would go off. I'd wake up soaking wet, my heart racing. If I was able to go back to sleep, I saw Danny looking up with lifeless eyes. I relived Vietnam *every single night*.

Finally Shirley said, "I love you, but I can't live with you like this. You're killing me too." She walked out, and God allowed me to hit rock bottom.

Several weeks before Shirley had left, some church people asked us to attend their couples' Bible study, and we accepted the invitation. One night they asked an icebreaker question to help us feel comfortable even though I knew I was *not* comfortable with these people.

As they went around the room, but before my turn, I felt as if I had been lifted up out of the room. Looking down into another room, I could see a man lying on a bed, bloody and bleeding. I heard him say, "God, if there really is a God, if You let me live, I'll do anything You want." Then I found myself back in the room with the Bible study group. I didn't share my vision with anyone that night, including Shirley.

I felt as if a mirror had been held in front of me. When I looked in that mirror I saw a phony. I knew God had spared my life, but I didn't understand why. During the ten days Shirley and I were separated, the Holy Spirit brought great conviction into my heart. Shirley returned, and while we were walking through a mall she looked at me and said, "Unless we put God first place in our life, we're not going to make it."

"I know, but how do we do that?" I said.

Although the people in the Bible study we had attended were loving, and we could see their lives were different than ours, they never confronted us by saying, "Roger and Shirley, you need Jesus."

After our walk at the mall that night, we returned to the apartment Shirley had moved into. We knelt by her bed, and I cried out from a broken heart. I didn't know that Scripture says, "Whoever calls upon the name of the Lord will be saved" (Acts 16:31). But I did cry out, "God, what's missing?"

The still, small voice of the Holy Spirit seemed to say, "Rog, Shirley, it's not what's missing; it's Who's missing. You need Jesus."

I told God that my life was a mess and that I had destroyed the love of the only person who had ever cared about me. "I don't know if You could use somebody like me, but if You can, here I am," I told the Lord.

Prior to praying that prayer, every morning for four and a half years I felt like I put on a hundred pounds of emotional gear on my back. But after I had prayed that simple prayer from a broken heart, the weight fell off. The nightmares I had experienced for four and a half years stopped that night. In almost thirty years and sixteen trips back to Vietnam, I've never had a nightmare of the war there.

God healed my marriage. Shirley and I celebrated thirty-three years together last September. I have two children, Joshua and Jamie, even though doctors said I couldn't have children. And we are in our twenty-eighth year of Teen Challenge, a ministry where God reaches into the lives of thousands of hurting people just like me.

Roger Helle is Executive Director of Teen Challenge International Mid-South Headquarters in Chattanooga, Tennessee, an international ministry founded by Rev. David Wilkerson and made famous by the book **The Cross and the Switchblade.** *Teen Challenge provides help for those bound by all types of life-controlling addictions. In cooperation with Vets With A Mission, Roger has travelled back to Vietnam to bring help and healing to the war-torn nation. They have rebuilt orphanages, built clinics and hospitals, shipped millions of dollars of donated medical supplies, taken in teams of doctors, and provided aid to the struggling Christian church. Roger and his wife, Shirley, live in Chattanooga, Tennessee.*

24

LIAR, LIAR

by Jim Preston

Jesus, full of the Holy Spirit, returned from the Jordan and was led by the Spirit in the desert, where for forty days he was tempted by the devil.

LUKE 4:1,2

I believe the hand of God rested on me from the beginning of my life. After five years of marriage, my parents were unable to conceive. A Catholic priest prayed for Mom, and she became pregnant immediately. My brother, Rich, my sister, Therese, and I were miracle babies in the Lord's hand.

At nineteen, after realizing my need for forgiveness, I confessed my sin to the Lord and accepted Jesus as Savior. Although I already felt He was in my life, I wanted to make sure, so I invited Him in and was born again.

About a year later while reading Harold Hill's *How to Live Like a King's Kid*, I learned about the baptism of the Holy Spirit. "You know my heart," I told the Lord in prayer. "I want the Holy Spirit and all of His gifts. I ask You to baptize me in the Holy Spirit." And He did! I began to speak in tongues almost immediately. Receiving the infilling of the Holy Spirit was one of the most powerful experiences in my life and a significant turning point for me.

Early in 1984 the Lord led me to two periods of fasting. I submitted to His prompting in an effort to turn from the desires of the world and more fully to Him and His Word. He made the starting and ending time of the fast clear to me.

However, soon after this initial fasting period, I started receiving strong impressions to fast more and more. I felt guilt and condemnation whenever I ate, and I could no longer enjoy good food. Deceived by Satan—yet thinking God was leading me—I fasted over a period of fifty days and lost forty-five pounds. At 6'3" I weighed only 145 instead of my normal 190. The longer I felt compelled to fast, an increasing spirit of oppression, depression, and confusion tormented me.

Next, I started receiving strong impressions to do strange things at my workplace. Again thinking the Lord was directing me, I knelt down among coworkers, lay on the floor to worship the Lord, and jumped up and down to praise Him. Although acting on these strange impressions made me very uneasy, I had dedicated myself to do God's will and felt I needed to obey Him.

Eventually my employer asked me to go home. After my supervisor called my parents, Dad and a family friend escorted me home from work. My coworkers, of course, didn't understand my odd behavior. I didn't understand it either, but knew I needed to obey God. Fellow employees thought I needed help—which I did—but not the kind of help they thought I needed.

My parents, confused by my behavior and deep depression, pleaded with me to seek psychiatric help at the hospital. When I resisted seeking help, my mom, Carol Preston, called the 700 Club and asked them to pray for me. When the person on the other end of the phone prayed, my dad and I felt the tangible power of God come into my bedroom and touch us. Instantly the depression lifted, and I felt happy and normal again.

Although the oppression had left, Mom and Dad still wanted me to be checked out at the hospital. Convinced that I had been delivered, I went willingly only to make my parents feel better. After being evaluated at Abbott Northwestern Hospital in Minneapolis, Minnesota, from Friday night until Monday I was released.

Apparently the *devil* wasn't ready to release me, however. On Sunday evening as I prepared to return home, the depression and oppression started coming on me again. Although I had started eating while at the hospital, I again felt condemnation about eating and felt compelled again to fast.

After returning home I also believed God wanted me to kneel for long periods of time and didn't want me to talk to anybody. Although I had been temporarily delivered from this demonic attack just days earlier, it had returned, but this time with a vengeance. The following week I had been kneeling for an extended time, and when I finally stood up, I heard an audible voice. "You disappoint me," it said. "You don't take your commitments very seriously."

Then the voice made it sound like I was asking a question, "What's going to happen to me now?"

The voice returned, "You'll go to hell." Because I assumed that every voice I heard was God's voice, I believed God had condemned me to hell. *I must have lost my salvation,* I thought, *because either I didn't fast long enough or didn't stay up and pray all night.* I thought God had completely given up on me.

Sinking deeper into depression and hopelessness, I knelt in my bedroom for about seventeen hours. Thinking I was obeying God, I refused to talk to anyone, quit drinking water, and began another fast. My parents and family became deeply concerned and didn't understand what was happening to me. Yet, I continued in deception, thinking I was doing God's will.

Because of my strange behavior, fasting, and refusal to drink water, my parents had me committed to the hospital by court order. When the hospital staff arrived, I tried to resist them, but I was too weak to fight. Against my will I was admitted to the psychiatric ward of Abbott Northwestern Hospital where I spent about three weeks.

Now at the lowest point in my life, the devil deceived me into thinking that I had committed the unpardonable sin and would spend eternity in hell. I didn't know what I had done to commit the unforgiveable sin; I only knew I had committed it. I wanted to die, thinking the longer I lived, the more sin I might commit and be punished for in hell.

Although I had decided to quit eating and drinking so I could die naturally, the hospital staff wouldn't allow it and force-fed me intravenously. When I finally agreed to eat, the devil whispered, "You're already under judgment for eating." Thinking it was God speaking, I thought I must be under judgment for not fasting long enough.

Immediately I lost my sense of taste and could barely discern 95 percent of the foods I ate. I devoured rich foods, trying to get even a slight taste of food. My lack of taste along with the depression led to a significant weight gain in a short period of time, about eighty pounds in eight months.

I considered suicide, especially after being released from the hospital. I lay awake at night sometimes contemplating how I'd do myself in. I drove to a gun shop on the way home from one of my required psychiatrist appointments. Although I had considered buying a gun, I sat in the parking lot of the gun shop, hesitating to go in. Because I was so depressed at the time, I knew my plans of suicide would be obvious to the people in the gun shop. Instead, I drove home, pulled into the garage, shut the door, and let the car continue running. I lay down on the garage floor, hoping to die from the toxic fumes. I changed my mind again, though, thinking this method was a dumb idea.

A deep oppression and depression blanketed me. I was unable to work for three months and felt I had to lie down frequently. Void of peace, I sensed demons surrounding me, whispering condemnation like, "The devil is going to get your soul." At times I sensed demons staring at me, a very irky feeling. Convinced that I had lost my salvation, I believed I no longer had authority over Satan or his demons. Thinking I had been stripped of spiritual authority, I knew I couldn't resist Satan or make him or his demons flee.

After I returned to work the devil spoke to me while I was driving home from work one night. "I have a surprise for you," he taunted. "You're not going to be tired anymore." Again thinking it was God, I assumed I was under judgment now because I didn't stay up all night to pray. Beginning that night, I no longer got tired and stayed awake most nights. Although my body felt run down, I couldn't sleep normally.

The devil led me to believe that I needed to work unreasonably long hours. Once I worked twenty hours straight, slept in my car for an hour and a half in the parking lot, then worked another seventeen hours. Since I wasn't growing tired, I was able to work fourteen to fifteen hours a day.

Although people I worked for didn't want me at work for extended hours and overtime wasn't available, I felt I should work anyway. When I called my supervisor at the home plant to give him my weekly hours, I told him to put me down for only forty hours, although I had worked sometimes more than twice as many. I didn't realize that God wouldn't lead me to go against the authorities at work, which would violate Romans 13:1. "Everyone must submit himself to the governing authorities, for there is no authority except that which God has established. The authorities that exist have been established by God."

Later in 1984 my brother Rich planned to get married, and I was supposed to be a groomsman in his wedding. However, the devil impressed me that I couldn't attend the wedding, and thinking I was obeying God's direction, I cancelled out at the last minute. Rich had to find someone else to take my place in the wedding.

After I cancelled my participation in Rich's wedding, the devil called me a fool. "Why'd you wait so long?" he taunted. The devil comes to harass, get you down on yourself, condemn, make you think you're a bad person, and convince you that you're worthless. It felt degrading to be called a fool. At the time I didn't know the difference between conviction of the Holy Spirit and condemnation from the devil.

While I was still in deception I asked my friend Dave Lehman if I could borrow a book I remembered seeing at a past book and tape sharing. The book had looked interesting at the time and now I wanted to read it.

Dave unknowingly brought a different book than the one I had requested. God hadn't made a mistake, though. In His perfect time He used Dave to deliver Dr. James Dobson's book entitled, *Dr. Dobson Answers Your Questions,* * a book God used to help me see the light. Although I knew it was the wrong book, I started leafing through the pages. Spotting a chapter titled "Interpreting Impressions," my eyes locked on the pages as I read about discerning right and wrong spiritual impressions.

In addition to Dr. Dobson's book, family and friends prayed unceasingly on my behalf during my journey through deception. The Holy Spirit worked through various people who faithfully persevered in sharing the truth of God. The Bible says, "You shall know the truth, and the truth will set you free" (John 8:32). When the truth of God's Word finally sunk in, I realized that I had not lost my salvation. After I sensed the Holy Spirit whisper, "Everything is going to be okay," I ran into Mom's room and woke her up to tell her the good news. I felt like I was born again—*again!*

Shortly after my spiritual eyes were opened, the devil took one last shot at me, impressing me to kneel in my room again. When I knelt down, Mom peeked in my room and recognized what was happening. The Holy Spirit rose up within Mom, and she charged into my room and laid her hands on me. With great authority she commanded, "Devil, in Jesus' name, take your hands OFF God's property!" The Holy Spirit anointing broke the devil's power. Finally free, my mind became clear and has been clear ever since.

Realizing that I had not lost my salvation and therefore still had authority over the devil, I sought the Lord and asked, "Why hasn't my taste returned? What am I supposed to do?"

The Lord spoke to my heart, "This kind comes out only by prayer and fasting" (Mark 9:29). When I began to pray in the spirit and fast, my taste returned 50 percent. The next day, as I continued to pray and fast, my tongue started feeling strange and thick and my taste returned 100 percent. I sure appreciate food now!

The Lord touched my sleep as well, restoring me from three hours to six hours, then to full restoration. It's so good to be able to sleep!

After sharing my story with my sister Therese for this book, I ordered a used copy of *Dr. Dobson Answers Your Questions,* one of the primary tools God used in my deliverance. Twenty years after God delivered me from demonic oppression, this book continues to make a strong impact on my life regarding spiritual discernment—it was as fresh today as it was then.

I believe God worked faithfully to deliver me throughout this time of testing and am fully persuaded that He who began a good work in me will also complete it in me.

Jim was born in Hopkins, Minnesota, where he has spent his entire life. He has worked as a manufacturing technician for over seventeen years in the industrial market. Jim has enjoyed serving the Lord for over twenty years through the ministries of Full Gospel Businessmen, Dinner at Your Door, and International Student Fellowship (ISF).

* *Dr. Dobson Answers Your Questions,* Dr. James Dobson, copyright 1982, Tyndale House, pg. 187.

25

RISE UP!

by Mike Drynan

Then he said to the paralytic, 'Get up, take your mat and go home.' And the man got up and went home.

MATTHEW 9:6,7

$\mathcal{A}$s the mid-winter snow swirled outside at *Mike's Home Bakery Coffee Shop* in Bridgenorth, Ontario, my eyelids grew heavy. I had worked close to a double shift at the bakery I had owned and operated since 1981. The weekend rush was coming, so I slumped upstairs to an apartment above the shop. My head throbbed with pain. It felt soothing to put my head on a soft-feathered pillow and slide between cozy, warm sheets.

Despite my fatigue and headache I sensed a good feeling too. After four years business was finally booming. Although I thought bakery sales would trail off after the Christmas and New Year's rush, instead they got busier. We were supplying goods for pizzerias, lodges, service clubs, and church dinners. Demand for cakes and tarts was up too.

This had spurred expansion plans. Because of a potential partner's enthusiasm, we had started building a small café next to the store. Unfortunately, a financial pinch forced him to back out, but I had continued on. Thus, visions of new challenges danced in my head as I drifted off to sleep.

A couple of hours later two construction workers came looking for me. They needed the blueprints. "Mike!" they called several times. When I didn't answer, they entered the apartment. Thinking I was asleep, they nudged my shoulder. Suddenly they realized that I wasn't asleep but unconscious. My skin color had faded to a dull grey.

"Mike's had an attack!" one of them yelled. "Call an ambulance! Hurry!"

Ten minutes later the emergency workers arrived. "This man has had a stroke," one attendant said. "One side is paralyzed." En route to the hospital they stopped at my doctor's office so he could check me. He phoned ahead so they had an emergency bed waiting.

Unfortunately that stroke was followed by several more. After eight hours in intensive care, they couldn't control the seizures. They flew me to Toronto by air ambulance. When I awoke the next day, I didn't know what had happened. My wife, Gayle, stood on one side of my bed. On the other side a nurse took readings from monitors.

This is a nightmare, I thought. *This isn't really happening.*

When I tried to speak, everything came out garbled. I tried to move but couldn't. My whole left side felt like a rock.

"It's okay, honey," Gayle soothed. "Just lie still. You've had a bad stroke, but everything is going to work out."

The sign on my bakery read: *Closed. Mike's Home Bakery on Ward Street is closed due to Mike Drynan's illness. He is in Sunnybrook in Toronto, but Gale, his wife, said it is hopeful Mike will be coming to Civic Hospital in Peterborough soon. Everyone wishes Mike a speedy recovery.*

As doctors predicted, I went through stages, including not wanting to live, depression, crying fits, and denial. Finally I accepted it and fought back. I had a lot of hard work ahead of me to gain back the use of my arm and leg. As I recuperated later at home, I had a hard time understanding what was happening. Hadn't God already healed me once? Many a day I thought, *Why, Lord? Why? What reason was there for suffering another disability at the age of forty-one?*

I recalled the first time the Lord healed me at age nineteen. I was partially deaf, a condition that had improved with a hearing aid in sixth grade. But I still struggled to cope in a world of silence. I was always left behind because of my handicap.

This changed the same night I accepted Jesus as my Savior. I had been invited to a Gospel Tent Crusade sponsored by Calvary Pentecostal Church. The pastor who invited me said, "I believe the Lord will heal you of this deafness."

I got a surprise when I arrived. People were clapping their hands; many sang loudly. Others cried. We didn't do that kind of thing in the dignified church my family attended. After an hour I muttered, "What did I get myself into by being here at this meeting? I've got to leave."

For some reason, I stayed. When the speaker, Rev. Franklin Walden from Lithonia, Georgia, finished, he said, "If anyone wants a healing touch from God, walk forward." The pastor who had invited me offered to accompany me to the front. Reluctantly, I agreed. Once there, Rev. Walden surprised me. First he told me to lay my hearing aid on the altar. Then he put his fingers in my ears and prayed. I had never heard anyone pray with such excitement!

"Do you accept Jesus into your heart and life?" he asked. "Do you believe God will heal you at this very moment?"

Suddenly I felt cold. Then a warm feeling came over me like a blanket of love. "Yes!" I grinned. "I do believe, and I do accept Jesus into my heart and life."

When he removed his fingers from my ears, it sounded like a rushing wind. In crystal clear tones I could hear people singing and praising God. Now, because of that experience, I found it hard to believe that in 1986 I was in need of healing again. Unable to walk on my own, I used leg braces and a cane when I was unable to go places where my wheelchair could go. I could walk, but with great pain and difficulty, so most of the time I used a wheelchair.

More misery followed. Over the next three years I suffered two more strokes and had two back operations. The latter forced me to take six Percocet (painkillers) a day. I had to give up my business.

Ten years passed. One of the things I hated during that time was when our oldest grandson, Micah, would ask me to play. It broke my heart to tell him I couldn't. Still, I never gave up hope that God would touch me again. When Gayle heard that evangelist Benny Hinn was coming to Toronto's Maple Leaf Gardens in September of 1999, we decided to attend.

Gayle brought a friend and her brother, Greg Howson, with us. We waited outside three hours to get into the Gardens and another four hours for the service to start. I was only allowed to have one person accompany me in the special section reserved for the handicapped near the front of the stage. Greg sat with me, and Gayle and her friend sat in another section. Approximately twenty-five thousand people were in the crowd.

During the four hours of waiting, I befriended an elderly lady, Mrs. Maria Tames of North York, Toronto. Maria, who sat next to me, was wearing a neck brace because of a car accident. She knew a lot of the Benny Hinn staff because she had made a trip with them to the Holy Land. Seeing all the other people around me—like a boy with brain cancer and crippled children—I felt unworthy and decided to pray for them instead of myself.

After the service began, Benny's brother, Henry Hinn, came over to pray for Maria. After praying he asked her to remove her neck brace. She took off her brace and moved her neck around. "I've been healed! Praise God! I've been healed!" she exclaimed. She was so excited, she touched me, and it felt like a shock of electricity shot through me. Feeling the jolt, I jumped.

Just then Benny Hinn asked everyone to be silent. "The Lord is moving," he said. "People are being healed while they are in their seats." He then asked everyone to stand.

When I stood, I felt God's healing presence surround me. My hands started to shake uncontrollably, and I knew God was touching me. Two staff members walked over. One said, "What's happening, brother? The power of God is all over you! We can see it! God is doing something." Later I learned that people sitting behind me saw a glow surrounding me.

"Take off those leg braces and start walking," a staffer said. "The Lord has just healed you."

I took them off, and there I stood. When he asked what I felt, I said, "No pain. There's no pain!" I felt like a heavy weight had been lifted from me. My legs were like feathers.

I wept openly, knowing God had touched and healed me. Again. As I started to walk, my legs got stronger with each step. When I reached the stage, I was completely healed. My brother-in-law, Greg, followed with the empty wheelchair and braces.

After Benny Hinn placed his hands on my head and prayed, I bounced back about five feet and fell under the power of the Holy Spirit. They picked me up, but the power of God was so strong, I went down two more times. Then I was led back to see the staff doctor who checked me over.

Rev. Hinn didn't heal me, but he was the instrument God used to work through. God healed me, and God gets the glory!

In September of 2001 I sold my wheelchair. I kept my two hand-carved canes, only because I want to pass them on to my grandsons as family heirlooms and remembrances of how Jesus had healed me.

Now I take our grandsons fishing and exploring in the woods. Most of all, I know that God is real. With every step I take, I thank God for His love, His mercy, and His miraculous healing power. I give all the glory to Jesus! I trust and pray that my testimony and my healing will move many to turn their lives over to Jesus Christ.

Mike and his wife, Gayle, were both born and raised in Peterborough, Canada. Mike is Provincial Membership Chairman for Ontario and Vice President of the Peterborough Chapter of Businessmen's Fellowship. He and Gayle have two daughters. They attend Elim Worship Centre.

26

BLINDED BY THE LIGHT
by Julie Greenfield

After they entered the city, Elisha said, 'LORD, open the eyes of these men so they can see.' Then the LORD opened their eyes and they looked, and there they were, inside Samaria.

2 KINGS 6:20 NLT

*E*arly on December 18, 2003, I woke up feeling uneasy in the pit of my stomach. I planned to send my eight-year-old daughter Haley on an airplane to Spokane, Washington. We had recently relocated from Spokane to Reno, Nevada, after my husband, Tom, accepted a new career position. Because we had no family or friends with which to spend the holidays and Tom could not get time off, we decided to fly Haley to Spokane to spend time with our families. Tom and I had never been apart from our daughter at Christmastime.

I despise airports. Although I understand the heightened security process travelers must go through to ensure safety, especially since the tragedy of 9/11, I wish I could somehow avoid it. Hoping I might bypass the frustrating delays of security procedures, I planned to leave my purse at home and instead bring only my wallet. However, I changed my mind at the last minute and took my purse. Later I wished I had followed my first instinct.

Hayley and I left the house later than expected, then got caught in road construction on the interstate. Even after getting a late start, we arrived at the terminal with about ninety minutes to spare.

At the airport I felt calmer than I had earlier that morning as Haley and I prepared to leave. My next task was to obtain an unaccompanied minor pass, which would enable me to accompany Hayley to her departure gate. Without this pass only ticketed passengers and airport personnel could go beyond the security area.

Pass in hand, we entered a fast moving line of passengers proceeding through the metal detectors. After removing my shoes and coat, I placed them, along with my purse, on the X-ray conveyer belt. Hayley and I breezed through the metal detectors without incident.

While waiting for our belongings to reappear on the conveyor belt, I conversed with the gentleman standing behind me in line. Engrossed in small talk, I didn't notice that the conveyer belt had stopped.

A horrifying thought hit me: I had a gun in my purse! With all of the scurrying around in preparation for Haley's trip, I had forgotten to take it out of my purse. Three months earlier I had received this gun as a gift. It had never been fired, I had not taken gun training, and I had no concealed weapons permit. I panicked, feeling as if my heart had stopped. "Oh my gosh!" I said to the man I had been talking to. "I forgot I had a gun in my purse!"

"Yeah, right," he laughed.

"No, I'm serious," I pleaded. "Am I going to get arrested?"

"Probably," he said in disbelief.

Terror struck me when an officer approached. After taking my purse and my belongings, he ordered me to follow him. I followed in silent obedience. As we walked, he told me I would have to answer a few questions. Although terrified inside, I kept my cool outwardly for Hayley's sake. I didn't want to frighten her any more than she already had been.

Four additional officers surrounded us and then escorted us upstairs to the police department. They sat down and wasted no time pulling information from me. First, they asked for my social security number. *Maybe they want to check to see if I'm a hardened criminal,* I thought. Then they questioned me about the gun. Why was it in my purse? Did I have a concealed weapons permit? Had I ever fired this weapon? Fully cooperative, I politely answered their questions.

While holding my gun, the questioning officer asked if I had the clip (the clip is often referred to as a magazine which holds the bullets). "I think I took it out of the gun when I got it," I said.

"Is it in your purse now?" he asked.

I told him, truthfully, that I wasn't sure what I had done with the clip when I took it out of the gun.

"Can I search your purse?" he asked.

While another officer searched through my purse, the questioning officer informed me that if they found the clip in the gun or on my person, it would mean an immediate arrest and felony charge. In that case, he said, I would be escorted downtown. The officer continued searching for the clip but came up empty-handed.

The officer asked if I would go through my purse to see if I could find the clip. I trembled. Although I was still uncertain of the whereabouts of the clip, in my heart I suspected it was in my purse. I halfheartedly searched my purse but found no clip.

After the officers learned that I was a full-time homemaker and home-school mom, it seemed that they realized I was not a threat. Close to Hayley's departure time, a kind woman representing the Transportation Security Administration (TSA) entered the room to question me. She said she planned to meet with an inspector in a few minutes to discuss the details of my case. After learning that Haley's flight was scheduled to depart soon, she offered to escort her to her gate. Her gentleness and under-standing comforted me.

Hayley cried hysterically, not welcoming the thought of leaving without me. I tried to calm her, explaining that we had no choice unless we postponed her flight. Sensitive to our obvious crisis, the kind woman agreed to allow me to accompany her and Hayley to the gate.

Hayley, the TSA security woman, two officers, and I proceeded to the gate. For the second time I was required to put my purse through the X-ray machine. I prayed a silent but diligent prayer, asking God to blind the eyes of the security people. Still unsure if the gun clip was in my purse, the thought of a possible felony charge echoed in my mind. My insides tremored, yet outwardly I remained remarkably calm.

What a relief to see my purse come through on the belt. As I reached for my purse the X-ray person in charge of monitoring grabbed it. "Is this yours?" she asked.

After I confirmed that the purse was mine, she said she needed to run it through the X-ray one more time. She laid the purse on the conveyor of the X-ray machine once again, my purse's third trip through X-ray that day. Smiling nervously I said, "No problem."

I waited patiently, praying again as my purse travelled through the sensitive cameras. When my purse exited the other end with no problem, Hayley, my escort, and I continued on to the departure gate.

After a tearful good-bye to Hayley, the TSA woman and the officers escorted me back to the police station. The inspector had arrived and continued questioning me about my gun and the mysteriously missing clip. He said I was very fortunate, even "blessed." The current fine for this type of violation ranges from $300-$10,000. After January 1, 2004, only weeks away, the minimum fine would be raised to $3,000.00.

After a few more grueling questions from the TSA rep and the inspector, they released me and I was free to go home. They said I could expect to see paperwork in the mail in the coming weeks. They seemed compassionate, giving me tips on filling out the paperwork and advising me to return it as soon as possible.

On the drive home a pent-up dam of tears broke. Once home, I emptied the contents of my purse and thoroughly searched every nook and cranny. I still wondered about the missing clip. In the front pocket where I had kept my gun, I discovered a small rip in the seam. Feeling around and between the purse lining, I froze. The clip had been in my purse the whole time, hidden from the security people, hidden from the X-ray machine, and hidden even from me.

God had answered my desperate prayer and protected me, even though I had mistakenly left my gun in my purse. I felt such gratitude for His divine hand of unmerited grace, but I knew I still faced consequences for taking my gun into the airport. At the airport earlier the officials made it clear that I would face a minimum $300 fine.

Knowing God could take care of the fine, I prayed repeatedly, asking Him for grace to get off without a fine. I thought receiving a letter giving me a simple slap on the hand sounded like a good resolution to me. I hoped God would accommodate my request, so I continued to pray and expected Him to get me off the hook.

When a letter came from TSA, I learned that I had been issued the minimum fine of $300. I knew I deserved the fine and was thankful that I had received the minimum amount. I would have preferred to pay nothing, as I had prayed, yet I felt peace in knowing that God knew best. So I paid the fine with thanksgiving.

A few weeks later I sold a car and bought a new car. After completing the paperwork, I discovered God's unexpected surprise. Through the car trade and loan transfer process, I skipped a car payment, resulting in a surplus of over $300! Even though I deserved the fine, God paid it for me, only in a different way than I expected. Case closed!

Julie Greenfield lives in Reno, Nevada, with her husband, Tom, and their daughter, Hayley. As a homeschool mom, she feels that teaching her daughter is the most rewarding job she has ever had. Julie says she is blessed with an awesome husband who supports and encourages her to take care of their home as a full-time wife and mother.

27

MARY, MARY, QUITE CONTRARY
by Pastor James Mutahi

Therefore I tell you, whatever you ask for in prayer, believe that you have received it, and it will be yours.

Mark 11:24

*M*y daughter Mary fell sick in July of 1988 during the season of heavy tropical rains in Kenya, East Africa. The episode started when Mary, two years old at the time, became uncomfortable one Saturday afternoon. She was not able to play with other children like she was used to. That evening Mary ate little and her temperature began to rise.

The endless fever and discomfort continued into the wee hours of the following morning. Her mother and I became restless, troubled, and concerned about what illness had befallen our daughter. We prayed, gave her Tylenol, and then tried to sleep. We got little sleep because her fever continued to rise even though we tried to cool her body with a cool, damp cloth.

At about 2 A.M. my wife, Jane, suggested that we take Mary to the hospital for medical care. Though we had come to this conclusion, I knew so well in my spirit that God was going to heal Mary even without going to the hospital. But because I also believe in scientific medicine and because I wanted to be in agreement with my wife, we set out to take Mary to the hospital.

I went outside to start our van, while Jane dressed the baby for the hospital. That night it had rained many inches, to the level that the vehicle tires were spinning and could not move at all. In Kenya the tropical rain can fall so heavily for a number of hours and sometimes throughout the night. Many a time this makes the vehicles not able to move at all because the tires become glued to the ground, making it impossible to drive through. This is due to the sticky clay soil in many parts of the country, and this was the case with us that morning.

We were stuck in the mud, unable to get to the hospital. I had Jane and Mary in the vehicle, all of us helpless. I didn't want to wake the neighbors to come out and push the van out of the mud. Besides, I didn't feel it was necessary to wake my neighbors because I believe in the God of miracles. Within my spirit I had an inner witness of the Spirit of God that God was going to heal my daughter regardless of the difficulty at hand.

In order not to damage the clutch plate of the van in trying to get out of the mud, all three of us went back into the house. Knowing prayer was our only alternative, we prayed and trusted God to intervene.

During the time Mary was sick I did a lot of praying in my heart and believed in the power of God to heal our daughter. Without any reservation my heart clung to the God of wonders, and I trusted Him to heal her.

God intervened. Mary's temperature started going down, and she fell asleep. Jane and I slept, too, until about 6 A.M. As we slept the Lord Jesus touched our daughter and healed her. We thanked the Lord for healing Mary and held our morning devotions. We took our breakfast and, together with our other children, headed for the church. Mary had eaten well and wanted to play, completely normal as ever before.

We enjoyed a lovely worship service that Sunday morning, sharing with the congregation our testimony of Mary's sickness and healing the previous night. We all glorified God together for healing her. Only the Lord is able to do such things!

This kind of miracle happening, like we saw with Mary, has always been an indication that we have a God who is not far away from us. He hears our prayers and desires to do good things for those who love Him. Mary's healing was a great encouragement to us and a reminder that God's promises will always be true. Jesus said, "I will never leave you nor forsake you" (Hebrews 13:5).

He didn't leave us or forsake us—and He will never leave or forsake you!

Pastor James Mutahi is a Kenyan national who relocated to the United States in 2000. He and his wife, Jane, have three daughters, Lydiah, Grace, and Mary. Pastor James felt the call of God early in life after making a commitment to follow the Lord Jesus Christ. He resides in Roseville, Minnesota, and pastors Faith Christian Center Fellowship, a young, growing church in South Minneapolis, Minnesota. He is also in partnership with International Student Fellowship (ISF).

28

SCENES UNDER THE SKY CATHEDRAL

by Evangelist Sammy Simon Wanyonyi

All of them were filled with the Holy Spirit and began to speak in other tongues as the Spirit enabled them.

ACTS 2:4

$\mathcal{G}$rowing up in a small, rural, and obscure Kenyan village where my parents, Justus and Rose, serve as lay Salvation Army evangelists does not exactly look like a place to conceive dreams of impacting cities and nations of the world, does it? Perhaps one would be quick to ask, "Can anything good come from a Kenyan village?"

The answer seems obvious that it could not be so, not according to the world of scholars and bureaucrats. Aristotle or the ancient Greeks would tell you otherwise, affirming that karma would never permit it. In an African environment famous for poverty and pestilence, where modern advantages of electricity, written or electronic media, and libraries lined with books of adventure stories are still scarce, the likelihood of such grand dreams are most improbable, leave alone the development of skills so vital and necessary to grand accomplishments. It would seem that the dreams, if any, should be those of mere survival from day to day.

Yet in such a setting God in His sovereign plan chose to shape my early life, hidden away from the rough and tumble of modern-day conveniences. Here I conceived of the sky as my cathedral, lined with works of art more splendid than the best of Michelangelo. These inspired in me limitless potential. Imagination stirred, and I was free to dream and to paint amazing scenes on the moon at night. I learned to count the stars in the clear sky, to enjoy the melodies of a lonely sparrow in the cool of the day and the welcoming tune of the dancing weaverbird at the break of the dawn.

I learned to listen to the whisper of the wind over the cornfields and the grassy Savannah; to listen to the rumble of the April storm as it approached, leaping over the hills from the east—a phenomena that seemed to emphasize my smallness. Life was a gift to be cherished every day as I drank clear drops of water from the petals of a freshly bloomed flower or washed my feet in the morning dew that reflected the piercing rays of the waking sun. The suspended and glittery dew drops served as mirrors of self-reflection.

Here I learned to quietly minister to the village's lovely people along-side my parents and siblings from day to day. Very early in life I had read the wisdom of the preacher in Ecclesiastes when he affirmed, *"The race is not to the swift, nor the battle to the strong, nor bread to the wise, nor riches to men of understanding, nor favor to men of skill, but time and chance happen to them all."*

This seemed to confront the lie of karma and to refute the Aristotelian maxim that some men are born to be hewers of wood while others are born to be philosophers and geometricians—and the two spheres should never cross within the same individual. Privately I nurtured dreams of personal achievement, especially the desire to develop a career in law.

In 1981, while a third grader and by all means an average and ordinary eight-year-old rural African kid of no extraordinary stature or brilliance, I encountered the Lord Jesus Christ in a very personal way. The encounter left a permanent mark upon my life and sparked an unquenchable spiritual passion.

My quest had started four years earlier with desperation in my young heart to know through personal experience the reality of God. With the innocence of a four-year old, I prayed with my mom to receive Jesus Christ into my heart as Savior. However, I had no intellectual understanding of what it actually meant, and nothing extraordinary seemed to have transpired.

At age eight I wanted to know Him tangibly in the manner I saw modeled by my parents, Justus and Rose, exemplified by my first-born brother, Titus, and to which the Scriptures—so often read in our family prayer times—testified and spoke openly as being the norm since Pentecost.

I expressed this effusive quest in songs as I harmonized familiar hymns with my sister Jane or in silent meditation while tending our family sheep scattered on our fifteen-acre farm. At other times it was in deep sighs of awe when captivated by the wonder and beauty of the setting sun as it descended on the horizons of nearby Mt. Elgon, or by the rainbow appearing in the sky before a fierce storm, or as I lay gazing at the roof of the heavenly cathedral adorned by the moon and the stars. I had begun a journey of self-discovery, a quest to know from whence I came and whither I would go.

Dad and Mom lived daily in pious devotion to God and exuded unequalled confidence while demonstrating loyalty to God and character of heart and mind that perfumed itself in prayer and through their bold testimony to the saving grace of the Lord Jesus Christ. In the African villages, whenever opportunity presented itself, they set up a pulpit and preached Jesus. Indeed, though not perfect—they never claimed to be—their genuine and loyal expression of faith was contagious.

In gatherings at our local Salvation Army Assembly or village funerals and weddings, Dad, although not officially ordained by our Salvation Army denomination, was often called upon to pray, preach, or translate for visiting preachers. His gift as an evangelist was clear to everyone, and he used it maximally to the glory of God.

I longed for such an experience and incontestable testimony of Christ's authority as they had. Often I would kneel long in the night after the lanterns on our farmhouse were out to offer up whispered prayers to the Lord in hopes of a sudden encounter. I did not know how to approach or formulate statements of piety toward God. My heart was not yet enflamed by the ambers of the Holy Spirit.

I longed to connect at a deeper level with the Source, so in quiet tones in our mud-walled, tin-roofed house I verbalized my longing to the invisible and intangible Supreme. Deep inside I knew God was more real than I perceived Him and that every gasp I made for spiritual fresh air would be heeded. I therefore prayed with expectation of a personal encounter with Him.

That hour arrived while praying with my brothers, Titus and Norbert, several months later. When I felt the Lord touch me in an unprecedented way, I knew something new transpired in my heart and personal expression of worship. Of course I had prayed that He would fill me with the Holy Spirit, but had no idea what I would feel or sense. I had prayed with my parents as a four-year-old to ask Jesus into my heart as Lord and Savior, yet I had had little understanding of what it meant. But this experience was different.

As I prayed with my brothers sudden, great joy swelled in my heart. It seemed as if the longing to touch God and fully discover myself was finally met. My physical surroundings seemed engulfed with a sense of spiritual luminosity, this time not drawn merely from the outside but from the inside. With no struggle to enter into God's presence, the distance between Him and me felt remarkably eliminated. It seemed I was discovering piety for the first time. Indeed, more than piety, I was given a blessed revelation of Jesus Christ in His imminent magnificence and splendid majesty.

Up to this point I had spoken no English and did not know how to read or write. In an instant I spoke perfect English, glorifying God and declaring His wonderful works such as took place on the day of Pentecost. Not only was I praising God in flawless English, God miraculously enabled me to read and write in English—just like that!

My life became a wonderful testimony as multitudes thronged places to hear me testify to the saving power of Jesus Christ. *That* was something new, and my faith suddenly became more vital, dynamic, relevant, and thrilling.

It seemed as if I had known only prose and discovered poetry, or had only read lyrics and now heard them sung. I felt like Dorothy in the *Wizard of Oz*, opening the door of her black-and-white home and looking out to a realm of color, or like the lucky actor in *The Purple Rose of Cairo* who discovers he can step down from the movie screen and live in three-dimensions. It was the difference between religion and relationship, and it *is* hard to explain.

Indeed, the spiritual experience of being in a relationship with Jesus Christ does not feel quite like anything else but feels *something* like a romance, which may account for the sensuality of the metaphors often used to describe it. For an eight-year-old, it was astoundingly blessed.

Still in his early thirties, Sammy Wanyonyi is an international evangelist whose ministry currently spans three continents: North America, Asia, and Africa. He is Founder and President of Sammy Wanyonyi International Ministries (S.W.I.M.), an evangelistic and teaching ministry based out of Minneapolis, Minnesota. His passion is reaching entire communities with the Good News of salvation through Jesus Christ by holding citywide evangelistic festivals, leadership seminars, and revival, evangelism, and mission conferences as a way of strengthening the church of Jesus Christ. In addition to his global travels, he is currently completing his master's of divinity degree at Bethel University Seminary in St. Paul, Minnesota.

29

ON THE MOVE IN AFRICA
by Terry Charlton

With shrieks, evil spirits came out of many, and many paralytics and cripples were healed. So there was great joy in the city.

ACTS 8:7,8

In February 2000 a large group of evangelists from England led by David Ballard accepted an invitation from Rev. Ivan Lugoloobi to visit Uganda. Participants of the mission slept on church floors in rucksacks and walked from village to village in teams of two or three, inspired by the witness of the first disciples.

As teams walked each morning from mud hut to mud hut in a rural area fifty miles north of Kampala, we delighted in seeing entire families give their lives to Jesus in nearly every home we visited. Each afternoon we held a crusade in the countryside where two tracks crossed. As the sound of worship filled the air, groups of people emerged from the bush to dance and to hear the gospel. Many hundreds surrendered their lives to Jesus during the two weeks we visited, and scores of people came forward each night needing prayer for healing.

While the gospel was still being preached, before an appeal was made to receive Christ, a constant stream of people approached team members asking to be saved. Such was the power of God moving people's hearts at these meetings, leaving a real sense that the harvest was ripe. Like walking through an orchard, not only was the fruit ready for the picking, it was falling into our hands! People responded to God in far greater numbers than we had ever experienced in the United Kingdom.

From this trip God led some of us from the original team to found *Mission Africa*, an itinerant evangelistic and Bible teaching organization. David Tucker heads up the Bible teaching trips, David Ballard (the leader of the original team) the discipleship training trips, while I have headed up evangelistic missions for the last two years. The three of us plus Pastor

David Sseruwagi formed the core team of *Mission Africa*. Others from the UK and Uganda with a similar calling quickly joined. The Lord called us to take the gospel into places of Africa unreached by the big city crusades: villages and small towns, slums, schools, and prisons.

From the first trip we witnessed God perform a wonderful work of healing. While Peter Stoneley and a friend were doing door-to-door evangelism, they encountered Paul, a cowman who sat by the side of the road suffering great pain in his leg. Cowmen like Paul drive herds of large, long-horned African cows with a stick throughout central and east Africa. Seeking help, Paul had visited the witchdoctor who had hammered red-hot nails into his knee. Paul's pain was so intense he wanted to die.

Peter led Paul to the Lord and prayed for his healing. That afternoon, Paul was the first to arrive at the crusade still with his stick, but testifying that most of the pain had gone. We prayed again. Two hours later we saw Paul worshipping and dancing, waving his stick in the air—totally healed and hardly able to contain his excitement about what the Lord had done for him.

Since those early beginnings the flow of healing miracles continued unabated. In February 2004 the *Mission Africa* team visited the village of Kibuara—fifteen miles from Fort Portal in the far west of Uganda, close to the Congo border—doing door-to-door visits. After I shared the gospel with a group of men outside the village bicycle repair shop, a number were praying the prayer of salvation when a lady was brought to me for prayer. Hobbling painfully with a stick, she was paralyzed from shoulder to foot on the left side. As I prayed with her, God healed her instantly and completely. Immediately she threw away her stick, declaring loudly that she no longer had any use for it!

This little scene deeply affected another group of onlookers, whom we also led to receive Jesus. With joy we watched a group of no fewer than one hundred and five people be baptized in the local river at the end of that week. To God be the glory!

While on that mission another member of the team, Terry O'Keeffe, felt led to deliver a serious prophetic word that indicated the current freedom people enjoyed to worship openly in Uganda and surrounding countries may be coming to an end. That night the team woke up when the bedroom walls felt as if elephants on the other side were shaking them.

Being the first earth tremor in the area for seven years, it seemed as if the Lord underlined the prophetic word spoken only a few hours earlier.

The following morning I preached the gospel to the inmates and staff at a juvenile remand home. Before I had left for Africa, the Lord had prompted me to prepare a message based on Acts 16, the story of Paul and Silas experiencing an earthquake while in jail, and the jailer falling to his knees asking what he must do to be saved. This was the appropriate time to share the message. As I made the appeal for salvation at the end, we heard a loud crash at the back of the room. A plaque of a distorted face with its tongue sticking out fell off the wall. All forty inmates plus staff members accepted Jesus as Savior!

At open-air crusades four blind people received their sight over three evenings. On his first mission trip, Mark Byard prayed for two of them. Overwhelmed by what God had done through him, he felt he also needed prayer!

We witnessed equally spectacular responses in our visits to Rwanda. At the end of 2003 I made a reconnaissance and planning trip with David. After a long journey traveling on bone-shaking, overcrowded buses on rough pot-holed roads (carefully stepping over chickens and sacks of potatoes in order to find a seat) we arrived at Kibungo in the southeast.

On entering the house of Paul Kamuzinzi, the local Pentecostal bishop and uncle of the country's president, he introduced us to his two brothers, the only family members not yet saved. When the bishop disappeared into the back of the house, we shared the gospel with his brothers and led them in a prayer of salvation using English and half-remembered French.

When I met the two men the following year their faces radiated. One, a farmer, previously battled a serious alcohol problem and had been selling off farm and roofing materials to raise money to buy beer. Since receiving Jesus Christ, he had not touched a drop of alcohol. Such is the power contained in the simple sharing of the gospel!

The next day, after meeting a group of pastors to discuss plans for the following year, David and I were invited to speak at a church in Karborunda, a small, one-street township eight miles away. This church gathering of about twenty people met under an avocado tree in an open yard.

After preaching the gospel and praying for the sick we returned to the bishop's car. Standing by the vehicle we saw a young man weaving dangerously in and out of the traffic. Seeing that he was mentally unstable, we talked and prayed with him. When a crowd of one hundred twenty gathered around us, David felt a nudge to preach the gospel. To our delight over sixty people accepted Jesus! Two years later we learned that the young man we had prayed for had been completely healed, the church under the avocado tree had grown to more than three hundred, and they now met in a permanent building!

The following year a small team from *Mission Africa*—David Ballard, David Potter, Gill Chadwick, and myself from the UK; and David Sseruwagi and Ivan Lugoloobi from Uganda—visited Mulindi, a remote township near the Burundi border. Mulindi was a small township with no electricity, running water, or telephone; and a bus that visited only once a week on market day. To get to our toilet we had to go out of the house where we were staying (just a mattress on the floor and a mosquito net), down a passage, across the main street, into a field, to a little shed, where we opened the door to see a hole in the ground. Personal washing took place in a windowless, candlelit shed across the yard. The heat was in the high 90 degrees Fahrenheit with equally high humidity.

Despite almost every inconvenience known to man, we feel drawn to these locations in the back parts of Africa where we see God make the greatest impact. One sick lady walked for nine hours over steep mountain paths to reach the crusade ground and was healed the instant she arrived—without anyone praying for her! Such was the power of God being released over the place and the result of people praying for us.

Thousands of people crowded around, many even climbing trees like Zaccheus to get a better view. An old man, who we later learned was a local witchdoctor, came forward one night and knelt down in front of the stage while the gospel was being preached and before the appeal was made. We also witnessed God restore sight to the blind, hearing to the deaf, and instantly clear the minds of the mentally ill.

The greatest miracle of all, however, is the transformation of a human heart. In 2003 our group (David and myself from the UK, Pastors David Sseruwagi and Nelson Kabuuka from Uganda, and Bishop Paul Kamuzinzi and Pastor Emmanuel Murangira from Rwanda) was invited to Rwanda to visit eight of eighteen prisons in the country, housing over 100,000 detainees suspected of involvement with the 1994 genocide.

God already at work, many of these prisons had churches, choirs, intercessors, evangelists, and pastors. The Spirit-filled choirs often sang unaccompanied in perfect four-part harmony. At other times prisoners playing homemade wooden guitars, and drum sets fashioned from food tins accompanied them.

During this trip we experienced a succession of vehicle breakdowns, accident near misses, tire blowouts, and brake failures (often when traveling down steep inclines as we crossed the mountains of Western Rwanda). The delay resulting from the second brake failure caused us to arrive much later than we intended. We left the Congolese border for a four-hour journey back through mountain forest occupied by armed groups of Interahamwe. The latter had the unpleasant habit of ambushing vehicles and killing all of their occupants. The delay meant a trip across the forest after dark on a very empty road. We pleaded the blood of Jesus over the vehicle and arrived back safely, ready to speak at the next prison the following morning.

As the prisoners were released for the meeting, each cellblock in turn, they raced each other to get the best positions. After speaking to a crowd of up to 2,500 pink-uniformed prisoners in the high-walled yard, we were thrilled to see a forest of hands raised indicating their decision to ask Jesus into their lives. In awe, we looked around the high walls of the yard and saw a mass of hands reaching through the bars from cells of those considered too dangerous to be allowed into the space below.

Prisoners here had committed an average of eight to ten murders. Joy spread across their faces as they realized their crimes could be forgiven and they could start again. It was an awesome sight to behold! Afterwards I was mobbed while handing out tracts and needed rescuing from the melee. The demand was such that it seemed as if we were giving out hundred-dollar notes!

In one prison no fewer than six hundred of the two thousand addressed on a Sunday morning accepted Jesus as Savior. We spoke to twelve thousand prisoners over eight days and saw more than twenty-four hundred give their lives to Christ. We distributed more than four thousand tracts, over nine hundred Bibles, plus some one hundred more Bibles the following year.

In 2003 a Mission Africa team comprised of David, Gill Chadwick, and myself from the UK, and Pastor Steve Trint and Esther Kalule from Uganda, visited slum areas on the edges of Kitale and Eldoret in Kenya. These two large towns in the western part of the country were large rabbit, warren–like places with open sewers. We preached in the marketplaces and parks, the latter seedy and neglected areas where drug dealers and prostitutes hung out and drunks slept under the trees. When we preached crowds gathered around us, and we witnessed many healings, including the deaf and paralyzed. One young man who had been unable to urinate without pain for twenty years was healed.

Each evening we held crusades in the slums and witnessed numerous healings, including a woman affected by evil spirits who suffered with a bleeding problem for many years. When we prayed for her no obvious change appeared, but the next evening she was the first in the queue to come on stage to share her testimony. Her face radiant, she testified of her total mental and physical healing.

In January 2005 during an evangelistic training session in Kayunga, Uganda, an overweight and lame elderly lady with a stick sat on a grass mat in the front. She approached Pastor Steve Trint, one of our speakers and an extremely valued Mission Africa administrator who lives on the outskirts of Kampala. She told him she had been converted eight years earlier after having been a witch doctor, but still kept her witchcraft equipment under her bed at home. While Steve preached she sensed the Holy Spirit tell her to burn it publicly.

A member of our team, Pastor Fred Mudde (a witch doctor before his conversion to Christ), and a local female pastor visited the woman the next day. Together they collected the items and set fire to them on the crusade stage that evening, accompanied by much cheering from the crowd. The following day she approached Steve, her face glowing with joy, and testified that God healed her leg instantly the moment she burned the witchcraft paraphernalia. She offered up her stick saying she had no further need of it. God is so good!

Terry Charlton worked for many years as a commercial lawyer with large international companies before receiving God's call in 2000 to work as an evangelist in Africa. He co-founded Mission Africa, an itinerant ministry that works in the remoter areas of the continent where the big city missions do not go. The ministry is non-denominational and works with as many churches as possible, seeing power and blessing coming as a result of the unity. He has a passion to see broken lives restored and a vision of seeing revival spread throughout Africa and into Europe. Terry and his wife, Carol, recently moved into a two-generation house along with their daughter, Merryn, son-in-law, Tim (a pastor), and two very lively grandsons. They live in the Channel Islands.

30

THE PROMISE

by Therese Marszalek

'Do not lay a hand on the boy,' he said. 'Do not do anything to him. Now I know that you fear God, because you have not withheld from me your son, your only son.'

GENESIS 22:12

*A*pril 26, 1996, started as a normal day. I was homeschooling our oldest son, James, while our two younger kids played. My husband, Tom, was at work and had plans to leave town that afternoon for a Promise Keepers event in Portland, Oregon.

Focused on teaching James a piano lesson, I was unaware that two-year-old Joseph and four-year-old Emily were jumping on the bed in the guest bedroom downstairs, play we didn't normally allow. When Emily crept up the stairs, I knew something was wrong. Joe followed behind, crying.

"What happened?" I quizzed Emily. "Why is Joe crying?"

Emily sheepishly admitted that they had been jumping on the bed. "He fell off," she explained.

"Did he hit his head on something?" I asked.

"Nope," she said. The guest bedroom floor had plush carpet so I knew he couldn't have hit his head on the floor. He couldn't have fallen into bedroom furniture either, as it was positioned far from the bed. Figuring that whatever happened couldn't have been too serious, I assumed everything was all right and continued teaching James his piano lesson.

Joe crawled into the rocking chair in the living room and stopped crying. When I glanced over at him about five minutes later, he was sound asleep. I sensed trouble, as he never slept this early in the day.

"Joseph!" I yelled. "Wake up!"

He didn't stir. With growing concern I ran to the rocking chair and tried to wake him. He opened his eyes, which were fixed straight ahead. When I waved my hand in front of his face, he didn't blink. Running to the phone I dialed his pediatrician, Dr. Melvin Morse, in Renton, Washington. "I need to bring my son in right away," I told the receptionist.

"Well Mrs. Marszalek," she said, "we could probably fit you in at 4:00 today."

"No, you don't understand!" I panicked. "I have to bring him in *now*. Something is wrong. I can't rouse him." Understanding my plea, she instructed me to bring Joe to the office as soon as possible.

I dropped James and Emily off at Kate and Dave Bemis's house, neighborhood friends in Renton, Washington. On the twenty-minute drive to the doctor's office I kept Joe in the front seat. Keeping one hand on the steering wheel and the other hand on Joe, I tried to keep him awake by rubbing his stomach and arms. Although his eyes opened intermittently, they remained glazed and fixed. His body was listless.

Dr. Morse saw Joe as soon as we arrived, putting us ahead of the others in the waiting room. Another young patient's mother fumed, not realizing the seriousness of our situation.

My thoughts scattered after Dr. Morse took Joe for tests. I waited for what seemed an eternity for their return. "I've made arrangements for an ambulance to transport Joe to Harborview Medical Center," he said. "He's suffered a serious head injury, and they have a neurosurgeon standing by." Harborview is the primary trauma center for all of the Pacific Northwest and Alaska.

I felt a wave of dizziness. "Why would they need a neurosurgeon? Joe needs surgery? What's going on?" I asked.

"With a head injury like this," Dr. Morse explained, "the brain can swell. If it swells, they have to drill into the skull to relieve the pressure on the brain."

"A head injury?" I thought out loud. My mind raced, picturing the downstairs guestroom. How could he have gotten a head injury? It didn't seem possible. Yet Joe's blank stare and nonresponsiveness reminded me that something indeed had happened.

After they loaded Joe and me into a waiting ambulance, we started the trip to Harborview, about a twenty-five-minute ride. I held Joe's limp hand while he lay on the gurney, motionless and staring straight ahead. "My baby," I sighed as the siren screamed our way through traffic.

When I called Tom to let him know of the accident he said he'd leave work immediately and meet me at Harborview. Later, he told me that on his way to the hospital he had told God, through tears, "If you heal Joseph, I'll do *anything* you ask of me. I'll go *anywhere* you ask me to go." He cancelled his trip to Oregon for the Promise Keepers meeting, thankful he hadn't left yet.

When we arrived at Harborview a medical team met us at the entrance. After whisking Joe off for a battery of tests, they questioned Tom and me individually about the details of the accident. My stomach sickened as I realized they were trying to rule out child abuse. The thought of someone thinking we could hurt our little Joe grieved my heart, but I realized later that this was necessary routine hospital procedure.

I called close friends from church and asked them to pray for Joe as I peered into the room where they were doing CAT scans and other tests. Joe stared ahead still unresponsive. An ER doctor explained to us that head injuries like this could result in Joe being wheelchair bound, brain damaged, or a victim of other permanent medical issues. Grim possibilities for Joe's future raced through my head.

Hearing the doctor's dark report, Tom and I embraced, unable to speak. I stared into the room where Joe still laid on the gurney. And we prayed desperate prayers.

Several hours later Tom and I stood at Joe's bedside, silently watching our motionless son. Suddenly, Joe sat up straight and with bright eyes said, "I want juice!" Our Joe was back! Our Joe was fine! Unspeakable joy swelled in our hearts.

Tom spent the night at the hospital with Joe, as hospital staff felt it was important to observe him overnight in spite of his miraculous recovery. It was an uneventful night.

When we returned to see Dr. Morse on April 30, we realized the magnitude of Joe's miracle. "Joe's X-rays showed an injury sustained at the base of his skull like that of one who had been dropped on their head onto concrete from at least twelve feet," he said. "It's an absolute miracle." We already knew that!

Several years later, while attending a church conference at Spokane Faith Center, Prophet Ruckins McKinley spoke a prophetic word to Tom and me. He said to Tom, "The Lord says, 'I have not forgotten the promise you made three years ago.'" Not understanding what it meant, we tucked the words away.

When I checked our medical files later, I realized that the day that Ruckins McKinley spoke the prophetic word (April 26, 1999) was exactly three years after Joseph's accident. God hadn't forgotten the promise Tom made through his tears on the way to Harborview Hospital that day: "If you heal Joseph, I'll do *anything* you ask of me. I'll go *anywhere* you ask me to go."

In April of 2004, when our pastor returned from a missions trip to India, he shared video coverage of the trip. I didn't realize it until later, but during the video Tom, who was ushering that day, stood in the back of the church weeping. Seeing his red eyes after church, I asked him what was wrong. He tried to tell me but was unable to talk without breaking down. Several days later, he explained. While Pastor Lonny was showing the video of the India mission in church, Tom sensed the Lord whisper, "Do you remember the promise you made to Me when Joe had his accident?"

"Yes," he answered in his heart, remembering his promise to go anywhere and to do anything for the Lord if He healed Joe.

"I want you to go to India in March," he sensed the Lord say.

Before that service Pastor Lonny had told the congregation that he felt the church elders needed to go on the next India missions trip. After the service Ray Flood, a church elder, approached Tom in the parking lot and, pointing to Tom's foot, said, "Is that foot going to be healed up by March?" Tom had recently undergone foot surgery.

"Probably," Tom said. "Why do you ask?"

"Because I made the recommendation that you be added to the elder team, and I think you're supposed to go to India in March." Tom wept, realizing God had confirmed His words immediately. He knew without a doubt he was going to India.

In March of 2003, as Tom stood in front of a room full of wide-eyed believers in New Delhi, India, he told the story of Joe's miraculous healing and how God brought him to India. They didn't realize that the last thing Tom had on his personal agenda was to travel to the other side of the world to experience the hopelessness and despair evident in that country.

Tom choked on his words and tears streamed down his cheeks as he tried to describe the indescribable. As the heart-wrenching story turned to sheer joy in God's glorious miracle of raising Joe up, Tom's heart felt like it was going to explode in his chest. Although anxious as these Indians were to hear the story about our son, they were hungrier for what God had for them through Tom and Joe.

Many shared in the tearful joy as they learned about obedience that day, just as Tom had learned obedience in fulfilling his promise to God. They learned of a father's love for his son, just as our heavenly Father loved His Son Jesus. God fulfilled His purpose for Tom in India, just as He did for those who experienced Tom and his miracle. Tom witnessed miracles take place before his eyes for people who, although they had little in this world, had everything in Jesus Christ. He learned that God wants obedience and loves us. And sometimes, He uses our circumstances to teach us just that.

Tom and Therese have been happily married since January 1, 1991. They have three children together (James, Emily, and Joseph) and Tom has two dearly loved grown children, Andy and Katy. Tom has worked for the industrial marketplace for over twenty-seven years, and Therese is an author and inspirational speaker. They live in Spokane, Washington, always on the lookout for God's miracles.

31

ANGELS IN THE LAST DAYS

by Flo Ellers

Do not forget to entertain strangers, for by so doing some people have entertained angels.

HEBREWS 13:2

The Bible recounts numerous instances when angels interacted with God's people. In Genesis 18:1-16 angels talked to and had dinner with Abraham. Angels cooked two meals for the prophet Elijah in 1 Kings 19:5-8, protected the camp of Israel from an invading army in Exodus 14:19-20, announced key events in Genesis 19, and prophesied Samson's birth in Judges 13. These are just a few places angels are mentioned in the Old Testament.

The list continues throughout the New Testament. Angels assisted the disciples, again making proclamation of historic events. In Acts 5:18-20 the angel of the Lord opened the prison doors for the apostles; an angel instructed Cornelius to send for Peter in Acts 10:1-3; an angel struck Peter to waken him in Acts 12:7; and Matthew 18:10 says that guardian angels watch over us. The Lord sent an angel to speak to Zacharias in the Temple, announcing the birth of his son, John the Baptist, in Luke 1:13-20.

Much angelic activity took place during the first coming of Jesus. God sent Gabriel to Nazareth to a virgin named Mary and told her she would bear the Son of God. After Jesus was born angels appeared to the shepherds living in the fields of Israel and proclaimed our Lord's birth. After their announcement they were joined by a multitude of the heavenly host praising God and saying, "Glory to God in the highest, and on earth peace goodwill toward men." Then they left and returned to heaven. (Luke 2:8-15, NKJV.)

When Jesus was raised back to life after His crucifixion on the Cross, the angel descended from heaven and rolled away the stone from the tomb where His body had been laid. The Bible says the angel's countenance was like lightning, and his clothing as white as snow. So awesome was his appearance that those guarding Jesus' tomb shook with fear and "became like dead men" (Matthew 28:1-7).

In these last days I believe there will be as much or more angelic activity for Jesus' Second Coming as there was during His first coming to earth. The term "angel" comes from the Greek word *aggelos,* which means, "messenger."* Hebrews 1:13-14 NKJV [brackets mine] says of the angels, "But to which of the angels has He ever said, 'Sit at My right hand, till I make Your enemies Your footstool?' Are they [angels] not all ministering spirits sent forth to minister for those who will inherit salvation?" The Bible says of these angels, they are "mighty" (2 Thessalonians 1:7). They are here to minister to *us* and for *us.*

Many years ago the Lord sent an angel from heaven in human form to assist me. In the late 1980s I lived in Everett, Washington, with my husband, Mike. While there an old friend I had met at Bible school in 1982 invited me to minister in a church in Grand Forks, British Columbia, Canada, for a week of revival meetings. I accepted the invitation, enthusiastic to preach the Word and equally excited to see old friends again.

I packed my three red suitcases, one large hard-sided, one medium-sized, and a small carry-on. They contained all I would need for the week, including some beautiful gold nugget jewelry my husband bought for me as a birthday and anniversary gift. Tucking the black velvet case with the gold jewelry in the outside pocket of the carry-on, I headed to the Seattle airport.

I had hotel reservations in Vancouver, British Columbia, for a one-night stay and planned to continue on to Grand Forks, B. C. the next morning. When I arrived at the Vancouver airport that evening, the sky was dark with ominous clouds pouring out sheets of rain. The airport was almost empty. Standing by the baggage claim carousel, I waited for my bags to come down the conveyer belt. Being the only three red suitcases, I spotted them easily. I picked them up, put them on a cart, and wheeled them to the waiting line of taxis outside the terminal.

When I stopped at the first cab the driver jumped out. Opening the trunk he put the big suitcase in, then the medium size one. As he reached for my carry-on, I thought, *What am I doing standing out in this rain?* I then stepped back on to the curb, opened the back door, and got in.

"Please take me to the Blue Bell Hotel," I told the driver.

When we arrived at the front door of the hotel the driver jumped out, opened my car door, then rounded the back of the cab to open the trunk. After he loaded my suitcases on a cart and wheeled them into the hotel, I walked up to the front desk and told the manager my name. He gave me a card to fill out and asked if I needed assistance with my suitcases.

"Yes," I said, as I finished filling out my registration card. Glancing down at my suitcases I noticed that my red carry-on was missing. I looked up to see the cab driver heading out the front door. "Wait!" I yelled, but he kept on going.

"He forgot to bring in my small carry-on," I told the hotel agent. "Please call the cab driver back." He picked up the phone and called the cab company. The dispatcher told him he would contact the cab driver and have him return to the hotel with my carry-on. Several minutes later the dispatcher called back and told the hotel agent that the cab driver pulled off the road as soon as he received the call to come back to the hotel. He claimed that he had checked in the trunk of his cab and found no carry-on.

I said firmly, "*Please* call the dispatcher back and tell him I want that cab driver to come back so I can question him." After I waited several more minutes, the dispatcher called and said the cab driver refused to return to the hotel because he had already given me my two suitcases from his trunk. By then, it was getting late and I had to get to bed to get a good night's rest for the next day's journey.

"Please call the police and tell them what happened," I told the hotel agent. He reluctantly called the police department and instructed me to wait in the lobby for an officer to arrive. By the time the officer arrived it was about 10:30 P.M., and I was becoming increasingly upset with the situation.

When the large-framed officer approached me, he asked the hotel agent for a private room to interview me then took me to the back office. When he asked me to tell my story, I offered him every detail. "I have thousands of dollars worth of jewelry that my husband gave me as gifts in a black velvet box tucked in the outside pocket of that red carry-on," I explained. "And I *must* get it back!"

"I've interviewed the cab driver and now have interviewed you, and between you and me, Mrs. Ellers, I believe you," he said with a kind look. "However, you'll never be able to convince a judge in a court of law, as it'll be your word against his. I'm sorry, but I'm afraid your jewelry is lost."

Thanking him, I thought, *No way! We'll see about this.*

I headed to my hotel room, and as soon as I got in the room I dropped to my knees and prayed. In closing I shared a passing thought, "…and oh, Lord, *You* know where my bag is, and so I ask You to send an angel to bring it back to me, in Jesus' name. Amen." I retired for the evening, and the next morning dashed back to the airport to catch my flight to Grand Forks, B. C.

After arriving at my friend's home I unpacked and prepared to preach. Before I brought the Word I mentioned my missing carry-on bag and continued with the service, not giving it a second thought. We enjoyed wonderful revival meetings, and the week flew by. Before I knew it, it was time to return home.

I boarded my jet and flew to Vancouver, this time arriving early enough in the day to catch a connecting flight to Seattle. My travel agent had scheduled my connections too close, so after going through customs I had to hurry to my airline check-in counter and get in line. A woman in front of me was smoking a cigarette and blowing smoke away from me. When the smoke still wafted towards me with its nauseating odor, I tried to look in the opposite direction from where she was blowing smoke. I moved up in line. *Only two more people to go,* I thought. *Oh, how I wish they would hurry! I don't want to miss my plane!*

When I looked at the sign above the agent working behind the counter, I suddenly realized I was at the *wrong* counter! I scanned the area, searching for the right counter, then took a quick glance back at the agent behind the counter. There were now two men standing behind the counter. The second one—who must have just arrived—looked at me with a glint in his eyes. Smiling at me, he lifted his arm up high—and in his hand was my red carry-on bag!

"That's my bag!" I squealed.

The other agent looked at this man, then at me, then back at this "agent," and said, "Lady, if you have your ticket for it, it's yours."

"I sure do," I said with certainty. I opened my purse and produced the ticket for him. He took it from the other man and compared the tickets.

"It's yours!" he exclaimed.

"Thank you!" I said, grabbing my bag. I wasted no time unzipping the side compartment, where I found my velvet case. I pulled it out and opened it up in front of the woman in front of me, who was at that moment taking a long drag off her cigarette. When I saw (and she saw) my jewelry intact, I said, "Oh, praise the Lord!"

"Yes!" she chimed in.

Remembering that I had a plane to catch, I took off running to find the right counter. When I saw the man who had produced my carry-on was walking toward me I thought, *I've just got to stop and give him a quick testimony.* Slowing down to a fast-paced stride, I approached him and looked into his eyes, so intense, shiny, and unusual. As I started to open my mouth I sensed the Holy Spirit speak loudly in my spirit, "He knows!"

I thought, *He knows.* Rather than stop to tell him my story I kept walking as quickly as I could. Not thinking anymore about it, I boarded my Seattle-bound flight, settled into my assigned seat, then sat in silent prayer thanking the Lord for bringing my jewelry back.

When I returned home I told my husband the story of finding my jewelry—still not fully realizing what had *really happened* but so grateful for recovering my loss. After sharing the story with Mike I decided to sit down and write my lady friend a "Thank you" card. I started out telling her how much I appreciated her hospitality and for hosting me for the week, then added a postscript: "Oh, by the way, an *angel... an ANGEL?*"

I stopped writing, then shrieked, "Mike! That man who brought my carry-on bag to the airport was an angel! Mike, he was an angel!"

Mike looked at me for a long moment. "Oh yeah, sure Flo," he said, then went back to what he was doing.

I thought, *No one is going to take away my joy of this moment,* then phoned my friend long distance. "Pastor Sam," I said, "you're probably *not* going to believe what just happened to me, but...." I told him the story, not leaving out one detail (as only a woman can do), and then waited for his response.

He immediately retorted, "Of course it was an angel, Flo! Do you think that agent was standing there for a whole week waiting for you to return to the airport at the *wrong counter?* Then at *precisely* the moment you looked up he lifted your carry-on bag so you could see it? Now what do you suppose the mathematical probability of that would be?"

With that question in mind, we both laughed.

"Sam, he looked like an Italian. He was short, stocky-built, and had black hair. Pastor Sam, that means an Italian-looking angel brought back my jewelry! Oh, thank You, Jesus."

Flo Ellers has been in full time ministry since 1982. She received her doctorate in ministry in 1998 from Shalom Bible School and Seminary in West Des Moines, Iowa. The primary emphasis of her ministry is to train and equip God's end-time revivalists. Flo lives with her husband, Mike, of forty-three years in Aberdeen, Washington.

*James Strong, Exhaustive Concordance of the Bible, "Greek Dictionary of the New Testament," (Nashville, TN: Thomas Nelson Publishers, 1984), #32.

32

THE OTHER GUY

by Gail Justesen

Are not all angels ministering spirits sent to serve those who will inherit salvation?

HEBREWS 1:14

"*D*rive safe and watch out for *the other guy* on the highway," Grandma warned. Stuffed with two days of her Thanksgiving cooking, we said our reluctant good-byes with hugs and blessings.

"Wasn't it great everyone could come this year?" my husband, Gary, asked as our little family settled into the van for the two-hour trip home. The kids, exhausted from holiday activities, smiled and nodded sleepily. Seated in the comfy captain's chairs, we shot up a prayer for travel mercies and slowly backed out of the driveway.

"I'll give them to the freeway on-ramp to stay awake," I mused. The snow, lightly falling, added to the "Ahhhhh" at the close of this special holiday. Normally the drive from Moses Lake to Spokane was serene and uneventful. I often succumbed to the monotony and slept. However, this evening weather reports on the radio went from bad to worse.

"That news isn't very encouraging," I admitted as an unexpected wave of anxiety washed over me. I reasoned it away, remembering that Gary had thousands of miles of driving experience through his work. Still, I found myself unable to drift off to sleep. The interior dash lights revealed the concern on both of our faces, as the snowfall increased steadily. I glanced back at the children sleeping peacefully. *Why can't I trust like that?* I wondered.

About an hour into our trip, the scenery before us became blurred with thick surges of blowing snow. It was accumulating at an alarming speed. We forged ahead. That sick feeling returned and the silent prayers became audible. In unison we called for God's protection, "Oh God, protect us and get us home safely!" But my faith in His covering was belittled by what I saw in front of us. Strung along the freeway, like the floor of our kid's playroom during Matchbox derbies, were vehicles sideways and stuck in the ditch.

We zigzagged around stalled vehicles as another wave of fear hit me. The wipers could barely keep ahead of the snow on the windshield. My hands gripped the arms of the velvet chair. I swallowed hard as I peered out of the window, trying to recognize our whereabouts.

Suddenly, on the front bumper of our tall van, the form of two fleshy, huge legs came into focus. *What was I seeing?* I gasped, thinking they would impede my husband's vision and send us joining others in the ditch. Alarmed and confused I sputtered, "Oh, my gosh...I think...uh...oh...wow"!

I looked toward Gary for his reaction. He was completely preoccupied with driving through the blizzard. He took my words as fear in what was before us on the highway. *Was he unaware of this most immediate obstacle?* The backs of the knees on this creature were above our eye-level! Like a figurehead on a ship it was cutting a path through the storm riding on our van. *How could he not see it?*

Oddly, an unexplained peace came over me. Looking back to the windshield, I discovered that the form was gone. Instinctively, I knew I had seen the angel assigned to our van to get us home safely. Again I looked over at Gary, steadily plowing through the white darkness. This time I calmly and clearly said, "We are going to make it home, honey. This time, *the other guy* is our angel and *he is BIG!*"

"Tell me about it," he said, not taking his eyes off the road but welcoming a diversion from the mesmerizing blizzard.

Reverently, I tried to describe our traveling companion to my curious spouse. As he persisted with questions I realized that I had only seen the angel's thick, tree-trunk legs. He was so tall that anything just above his knees—covered with an armor-like skirt—was out of my view. My glimpse into the spiritual world was only momentary, but I was changed forever. For certain, I now know God dispatches His servants to protect and guide His children.

One other time my celestial visitor made himself known. Again, I felt the sense of a peaceful presence in my bedroom. The sight of those cedar-like legs, the rest of his body concealed by the ceiling, brought reassurance as I quickly recovered from a horrible fever. My bedroom became a doorstep to the unseen kingdom of tranquility. Fear subsided in the presence of God's messenger of peace and healing.

Several years have passed since my last encounter with *the other guy,* whom I affectionately call "Legs." His partial image was so implanted in my mind and heart that I may never *need* to see him again. I simply know he is here, a constant watch and guard over me, a sentinel from my heavenly Father.

Gail Justesen is a writer and speaker. Currently, she is also a driver's education instructor. She enjoys encouraging people of all ages to fulfill God's unique purposes for them. Gail and her husband, Gary, have been married twenty-nine years and have two grown sons. Together they minister at marriage retreats at home and abroad.

33

AN EXTRAORDINARY JOURNEY
by Sue Reeve

God, who has called you into fellowship with his Son Jesus Christ
our Lord, is faithful.

1 CORINTHIANS 1:19

It was just another ordinary day in autumn when I, an ordinary woman, drove to work. Each year I exult in the colors, smells, and clear, crisp days of fall, yet I also see the melancholy side of autumn. The dark cloud of a looming winter plagues me. Winter in my home of Coeur d'Alene, Idaho, is magical, with snow blanketing abundant evergreens and mystical fog hovering over beautiful lakes surrounding our lovely resort city. It loses its magic for me, however, because winter means day after long, dark, dreary day, commuting in often-hazardous driving conditions.

On that ordinary workday, the conflicting emotions associated with autumn and winter were on my mind as I drove forty miles to my job in Spokane, Washington. It's a good job, and I enjoy stimulating, rewarding work. The job wasn't my problem—my problem was the daily trip I abhorred. In fact, my commute was frequently the subject of my morning prayer. I whined to God, declaring in no uncertain terms that I wanted to be delivered from commuting. I often tried convincing Him to see things my way. That day was no different. I told Him to change my circumstances.

Prayer has always been part of my life. I've never doubted God's availability to me through the avenue of prayer. But my requests were often self-centered, "Gimme, please" prayers. Prior to that morning, I'd never developed a consistent and disciplined prayer life.

On that ordinary autumn workday, I imagine God may have said, "It is time I reveal to My child that while she may be ordinary, I am not."

The Old Testament prophet Elijah described hearing God in a "still, small voice." That morning, while driving to work in my Toyota Camry on I-90 somewhere between Idaho and Washington, I also heard that still, small voice. The message was unmistakable. I knew in the depths of my spirit what God was saying. "I want you to live in Coeur d'Alene; I want you to work in Spokane; and furthermore, I want you to turn this car into your prayer closet."

To many the term *prayer closet* would seem strange, but it was familiar to me. Hearing it often while growing up in church and Sunday school, I knew it was a special place where one retreated to pray seriously. The still, small voice giving me the prayer-closet instruction in old King James vernacular was unmistakable, credible, and convincing. Accepting His direction, I said, "Okay, God. I can do that!"

As well as being very ordinary, I'm also inclined to be a project person. I approach tasks in the beginning, assuming each has a middle and ending. Somehow I knew my new commitment to prayer must not become another project. Never before had the still, small voice prompted me to pray. I knew this life of prayer was not merely a process—another project. This was a special, unique journey. That it began during my daily commute was only symbolic of a greater life journey that I knew was beginning.

I determined that since God had taken time to speak to me, He also wanted to be my travel companion. I confessed that I had been haphazard in my relationship with Him. I told Him I wanted to learn to be an obedient, godly woman and confessed that I had let the noise of the world and my own thoughts drown out His voice. I wanted to quiet down and learn to listen. For too many years I had tried to be what I thought I should be or what I thought someone else thought I should be. Now, I wanted to be an absolutely authentic woman. God's approval was all that mattered.

Remaining focused on prayer presented a distinct challenge. A word or thought easily triggered my active imagination. Before long, a prayer took on a life of its own, becoming another of my fantasies! I needed a plan to keep me on track, so I determined to pray according to exit markers. Since my husband had started working in a new sales territory between Exits 287 and 283, I started praying for Ron daily from exit 287 to exit 283. It fit perfectly with my penchant for projects!

Each daughter, son-in-law, and the grandchildren soon had designated exits. I prayed for other family members, friends, our church, the nation, and my needs accordingly. Although it seemed weird and I'd never heard of anyone praying in this manner, it felt right. I sensed God was pleased with me, possibly even smiling. The thought of pleasing Him felt great.

The journey continued—day after day—week after week—month after month. Instead of detesting the commute, I looked forward to it. My circumstances didn't change, and I continued to drive on the same freeway with the same road conditions. Yet, I was changing. It was through a sincere transformation occurring from the inside out. My traveling prayer closet became a haven where intimate soul talk occurred. I spent less time focusing on my preferences and focusing more time thinking about the awesome wonder of God. I whined less and worshipped more.

After several months I felt I needed a partner to support my new spiritual journey, so I asked my friend Jackie if I could routinely check in with her. We began meeting weekly. One week we discussed her surgeon husband's request that Jackie accompany him on his next short-term mission trip to Africa. While Duane spent long hours in a Cameroon mission hospital, Jackie joyfully conducted Bible studies for hungry, native women. She kept me up to date with e-mail messages that provided glimpses into rich African culture.

One of Jackie's messages altered my life.

After writing about teaching a study on The Lord's Prayer, as an aside she shared the story about how her friend in the United States prayed according to the exit markers while commuting to work. Afterward an excited woman approached Jackie, sharing that she too prayed according to the markers along the road as she trekked one hour a day to work. She told Jackie that because she didn't think another person in the world prayed like I did, my story encouraged her.

Tears welled and splashed down my cheeks as I re-read Jackie's e-mail. Coincidental? I think not. I believe that God in loving wisdom linked the hearts of two ordinary working women who lived continents apart. A plethora of emotions erupted as I pondered the African woman with whom I shared this unusual bond. I felt humbled recalling the times I complained to God. While I commuted in a comfortable car, with heat in winter and air-conditioning in summer, the woman in Cameroon walked unprotected during dreadful summer heat and torrential monsoon rains.

The African woman's story reinforced a sense of God's divine love for me. In turn I felt greater love for Him and a deep love for this woman, whose skin color was different than mine, whose culture was unfamiliar, and whose name I did not know. I knew He understood when I added my commuting friend from Cameroon to my freeway prayer agenda.

An awareness of a larger meaning for my existence dawned. As I prayed for my Cameroon friend, I felt a deep sense of global connectedness even though I had never travelled internationally. The next year, after sending my friend a letter and bookmark with a poem I'd written, Jackie returned with a letter and family picture. My friend now had a name, Pauline, a husband, and three sons about the same ages as my grandchildren.

I often prayed for Pauline and her family right after praying for my married daughter and her family. She became not only my commuting friend, but also my spiritual daughter in Africa. Each year since, Jackie and Duane have taken pictures of our family, gifts for each family member, plus a check to help with the boys' educational expenses. Pauline tells me the little boys ask when they will see their "Grandmom from America." The journey of prayer, begun in my car when I said, "Okay, God. I can do that," had miraculously spanned the globe.

Several years have passed since my journey began. My Toyota prayer closet—now with over two hundred thousand miles—often feels as holy as a beautiful cathedral, a sacred sanctuary where my spirit joins with the God of the Universe. Looking in the mirror, I realize that I'm still a very ordinary woman, but I am intimately and miraculously connected to an extraordinary God who knows my name. He cares so much about me that He whispered gently and convincingly, inviting me to take a journey with Him—an exciting lifelong journey—sure to be filled with many miraculous moments.

Sue lives with her husband, Ron, in beautiful Coeur d'Alene, Idaho. She is mom to two grown daughters and has three amazing grandchildren. Sue has worked in the public marketplace as a certified employee assistance professional. She is an active member of New Life Community Church in Hayden, Idaho, where she served as women's ministry director for several years. Sue has actively participated in the leadership of a regional inter-denominational women's ministry networking group. She has spoken for several Christian women's events. Since 2003 she has felt privileged to partner with an inner-city women's ministry program in Washington, D.C. In August 2005 Sue and her husband made their first international missions trip to South Africa.

34

ON THE THIRD DAY

by Marta Nelson

He told them, 'This is what is written: The Christ will suffer and rise from the dead on the third day, and repentance and forgiveness of sins will be preached in his name to all nations, beginning at Jerusalem.'

LUKE 24:46,47

The winter of 2003-04 was frigid in Spokane, Washington. Temperatures dropped below ten degrees for a week at a time, which is especially cold for this area of the country. Our home is very old, and at the time still had its original windows. Most of them were broken, at least one in each bedroom. Upstairs, downstairs, and on the main floor the windows were not just cracked but broken, with a chunk of glass missing. Because it was such old glass, when the windows cracked a corner would fall out, and in many cases the whole pane fell out because the old caulk had chipped away, leaving nothing to hold the pane in place.

My husband, Stephen, and I could not afford to replace the windows, nor did we possess fix-it skills or even an inkling of how to do that type of handyman work. I covered most of the broken windows with cardboard and tape, but air continued to flow through. Although it wasn't a permanent solution, we believed that Stephen would soon make enough money to allow us to replace the windows. In hindsight we probably could have replaced the windows with the money we spent on increased heating bills!

We had applied for and had been approved for a low-income housing rehabilitation program available to Spokane residents. Kiemle & Hagood, the organization contracted by the city of Spokane to run the housing rehab program, issues a list of homes in the rehabilitation program needing contractors. After several contractors had come to our home to bid the job, we chose a contractor—*so we thought.*

The windows in Stephen's and my bedroom, a large old-style window and a second standard window, were the best windows in the house. In the summer of 2004 while we were on vacation, my neighbor had caught another neighbor's kid climbing through our bedroom window. Using a power tool and screws, he screwed all of our windows shut. When we returned, I left the screws in the windows with the exception of two: the boys' room in case of fire and the large window in our bedroom so I could install the window air conditioner.

One day in the early part of winter, our cat Sonic found herself locked in our bedroom. Desperate to get out, she pushed on the windowpane of the large window where the air conditioner had been during the summer. Pressing the glass with her paws, the entire pane fell out and broke, leaving a gaping hole.

Although replacing a few of the windows or at least putting card-board over the large window in our bedroom would have seemed reasonable, we didn't do anything to correct the situation because we knew the windows would be replaced through the housing rehabilitation program, slated to start in February or March. Our broken and missing windows weren't very attractive, yet it didn't seem like a big deal to me. It simply never bothered me.

Because Steven worked nights as a nurse at Holy Family Hospital, my bedroom became the preferred sleeping spot for our family. The kids— Marquita, Dakota, and Parker—wanted to be with Mom while Dad was working. Amazingly, although we slept in my bedroom throughout the winter with cold air flowing through the paneless window, we never felt too cold. Even when the temperature dropped into the low teens or below, we slept comfortably while everything was frozen solid outside. It seems strange, but the colder the weather got the more we liked the window open and the better we slept.

Marquita slept upstairs some of the time, but her bedroom windows were nonexistent. Her bedroom is in the converted attic, a long narrow room the full length of the house. It had a small window at either end, one with no pane and the other missing a quarter of the pane. Both had a makeshift cover of cardboard. Normal airflow through that room makes it freezing in the winter and hot as Arizona in the summer.

Pastor Randy Klein, Senior Pastor of Living Water Church, is also a contractor in Spokane. He had worked on houses in the rehabilitation program in the past, but because he had been building a new home he had not accepted a housing rehab job in over a year.

One day when Pastor Randy stopped in at the Kiemle & Hagood office downtown, he saw the flyer listing the houses needing contractors in the rehabilitation program. God whispered to him, "Pick that up!" So he did. Thumbing through the listing, he felt prompted by the Holy Spirit to call us. After calling us immediately, he came right over. We knew the moment we met Pastor Randy that he was supposed to be our contractor. And he knew it too.

In March 2004 Pastor Randy arrived to replace our windows—and what a beautiful job he did! In less than three days he replaced all windows, including two huge egress windows in the basement and one in the attic. Suddenly our house was sealed tight! Noise we normally heard from outside could no longer be heard. With the windows shut, I couldn't even hear the kids playing outside.

A remarkable series of events occurred over the next three days. The day Pastor Randy installed the windows my mom, Marquita McIntire, called me from California. "Marta," she said, "although I don't understand the reason, I know I'm supposed to put some money into your bank account. I don't know why, but I feel you need some money. I happen to have some money right now, and I'm going to put it in your bank account." She had received money from an old debt owed her.

"Okay, Mom. I'm good with that!" I said. "I don't know what it's for either, but…cool!" So Mom deposited ten thousand dollars into my account. Little did either of us know that God had divine plans for that money.

The next day Pastor Randy said, "Marta, we can get you a really cheap air conditioner right now because it's off season, and there's not a lot of work right now. You can think about it."

I thought, *Well, that's kind of a weird thing to spend Mom's money on.*

I called her. "Mom, how does this sound?" I asked. "I can get an air conditioner for less than half price right now, but it sounds like a weird thing to spend your money on."

"That doesn't sound weird at all," Mom answered. "I think if you need an air conditioner, and you can get it for half price, then that must have been one of the reasons you needed the money. Go ahead and do it!" At that moment I thought, *Great! An air conditioner!*

I called Pastor Randy. "We're going to go ahead and get the air conditioner!" On the third day representatives from Hurliman Heating installed the system. When one of the service people got to the final step of connecting it to the household furnace, he opened it up and realized that our furnace was severely damaged. The heat exchanger was cracked, he said, and the amount of carbon monoxide leaking from it was absolutely deadly. When he removed the heater core he had to tag it. Because of the dangerous condition of our furnace, it wasn't even legal for him to walk away from it as it was. If he left it that way, he could be responsible for our possible deaths.

After removing the heater core, he talked to Pastor Randy and the two of them sat down with me to explain the situation. "The amount of carbon monoxide that's been leaking into your home is deadly," he said. "The only reason you and your family are still alive is because your broken windows vented the carbon monoxide to the outdoors. But now that your windows are sealed shut, the first time that heater kicks on, you could all die." Then he added, "There's absolutely no doubt in my mind about this. It's not a situation where a little carbon monoxide might make you sick; this amount would have killed you all."

When I realized the representative from Hurliman felt bad about having to take my heater core, I said, "Don't feel bad! You can have it. Take it!"

We now had an air conditioner but no furnace; but we still had our lives, and that's what mattered. That night the temperature dropped, and if our furnace had been connected it would have kicked on. I called Mom and shared the situation with her. "Mom, this is outrageous what happened here," I said. "Because God allowed the whole broken window thing, we're alive!"

God had given Mom unexpected money, prompted her to give it to us, then within three days of the windows being sealed we decided to take advantage of purchasing an air conditioner. In the process of installing the system, we learned about the life-threatening condition of our existing furnace, which saved our lives. With Mom's approval, we spent the rest of her money on a new furnace.

When God prompted Mom to give us the $10,000, she didn't know the details or the reasons, but she obeyed God anyway. The air conditioner cost $1900, the furnace $2000, we had been about $4000 behind on the mortgage and other bills, and $2000 was needed for extra work in the house. God provided for *all* of our needs.

The next winter of 2004-05, although I realized it wasn't rational or possible, I said, "It's colder in the bedroom this winter with windows closed and a new furnace than it was last winter with the windows open!" Everyone agreed. In spite of our eyesore broken windows, God had kept us warm supernaturally, then in His time made provision for new windows, an air conditioner, and a furnace—and saved our lives in the process.

Marta Nelson is blessed with Stephen, her loving husband, and their three children, Marquita, Dakota, and Parker. They live in Spokane, Washington, and attend Spokane Christian Center.

35

OH BABY!

by Lydiah Parkinson

*So in the course of time Hannah conceived and gave birth to a son.
She named him Samuel, saying, 'Because I asked the LORD for him.'*

1 SAMUEL 1:20

I arrived in Minneapolis, Minnesota, from Kenya in February 1996 to pursue nursing studies and graduated from Hennepin Technical College in Eden Prairie, Minnesota. My husband, Terry, and I met through Equally Yoked Christian Singles, a national organization that brings Christian singles together. We were married June 23, 2001, in Minneapolis.

Terry and I had been married about a year and a half when we decided to start a family. Since our friends seemed to be having babies effortlessly, some even unplanned and caught off guard, we felt confident we would conceive instantly. News of a pregnancy at any time would have been welcome news for us too.

After six months of trying to conceive proved unsuccessful, we enlisted the help of a fertility doctor who came highly recommended by our family physician, Dr. Benny Walker. Dr. Kopher, from Como Clinic in St. Paul, Minnesota, started medical procedures on both of us. We underwent extensive tests—blood work, labs, urology tests, a laparoscopy procedure on me—to rule out any medical condition that might be preventing us from conceiving.

After learning that all test results indicated no physical abnormalities, our anxiety over our inability to conceive only increased. In my mind I caught myself asking, *Why God? Why can't we just have a baby? Just one is all we ask for.* God had blessed us in so many ways. I had graduated from nursing school several years prior, Terry and I had good jobs, and we had built a beautiful home. All we needed to make the house a home was a baby.

With each passing month of no pregnancy, my heart dropped further into despair. The precious gift of a baby seemed to become an increasingly distant dream. In my disappointment I avoided anything that reminded me of my desire for a baby, including baby showers and birth announcements. I envied expectant mothers, as they had the one thing I could not have.

One Sunday evening in August of 2003, I attended a service at Abundant Life Church in Blaine, Minnesota, where a visiting evangelist from Russia was scheduled to preach. As he ministered that night, the evangelist (whom I had never met) unexpectedly called me to the front of the church. He delivered a word of knowledge by the power of the Holy Spirit, saying that my desperate prayer would be answered within the next year.

In the meantime depression and migraine headaches had set in, and we became increasingly desperate to conceive. We started rounds of fertility treatments through artificial insemination. Our insurance company would only cover seven rounds. If unsuccessful after seven attempts, they declare a couple infertile and will no longer provide further insurance coverage. After our sixth unsuccessful insemination attempt, I became restless and started considering the option of adopting a baby from overseas.

I had prayed, fasted, and believed God for so long but saw no answer to my desperate prayer for a baby. I felt it would be easier to adopt a baby than to suffer repeated disappointment while I waited for my own baby. I started gathering the necessary paperwork to pursue adoption.

In the process of looking into adoption, my father, James Mutahi, pastor of Faith Christian Center Fellowship and a prayerful man of God, spoke out in faith. "I believe God has a greater plan," he told Terry and me. "You will have a baby of your own." He encouraged us not to lose sight of faith, and he prayed.

One month later, in August 2004, God answered our desperate prayer. I was pregnant! I experienced a tough pregnancy with many complications. Suffering from Hyper-emesis Graridum made it difficult to keep fluids and foods in my stomach. I lost forty pounds during the pregnancy. The doctor inserted a pick line, which is a permanent IV, in my right arm in order to transfuse a liter of hydrating fluids and medication into my system daily. In spite of the difficulties, God saw me through the pregnancy and protected my baby from any harm.

Our beautiful daughter grew healthy to full term. On May 28, 2005, I delivered a beautiful baby girl whom we named Kimberly Elizabeth. She weighed 7 lbs. 3 oz. and was 19 inches long. Terry and I feel truly blessed for this miracle God performed for us. We know without a doubt that He hears our desperate prayers and is always there for us.

Lydiah Parkinson was born in Kenya, East Africa, and relocated to Minneapolis in 1996 to pursue studies as a licensed practical nurse. She works in nursing at Mount Olivet Home, a long-term geriatric care facility. Lydiah, her husband, Terry, and their daughter, Kimberly, live in Blaine, Minnesota.

36

SOS

by Della Walton

However, when He, the Spirit of truth, has come, He will guide you into all truth; for He will not speak on His own authority, but whatever He hears He will speak; and He will tell you things to come.

JOHN 16:13 NKJV

In April 2004 my parents, Leonard and Ruth Meier, joyfully anticipated a vacation they had planned to the Oregon Coast. Although I shared their excitement over an opportunity to get away for some rest and relaxation, I felt increasingly concerned about their pending trip. I knew Mom and Dad had travelled numerous times without incident, but I sensed an undeniable urgency to pray for their protection. Not wanting to alarm them, I expressed my concern only to my husband, Tim. I didn't understand what I was feeling, yet I continued to respond to God's prompting to pray.

Friday evening, the night before Mom and Dad headed out of town, I sensed an urgency to visit them, still unsure of why I felt an impending danger. At Mom and Dad's house I kept my concern to myself, but asked some casual questions to silence the alarm clanging in my spirit. First, I asked Dad how he was feeling. "I feel great," he said, explaining he had just been checked out by his doctor. Mom assured me that she felt good also. *No red flags in the health arena,* I thought.

After chatting further about their trip to the coast and asking about the details of the travel plan, I quizzed them about the condition of their car. Dad had always been methodical about maintenance and faithful about servicing his car. He explained that he had just picked the car up after having the transmission adjusted.

Okay, I thought. *I've asked what I can without alarming them.* After kissing Mom and Dad and saying, "I love you," I advised them to be careful and encouraged them to enjoy their vacation.

As Tim and I pulled away, I told God that I trusted His ability to keep Mom and Dad safe. Again, I prayed. "Lord, thank You for Your divine hand of protection that covers my parents," I said. "I trust You to keep them safe from all harm. You're always in control and always on time, even when I don't know exactly what to pray."

The weekend passed and the next week came and went without a 911 call from Mom and Dad, so I felt confident they were enjoying their vacation. I thanked God again for His faithfulness in taking care of my parents.

On Wednesday evening Mom called to let us know they were home. When I asked if they enjoyed their vacation, she said, "We had a great time, but…didn't you hear what happened?"

My heart skipped a beat. "Hear *what*, Mom?" I said. "*What* happened?"

Enroute to Oregon Mom and Dad had noticed a faint thumping noise erupting from under the hood of the car. Initially the strange sound didn't concern them because their car had been serviced before leaving on vacation. As they pulled off the Salem/Kaiser exit in Oregon, however, their car lurched and sputtered to the stop sign at the end of the ramp.

Dad tried to take off again, but the car wouldn't move at first. Revving the motor to 3000 RPM, he finally got the crawling car going and coaxed it to the side of the road. By the time the car stopped, dark smoke billowed from the hood of the car. The transmission fluid had spewed over the engine and had caught fire.

A man passing from the other direction saw Mom and Dad's crisis and called the fire department from his cell phone before my parents' car had even come to a stop. The Good Samaritan pulled up behind Mom and Dad's car and before getting out of his car or talking to my parents, he dispatched a tow truck and repair services from his cell phone.

When the man blew on the fire, it went out! The Good Samaritan, who *happened* to own an auto repair shop, had instant access to the towing services. After talking to Mom and Dad, he said he would have Dad's car towed in to the auto shop for repair.

When Dad called his insurance company from the side of the road, they delivered a rental car to the roadside location within thirty minutes. Everything was taken care of for them, without them having to lift a finger.

Not only did the insurance company cover the cost of the rental car, they covered all motel and gas expenses for the entire trip, plus the car repair as well. Mom and Dad learned later that the insurance company covered the repairs because there had been a fire involved. Without the fire, repairs would not have been included.

Mom said that when the fire started, she got out of the car, grabbed her shoes and purse, and headed away from the car. The Good Samaritan asked Mom if she would like to wait in his car while the commotion was going on. She took him up on the offer and told him she thought he must be an angel. Although he assured Mom that he wasn't an angel, she knew God sent him to help in their time of need.

Getting in the car, she discovered two little boys in the back seat, about ages six and three. While they waited, the older boy read Mom a storybook, then the younger boy pretended to read to her. When the older boy told Mom that his mom and dad were divorced, it became obvious to her that his parents' divorce burdened his heart. Mom told him about Jesus, telling him that he can pray and talk to Jesus any time. She was thankful to have the opportunity to tell him about Jesus, her source of hope.

When Mom and Dad picked up their car at the auto repair shop, the repairman explained that when Dad's car was serviced before their vacation, a vital part of the transmission had not been tightened properly. This caused the transmission fluid to leak out and the part to come loose. What a disaster it could have been if the car fire had spread or if it had started while they were on the freeway, far from needed help! God's mighty hand of protection had covered Mom and Dad.

After Mom finished telling me about their Oregon vacation adventure, I confessed that God had warned me of their pending danger and compelled me to pray for their protection. Mom and Dad were glad I had prayed and thankful that God had answered.

God is so good and is always on time!

Della has been married for more than twenty years to her wonderful husband, Tim. They have two beautiful daughters, Jana and Amanda. Della's passion is to love Jesus and serve Him by serving others. She has worked in the medical field for many years and is a currently a scheduler for a vascular medical facility. She enjoys cooking and spending time with friends.

37

NO LONGER DEAD—AND A NEW LEG!

by Carole Miller McCleery

*Believe me when I say that I am in the Father and the Father is
in me; or at least believe on the evidence of the miracles themselves.*

JOHN 14:11

*W*hen my husband died of emphysema in January 1981, I sunk to
the lowest point of my life. Not only did I have three daughters to raise, I
was dying of lupus. Six months after my husband's death, while driving to
West Palm Beach, Florida, I was involved in a horrible automobile accident
when a back tire blew out as I crossed a small bridge. At the same time, an
eighteen-wheel tractor-trailer loaded with two earth-moving machines
turned to cross the road. A bar sticking out through the trailer hit my car,
tore off the windows and roof, then threw the car into a spin. I was ejected,
landing a good distance from the car. The truck hit my car again, cutting
it in half. I was told later that my car looked as if a chain saw had separated
the front from the back, then threw it to the side of the road.

Before the ambulance arrived the highway patrol found a name and
phone number in my purse. It was my daughter's grandmother, known to
family and friends as Big Mama. When the patrolman called Big Mama, she
fell to her knees and asked God to spare my life. However, I was
pronounced dead at the scene.

When medical personnel lifted my body into the ambulance they felt
a weak pulse, so they worked to revive me until a helicopter arrived to
airlift me to the nearest hospital in Belle Glade, Florida. I was again
pronounced dead on arrival, covered, and brought to the morgue section.
Only God knows how long I remained in this state until someone heard a
noise, ran into the morgue, and found me alive and trying to talk.

The left side of my body was mutilated, my left leg split open from the
ankle to the top of the backside. Above the ankle and below the knee flesh

had been ripped away, exposing bone. My left arm, wrist, and hand had been cut severely, my thumb almost severed. Ribs were broken and my face and mouth smashed. Gangrene soon set in and spread throughout my body, causing a high fever.

Four days later I was airlifted in a coma state to West Palm Beach Community Hospital where I remained in the critical care unit for over three months and underwent twelve major surgeries in eleven weeks.

When my left leg died from gangrene, doctors told my brother that they had to amputate the leg, as it was dead flesh. They wanted to take it off above the femur bone that was broken and separated over two inches. My brother only gave permission for amputation below the knee, less than two inches below the kneecap.

After many weeks on total life support, doctors believed I was brain dead due to the dying experiences and lack of oxygen, so the decision was made to disconnect me. I could no longer take IVs because all of my veins had collapsed. When taken off the respirator, however, I took a breath and continued breathing on my own!

I was still unable to take fluids after IVs were removed. Big Mama, the hero of my survival, moved into our home, cared for my girls, and drove 120 miles round trip daily to the hospital with broth and soup. She said that when spoon-feeding me, two spoonfuls went down and three came back—but she would not let me die.

Through Big Mama's love, prayers, and determination I started to revive. This sweetest mother and sainted friend had faith for me, led me to my full gospel walk with God, and remains precious in our memories to this day.

In late November, two months after the accident, I began coming out of the coma. I didn't know who I was, where I was, or what had happened. When I was thrown from the car the memory part of the brain hit the pavement. Memory of two years preceding the accident, the accident itself, and the months following were gone.

One day I heard the television announcer say, "Danny Miller has been selected as All American," and realized the University of Miami football game was on. I started crying, as I knew Danny Miller. Danny, my nephew whom I loved, was the kicker for University of Miami.

The nurse came in and saw me crying. "You're suffering. You need your pain medication," she said.

"No," I told her. "I'm proud of my nephew because of the honor that was just given to him." I realized who I was! Later a brain scan and other tests confirmed that my brain was perfect and new. I suffered no damage from the restriction of oxygen of being dead twice or from being on life support.

For a year I was hospitalized and took trips home and back again. In the final stage I underwent plastic surgery on my face, including my mouth, chin, and lips. They even created new lips that now proclaim the glory of my God.

God healed me of the lupus and rheumatoid arthritis after the accident. He moves in mysterious ways! The doctor told me I would only have lived a few months if I had not been in the accident. Either the shock to my body from the dying experiences or blood transfusions arrested the medically incurable autoimmune diseases. More than twenty-four years later, I'm still healed of these diseases.

With the femur bone of my left leg over two inches apart, I could have chosen a body cast for a year, but doctors concluded that nothing would bring these two bones together. They suggested that I accept the fact that I would be in a wheelchair for the rest of my life and wear an artificial leg only for cosmetic purposes.

I asked the specialists, "How am I alive?"

"Medically," they said, "you can't be alive."

"The same way I'm alive is the way I will walk again," I said. My faith was in God—and not in men. The doctors could only see that medically it was impossible, but all I could see was Matthew 19:26, "But Jesus beheld them and said unto them, with men this is impossible; but with God all things are possible."

I was sent home to recover, as medical science could do nothing more for me. Eventually I was able to stay alone without nurses or family. Able to get around on crutches, I wanted to start driving again. Family and friends had faithfully taken me wherever I needed to go, but I wanted to make every effort to become independent.

Unable to find my driver's license, I contacted the Florida Highway Patrol to ask how I could get a new license issued. The officer put me on hold to pull my records, then came back to the phone. "Lady, I don't know what you're trying to pull, but Carole Oglesby is deceased," he said. "She was killed in a car accident. It's stamped on her file, and I have her license, so why are you trying to get it?"

I told him I was deceased, but I was not now! I visited the police station for intense questioning to prove I was Carole Oglesby—and indeed alive! Paperwork completed at the accident site indicated I was officially deceased, and their policy is to keep the deceased person's driver's license with the report. When officials were finally convinced that I was Carole Oglesby and had been brought back to life at the hospital, they retested me and issued a new driver's license.

In April 1995 I again faced the word "impossible." The trauma arthritis had caused the knee joints to severely deteriorate, leaving bone against bone. Doctor Kenneth Levy of Advanced Orthopedic Center in Port Charlotte, Florida, performed surgery on both knees, with radical amputation below the left kneecap. Again I was told that nothing more could be done.

Years later I was invited to share my testimony at a ministers' conference held at New Harvest Ministries Church in Holiday, Florida, near Clearwater. After praying for almost everyone, the power of God was moving mightily when Rev. Tyson Prater said, "Carole, may I pray for you? God just spoke to me in an audible voice and said, 'Tell Carole her leg is growing.'"

"Certainly!" I said. When Rev. Tyson touched my head, I knew that just as God "spoke" the world into existence, God spoke that my leg was growing, and His Word could not fail! As Abraham did not waver through unbelief regarding the promise of God, but was strengthened in his faith that he would become the father of many nations, I called my new created leg that was not as if it were by faith and gave the glory to God.

Putting my faith into action, I asked my friend Mrs. Billie Moore to take Kodak pictures of my left leg, showing nothing existing below the knee. I bought a pair of sandals, planning to walk the sandy beaches of Florida again.

Three weeks later, while talking to a friend on the phone, I looked down and saw my left knee come down level with the right knee as my hips came together. From the broken separated femur bones, which had fused together and caused shortage to my left amputated leg, instantly a new femur bone was created and the broken, smashed femur vanished. Seeing this creative miracle before my eyes, my shock turned to overflowing joy and excitement!

When I had X-rays taken the next day, the doctor said, "It's a beautiful healthy bone!" Due to the artificial left leg having been made taller to compensate for the shortage of the femur, the prosthetic was cut off at the ankle area, allowing me to walk level again.

The radical amputation surgery to my left knee in 1995 had removed all the fibula and tibia bones leaving almost nothing to walk on. It amazed doctors that I could even keep an artificial leg on. I did sustain many accidents, as it would slip off and cause me to fall.

After the completion of the new femur, masses of new bone began forming around and under the knee for several weeks. Then growth started down and around with shaping on both sides. The new growth to the knee area made it painful to wear the prosthesis, so I made an appointment with Dr. Levy, the orthopedic specialist who had performed the drastic amputation. He had treated me for fifteen years and had witnessed the other healings and miracles.

I prayed, "Father, how do I explain the new growth below the knee to this man?"

Realizing he was Hebrew, I knew what to say! As he sat down, I said, "'Doctor, prophets of the Old and New Testament said that before Jesus returned again the maimed would be made whole, and that's amputees!"

"Let me see," Dr. Levy said as I slipped off the prosthesis. "I don't need the prophets of old or new but only my own two eyes—your limb is growing into a leg! The only explanation for this is a creative miracle from God."

With God's direction I chose the largest orthopedic and prosthetic corporation to design the first prosthesis for this miracle. They were of Christian origin with offices in nearly every country in the world. I was the first medically documented amputee to be receiving a new creative leg.

The new prosthesis was designed to grow with me. Not enough room was allowed for the newly created fibula bone "head" when it was created. The specialist designer cut a large round hole out of the prosthetic's hard wooden material and replaced it with soft leather. This eliminated the pain and offered a comfortable solution. As growth continued, leather liners, jell plugs, and thicker jell contoured liners were replaced with thinner but larger ones. Wool socks were decreased in thickness until eliminated completely.

After the new creation to my amputated left leg had begun, Dr. Levy said that he and his associates felt this new growth was "holy" and like "touching the face of God." When they said they wanted me to make all future decisions, I told them I wanted an MRI to see what God had created up to this point. An MRI taken January 4, 2001, along with the other X-rays, confirmed the creation of the tibia and fibula heads and hamstring muscles, which came in off the hip, down the pelvis, and attached to the newly created tibia and fibula heads.

In September 2001 I flew into Arkansas for an outreach. I had received a new prosthesis on Monday, a week after the 9/11 attack, flew on Tuesday, and by Wednesday the new prosthesis was so tight it was cutting off circulation to the limb. I spent seven hours in prosthesis shops before Dr. Zooberg, the specialist who had taken over my case, called to tell the prosthesis specialist that he realized what had happened. He directed them to make me as comfortable as possible until I returned to Florida.

Upon my return X-rays documented that the separate fibula bone had been created and came out of the head on the tibia bone, which had been created in three days. God blessed *me* during the outreach to Arkansas!

An MRI taken July 25, 2002, documented new formation of quadriceps muscles, anterial tibaus, and gastrocnemius muscle. Currently my leg has grown to approximately three inches above the ankle. Medical doctors claim the foot will be created since the muscles necessary to support the foot have already been created. The new growth of my "new" leg is exactly like my other leg. MRIs, X-rays, and the complete story of the miracles God has done in my life can be found in *Healing and Miracles to My Life From the Father.*

All glory and praise to God who literally grew a miracle right before my eyes!

Rev. McCleery is an ordained minister through Kingsway Fellowship International. Carole's fifty-year ministry includes prisons, nursing homes, migrant workers, television, crusades, missions, feeding centers, and praying for the sick in hospitals. She has distributed her testimonial book entitled, Healings and Miracles to My Life from the Father* to many priests and pastors in other nations to share her miraculous testimony. Carole, who presently resides in Sprill Hill, Florida, wants the world to know what a mighty, miracle-working, loving God she serves.

* *Healings and Miracles to my Life from the Father,* Copyright 2005, Carole Miller McCleery, Fourth revised edition, ISSN 1521-2343.

38

FROM DEATH TO A MIRACLE
by Kay Ritchey

He said to them, "Let the children come to me. Don't stop them! For the Kingdom of God belongs to such as these. I assure you, anyone who doesn't have their kind of faith will never get into the Kingdom of God."

MARK 10:14,15 NLT

A Spokane, Washington, veterinarian declared our baby kitten dead just weeks after its birth. But when a child put his faith in God and was unwilling to let his pet die—God answered his prayers with a miracle.

On April 30, 1994, my son, Jonathan, my mom, Bonnie, and I were sitting in the bedroom waiting for our cat Scampers to give birth to her kittens. Jonathan's excitement and endless questions typified a four-year-old. Watching five kittens being born was a blessed event for all of us. After a long labor, Scampers was exhausted.

Five weeks after her kittens were born we couldn't find Scampers anywhere. She appeared to be a good mom, so it was hard for us to believe that she would just leave them. Yet we never found her. As the weeks passed we became concerned when we noticed that the kittens looked sickly. When a friend of ours expressed a desire to take the two eight-week-old white kittens, we hesitated and told her they were sick. She assured us she would take good care of them, so we let them go to their new home. Three days later they died.

A veterinarian later determined that the kittens were afflicted with a disease affecting the muscles and spine. With a high mortality rate, it results in a torturous, painful death. Later that week another kitten suffered for several hours then died. After holding a funeral at Jonathan's request, we buried it in our backyard. Its death hurt Jonathan emotionally and caused nightmares for several nights. He repeatedly asked, "If God is so loving and doesn't want us to suffer, then why did our kittens suffer? Doesn't He love them like He loves us?"

By June 6 only one playful gray and white kitten remained, which we named Scampers. On the morning of June 7, we found Scampers lying on her side, motionless. Mom screamed, "Scampers is dying!" Seeing Scampers' lifeless looking body, I agreed.

Using a low-sided cardboard box, sheets, and baby blankets, I made a cozy bed for Scampers on our dining room table. Picking up the limp kitten, I set her in the safe haven so she could be close to us and know she was not alone.

Knowing we could only wait, I felt helpless. Since the other kittens had died, I felt there was little, if any, hope for this one. Throughout the day, whenever Jonathan walked by the suffering kitten, he lay his hands on Scampers, looked toward heaven and said, "Dear Lord Jesus, You are the Great Doctor, so I just ask that You heal my little Scampers in the name of Jesus. Amen." How do you tell a four-year-old that death is certain?

Hours passed as we watched and waited. Jonathan continued to pray. When my mom and dad left the house for dinner at a friend's home, my brother Steven and I decided it would be best to bury Scampers before they returned home. Something, however, kept me from following through.

As my brother Tom passed by the table, he reached down, kissed her on the head, and said, "It's okay to go, Scampers. We love you and don't want you to hurt anymore."

At 9:30 P.M. I called the pet emergency clinic and talked to a vet. "Everything has shut down," I told him. Scampers' body had become stiff and had already started to smell. The vet felt certain that Scampers was dead. With no sign of life, everyone agreed that she was dead. All, that is, except for Jonathan.

I decided to talk to Jonathan before burying his kitten. "Scampers is already dead," I told Jonathan upstairs. "She isn't going to come back, but she's gone to be with Jesus."

Looking up at me, he said, "Mom, you can't bury her because Jesus doesn't want her yet!"

After I tried to explain that keeping a dead cat in the house could make us sick, Jonathan cried. "Mommy," he sobbed, "you said we should always listen to what God is saying to us, and that we should always do as He says. Right, Mommy?"

I agreed.

"Then why won't you listen?" I tried to calm Jonathan down. After awhile he became calmer, but he remained steadfast in his faith for his little kitten's life. "Mommy," he said, "just pray with me and then maybe you can hear God too."

Tired of trying to reason with him, I agreed to pray with him for his poor dead kitten. "Dear Lord Jesus," Jonathan prayed, "will You tell my mommy what You told me so she'll know what You want us to do for Scampers? Help my family know how to save her."

While we prayed, Mom and Steven stood in the next bedroom talking. Suddenly Mom remembered a story she had heard about a pet rescue where they saved a dog from drowning in a river. He wasn't breathing, Mom said, and after being artificially resuscitated, he lived.

Steven ran into my bedroom. "Can you set up Jonathan's nebulizer?" he asked. A nebulizer is used to open the upper respiratory system using steam and steroids. Although the thought of using the nebulizer on the kitten seemed foolish, I agreed.

Moving with an unforeseen sense of certainty, we eventually discovered a heart rate, which rose from zero to two hundred. As Scampers started to move slightly, her heart rate normalized. Just one hour later she tried to push the mask away from her face with her paws. We used the nebulizer hourly while simultaneously using a blow dryer to increase her body temperature. Along with a warm water baggy wrapped in a towel we believed we were making progress.

At 5 A.M. Mom frantically searched for Scampers. Somehow she had managed to move and make her way out of her bed. Finding her curled up under Mom's bed, we wondered if she had gone under the bed to die. We woke Steven up so he could crawl under the bed and get her. After Steven pulled her out from under the bed, Scampers looked up at us as if to say, "I was just sleeping! Can't anyone get any sleep in this place?"

Although weak, Scampers was alive. Later that morning she ate some fried chicken and cold macaroni and cheese. We called the vet again to ask what we could expect. The vet said the kitten would suffer retardation and partial or complete blindness. The vet's report didn't phase Jonathan. He kept praying, believing, and trusting God.

The first two weeks Scampers was slow to respond and acted as if she had difficulty seeing. But as she gained weight and strength, she acted as any normal kitten would act. In three months, completely recovered, Scampers became alert, playful, and smart!

Now ten years old, Scampers is healthy and a continual joy to our family. We call her Baby Scamp Miracle—a miracle because a little child refused to let go of a pet he felt God wasn't ready for yet. When we have the faith of a child, miracles happen!

Kay has lived in Spokane, Washington, all her life and is the oldest of eleven children. She accepted Jesus Christ as Savior November 17, 1988. She is a single mom to Jonathan, her fifteen-year-old son. Kay is a Sunday school teacher and sings with the worship team at The Rock of Ages Church, where she has attended for more than fifteen years. Her life's desire is to serve God and to let His light shine through her.

39

MIRACLE IN THE REARVIEW MIRROR
by D. F. Higbee

Yea, though I walk through the valley of the shadow of death, I will fear no evil: for thou art with me; thy rod and thy staff they comfort me.

PSALM 23:4 KJV

Sunlight streamed through the stained glass windows of Living Faith Church in Spokane, Washington, like a beckoning call to come outside and play. On a bright spring morning in 1978 the members of the "Bishop's Motorcycle Club" excitedly gathered their gear. Finally, the end of a cold, gray winter had come. Motorcycle engines roared their expectancy as ten members stomped pedal to the metal out of the church parking lot in anticipation of freedom, fun, and fellowship.

What awaited them was far outside of their expectations.

Pastor Richardson led the way up the Elk-Chattaroy Road just outside of Spokane. Ten people on motorcycles followed him, with Jack Lyman and Douglas Durheim bringing up the rear of the group. As they pulled through a turn in the road, Pastor glanced in his rearview mirror. As if in a slow motion disaster movie, the last two motorcycles careened off the curve and over the embankment, smashed through a barbed-wire fence, and disappeared in a cloud of dust and debris.

Stunned, Pastor immediately turned around and sped back to the spot. A few members had jumped off their bikes and slid down the bank to see about their friends. Pastor Richardson left some people at the top to obtain help while he also ran to his friends. The sight that greeted them was terrifying. Jack lay bleeding under a pile of barbed wire. Broken bones and gashes in his legs and arms showed a horrific crash.

The sound of weeping caused him to move over to Doug. "How is he?" he asked the small crowd.

"He's dead. He's not moving, there's no pulse, and his eyes…they're not…he's just…gone," their voices choked through the tears. Doug indeed was gone. He was tightly wrapped in the same barbed wire his bike had struck on its way down the hill. His leg, arms, and collarbone stuck out at angles not possible in the human body. Blood and gashes packed with dirt and brush made him almost unrecognizable. His motorcycle helmet was smashed and lay in pieces beside his head. He did not respond to verbal stimulus or physical touch. His eyes were fixed and unmoving. No breath came from his nostrils. They had all lost a friend who had served in the house of the Lord with his whole heart.

Pastor Richardson abruptly felt anger overtake him. "This will not end here like this. It will not!" As faith rose up in his heart, he told everyone to start praying. Reaching down, he touched Doug's lifeless body, and in a loud voice commanded him to live in the name of Jesus!

Suddenly Doug pitched upward, groaned, and opened his eyes. Everyone moved back a few steps as great fear washed through them. Then they erupted in a loud cheer!

Within seconds, a nurse who had seen the accident scene from the roadway scrambled down the side of the road, followed closely by EMTs from Spokane County. They gathered around Doug as their equipment was pulled from the truck. Could this man really be alive? The injuries were extreme: broken arm, leg, and collarbone, internal bleeding, severe concussion. The EMTs cut away the barbed wire, gently moved Doug and his friend Jack to stretchers, then pulled them up the hill to the ambulance.

One EMT turned to Pastor Richardson as Doug was being loaded into the ambulance and said, "This is a miracle, sir. There's no logical reason why this man should be alive. And that other guy is really lucky to be alive too. This is one I can't explain."

After several weeks of recuperation, Doug Durheim and Jack Lyman completely recovered from their injuries. When Doug is asked today in 2005 what it was like to be dead and if he saw anything, he simply responds with a soft smile and shake of his head, "Nope. Don't remember a thing."

Pastor Richardson often ponders that day. What seemed a total disaster displayed in the rearview mirror turned into a demonstration of the power of the Living God and His love for His children. And Doug? He is a living reminder that the opposite side of the valley of the shadow of death is a place of victory won by the risen Savior over two thousand years ago.

Dorothy Faye Higbee is Pastor of Raven Ministries, a home church based in Post Falls, Idaho. She is also currently a local leader of A Company of Women Ministry in Post Falls and has been involved in leadership for numerous other ministries since meeting the Lord in 1978. She has served as drama coach and worship leader. Pastoral care, prayer, and administration are also just a few of the areas that occupy Faye's time. She has been married to Myron Dennis Higbee for over fourteen years. The couple has two deeply loved stepchildren and one grandchild. Faye retired after thirty-one years in law enforcement in 2004.

40

HAPPILY EVER AFTER
by Jeri Erskine

Then Samuel said, "Speak, for your servant is listening."

1 SAMUEL 3:10

I had lost count of how many times my husband, Clyde, and I attended marriage counseling. I couldn't remember how often I wanted to file for a divorce. We had read books on becoming the perfect couple and attended weekend marriage retreats, but like a bad diet, after a few weeks of progress in the right direction we'd fall right back to where we had started.

Twenty-four years of this misery seemed ridiculous to me. I often asked myself why I stayed in a marriage where I felt so dismal. Miserable as I was, I knew there were some positive aspects of our marriage—after all, I wasn't being abused. Clyde had a good job with great benefits, and I wanted for nothing monetary. Although I couldn't buy a sports car on a whim, I usually got everything I wanted.

Something I desperately wanted and didn't have, however, was a close relationship with Clyde. We got along most of the time, and surely conversation wasn't a problem for us. As a result of raising two growing teenagers, being active in various church projects, involved in daycare, and Clyde's work as a cook for a state institute in Medical Lake, Washington, we had plenty to vent or to laugh about. Yet, I yearned for an intimate relationship with Clyde.

To fill the void missing in my marriage, I took up various hobbies: rock climbing, scuba diving, skiing, roller blading, working out at the gym, and learning to ride a motorcycle. But nothing filled the empty space.

On July 4, 2001, Clyde injured his back at work. Although he wasn't hospitalized, he was off work for an undetermined amount of time until his back improved. Intimacy was even more out of the question now, and cuddling and snuggling became impossible. Clyde started sleeping on the futon in the other room, claiming that mattress was firmer for him. I felt even further rejected by my husband.

In November of 2002 we were invited to a Christian retreat at House of the Lord in Tumtum, Washington. After Lorelei Salvatore laid her hands on Clyde and prayed for him, she told him to bend over, then to stand up straight, which is something he couldn't do since his back injury. That night, when Clyde bent over and stood up with ease, we chalked it up as a miracle from God. By February, seven months after his injury, Clyde returned to work. Life started looking and feeling better.

Clyde wanted to be geographically closer to his family, who lived in Ogden, Utah, so we started looking into the possibility of relocating. We flew to Ogden to check out the area, then drove a second time. We found a great church, a beautiful home, and submitted several promising job applications. Things seemed to be falling into place for us to relocate.

The prospect of moving to Utah felt so right; it felt like God was in the move. When Clyde and I prayed, I sensed God whisper, "You're going to move here." Thinking God meant the move was to take place immediately, I acted in faith and started planning the details of the move, including plans to develop a ministry to deliver groceries to the elderly and shut-ins.

On the drive home from Utah, Clyde's back started hurting again, and by the end of the drive he could hardly move because of the spiking pain. The doctor X-rayed and examined Clyde, finding two herniated disks and one ruptured disk. He told Clyde that once again, he could not return to work.

The living room became Clyde's room and the TV became his best friend. Our plans for moving to Utah came to a screeching halt. Confused by the unexpected circumstances, I sought counsel from a Christian leader whom I trusted wholeheartedly. When I asked what he thought might be wrong, he asked, "Are you *sure* you heard from God about moving?"

"I'm pretty sure I heard from God," I said. He explained that after praying he hadn't received any confirmation or direction from God about me or about Clyde and I moving to Utah. As an active member of the church, plugged in to numerous parts of the ministry, I figured God would have indicated to this leader if a major move in my life was part of God's plan. After our conversation, it crushed me to think I had missed God. Everything I had prayed for—a new house, a new job, moving—now seemed a whimsical thought, dream, or even a selfish desire.

I was wrong, I thought, convinced that I had totally missed the mark and didn't hear or discern God's voice. Then I questioned whether I had *ever* heard God. Did I really hear the Lord when He told me to give someone cookies? *Did I hear Him when He told me to give Therese my socks so she could visit a person on death row at Walla Walla State Penitentiary? Did I hear from God when He told me to hug someone? Was it really God when I heard Him whisper, "I love you, Jeri"?* Doubting if I had *ever* heard God tormented me.

I started questioning everything. *Have I ever heard God tell me to stay in the marriage?* I wondered. *Was I supposed to stay in the church I was in?* I had no idea where I was supposed to be or what I was supposed to do. I felt helpless and alone, like an empty shell. Although I went through the motions of everyday life, I felt dead inside. My only glimmers of life sparked when I was working with children in the daycare.

By March of 2004 I felt it was time to move on with my life. I talked to Clyde about divorce, quoting facts and rattling off a long list of reasons it would be best to end our marriage. I purchased the book *Divorce for Dummies* to learn how to arrange an easy divorce and was ready to comply with everything Clyde wanted. I simply didn't care anymore and was ready to move forward.

Even in this wilderness season, I clung to God for strength. "God," I prayed, "You said You would never leave me or forsake me. Even if I can't feel You or hear You, I know You're with me. God, Your Word says You're faithful, even when I'm not faithful. God, Your Word says You're a lamp to my feet and a light to my path." I opened my heart to Him and expressed my misery. "I feel like I'm dying, Lord," I told Him. "I have to leave so I can have life."

In one discussion with Clyde, I said, "If you'd just wooed me, or even showed some interest in me, I might have thought about staying." I assured him, though, that it was too late anyway. "We might as well accept the inevitable and get on with the divorce," I said.

A week later Clyde and I decided to go to a local baseball game. Surprisingly, we had great fun together. I felt a little sad knowing we were ending our marriage. We attended another game and saw a few movies together. But as far as I was concerned, our marriage was still over.

In August, after deciding it was time to move on with my life, I called Sarah Emery, a friend in Palmdale, California, who connected me with a nanny service. I planned to divorce Clyde, move to California, become a great nanny, make lots of cookies, and live happily ever after. Sarah and I planned to share a house together and be in ministry together. I sighed with relief, thinking I was now heading back into God's will for my life.

When an interview was scheduled with an actor and actress to be a nanny for their little boy, I drove from Spokane, Washington, to Palmdale, California, in record time. I stayed with James and Andra Phelps, who offered to let me stay as long as I needed. While I was in their home, I read *Redeeming Love* by Francis Rivers, a book about a woman being restored to her husband. This book impacted me greatly and made me think more about my marriage.

I sensed the still, small voice of the Lord. "You're running away."

I'm not running away; I'm just moving on, I reasoned in my head.

"You're running away," He whispered. My heart squeezed, and I began to cry, something I hadn't done in months.

At the time, Clyde was in Utah to celebrate his dad's eightieth birthday. He planned to relocate to Utah after the divorce was final. Few of his family members knew about our plans to divorce. The ones who knew about our marital problems prayed.

The landscape of Southern California was breathtaking. Seeing the Joshua trees almost as thick as pine trees, I started taking pictures to capture the beauty. One scene I viewed through the camera lens caught my eye. As I clicked the shutter, I thought, *This looks a lot like the mountains in Utah.*

I sensed the Lord's voice: "You should be in Utah with your husband." I knew the familiar voice of God and knew in my heart that I was supposed to be with Clyde. I realized at that moment that I *had* heard God in the beginning when He spoke to me about moving to Utah. It *wasn't* my imagination. It comforted me knowing that God had spoken to me and that I hadn't missed His voice. I had only missed His *perfect timing*.

Pastor Brek Ruiz, Senior Pastor of Destiny Faith Center, prayed with me on August 8 while I was in Palmdale. I desperately wanted to know God's will for my life. When I told him that God had given me my answer and that God still had plans for me in Spokane, Pastor Brek told me that God had told him the same thing in prayer.

Although my nanny interview had gone very well, I strangely never received a call back with any response. Even if I had received the job offer, I knew I could not accept it as God had made His plan clear to me.

I drove back to Spokane safely, wondering how Clyde would take my news that God had revealed His plan for us to stay in our marriage. He received me and my news with great joy. We had a long, drawn out conversation and started making plans to move to Utah.

Clyde's doctor sent him to a chiropractor who suggested unusual exercises and stretches that he had never tried in the past. As a result of the exercise and treatment, he was able to return to work part time while his back improved daily.

Shortly after God restored our marriage, Clyde had lunch with Pastor Ron Doyl, Associate Pastor of Spokane Faith Center. Pastor Ron shared biblical revelation with Clyde, including God's plan for giving. The next Sunday, September 26, Clyde wrote an offering check for $100 even though we had only $130 left in our account. Seeing the amount of the check, I thought, *Holy Moly, that's most of our money!* But the Holy Spirit spoke to my heart and calmed me with His peace. I knew Clyde was learning obedience and that God would take care of all of our needs.

The next week Clyde called Mike Baumgarden, a realtor from Nvest, who originally sold us our home. Clyde asked the realtor to give us a list of home improvements we needed to make to prepare the house for the market. We knew we had a great deal of work, which we estimated at approximately $5,000, to make our home presentable to potential buyers.

When Mike met with us at our home, he said, "Don't do anything. People will be looking mostly at the property, twenty-one acres on a forested hill, not the house." His advice surprised us because our house had "issues": ugly, smoke gray carpet with burn marks and holes, holes in the doors, laundry strewn on the couch, six cats, three dogs, dust, not to mention twelve abandoned cars outside.

Before the realtor arrived back at his office, he called from his cell phone and asked if he could show our house the next day. We thought he was kidding! Clyde cleaned and I made cookies. Because I was working at the daycare the next day, Clyde had to take our three dogs, who were not used to being in a car, for a drive during the house showing. The people viewing our home stayed for several hours so Clyde had to drive around with dog fur flying everywhere.

When I got home from work, the realtor called with an offer on our home. His news floored us. The offer was more than we had expected, especially considering we did nothing to prepare the house for showing other than cleaning up the outside. Clyde and I went out for pizza, talked about the offer, prayed, and decided to accept it.

Everything fell into place for our move to Utah, where we knew in our hearts God wanted to plant us in ministry. And because of God's faithfulness, we left Spokane for Utah debt free. And our marriage, which had been headed down a slippery slope of disaster, is now better than it has ever been in the past. Clyde and I talk, dream, plan, pray, and genuinely enjoy being together. I now have the intimacy I always desired with my husband. God completely restored our marriage and was faithful even when we weren't.

I won't ever doubt God's voice and will never doubt that I'm supposed to be married to Clyde, my lover and my best friend. And because of God's love and faithfulness, we *will* live happily ever after.

Jeri and Clyde, now married over twenty-five years, have two grown children. Jeri enjoys working with children through daycare and church ministries. Her heart's desire is to be trained in clowning to bring sunshine to other lives. She also hopes one day to be active as an Emergency Medical Team. Jeri and Clyde live in Ogden, Utah.

41

THE LORD DIRECTS OUR STEPS
by Gena Bradford

A man's heart plans his way, but the Lord directs his steps.

PROVERBS 16:9 NKJV

*W*hitworth College in Spokane, Washington, is a pristine sanctuary where pine trees guard the peace of searching souls coming as students to learn and, in my case, to heal. Looking back, I can follow the thread of events God wove together to lead me to this intimate Christian community, where depression would no longer consume my joy, hope, and will to live. Until then a small stumble, heartache, or a critical word would cast me down headlong into the black slippery well of despair.

I can trace the path back to before I was born, with my father's decision to enlist in the Army. When Dad was stationed in Munich, Germany, during my early school years, I met my first best friend Hedwig, who was living with her German grandmother. Hedwig and I attended the same school, but she returned to her home in Hawaii after a year. We spent many hours talking about her tropical paradise, and I vowed to one day visit her there.

In the following years I said many good-byes to friends like Hedwig, but also to every child's dream of having my parents stay together. Mom and Dad divorced when I was twelve and a great sadness entered my life. I chose to live with Dad and finished high school in Northern California. I met Jesus Christ as Lord and Savior at a Billy Graham Crusade, then became actively involved in Young Life, a Christian organization for teens.

Dad was all I had for family, so it shocked me when he said, "Gena, I'm getting married to a woman I met in Germany. She'll arrive soon and it would be best if you didn't live with us. I'll help you with your education. Pick a school, but you need to leave."

Searching for a new home and college, I remembered my vow to see Hedwig again and to experience her beloved Hawaii, though it had been ten years since we'd shared dreams. She always wanted me to visit, but I could never afford it. Now was my opportunity. I chose the University of Hawaii and registered for summer school. "Try to make this your home," Dad said. "Hawaii is just as good a place to live as any." But I didn't know; I'd never lived away from family before.

I called Hedwig as soon as I arrived at my dorm in Hawaii. We met at the beach, but she acted distant and didn't offer to see me again. She was married and had a child. *Had she forgotten how close we were as kids?* I wondered. We seemed like strangers.

Returning to my dorm, I met my new roommate, Carlotta from Vancouver, British Columbia. The bond instant, she felt like the old friend I had been looking for. We hiked to the beach daily and shared the joys of schooling in Hawaii like ukulele and hula classes. But at the end of the summer Carlotta left, and I was alone with no friends or family. Feeling lost again, I had no home to return to. I knew I would not stay in Hawaii, as the loneliness and bouts of depression were too great.

An airline strike hit Hawaii, grounding flights to the mainland USA. Hearing that the only planes flying out were to Canada, I thought of Carlotta. *Perhaps, I could stay a while with her in Vancouver.* I made the call. "Carlotta, I'm miserable here without friends or family," I said. "I wonder, since I can't get back to California with the airline strike, could I come and stay with you until I can figure out how to get home and what to do with my life?"

"I'd love to have you here," she said. "Come! Just give me the details, and my family and I will pick you up at the airport."

Carlotta's family treated me like a daughter and bought me a wonderful dinner where I tasted my first baked Alaska dessert with mile-high meringue. They drove me to their summer home on the water in the Puget Sound area of Washington where I stayed for the week. Daily Carlotta and I walked in the warm August sun, this time along the board-walk lined with red geraniums in wooden flower boxes just steps from their spacious bright summer home.

One day when we saw the college age Young Life crew on a large boat preparing to embark, I introduced myself. "Hi, you must be Young Lifers from your t-shirt logo," I said. "I belong to Young Life in California. Where are you going?"

"We're on our way to Malibu for our annual camp," one of the college boys responded. I had heard of this beautiful camp. Many high school students saved all year so they could enjoy a summer week there. I'd always wanted to go there myself.

With nothing to lose I boldly asked, "Could I go with you? I have nowhere to go, and I'd be willing to work or counsel kids or do anything."

They motioned to Abby, the camp counselor for the college age volunteers who was also on staff for Young Life at Whitworth College, in Spokane, Washington. She paused, taking a reflective look at me as if asking the Lord what He thought. "Sure," Abby said. "Can you stay two weeks?"

I ran back to Carlotta's, grabbed my bag, and bolted for the boat while hugging and thanking my friend for taking me in. Ready for a new adventure, I sailed up the inlet toward the haven called Malibu.

During the hours we sailed, Abby talked to me about Whitworth College. Hearing my story, she felt Whitworth would be a good place for me to attend school and tie in with a Christian community. Abby discerned that I was suffering from a bad case of believing that I must perform in order to be loved and accepted. Wanting to prove to me that God loved me even if I did nothing and counseled no one at camp, she said, "Be quiet for a week. Don't give anyone advice, don't lead. Just *be*."

Being quiet was one of my life's greatest challenges, but I obeyed. By the end of the week, I felt rested. Campers threw their arms around me and said, "You're so wonderful, and you've helped us so much!"

I laughed in disbelief because I had done nothing except pray for them. The Holy Spirit helped them and taught me that it wasn't about my "doing." I was used to striving to hold my world together. Seeing God rescue lives at camp without my help, I marveled that He could do it without me.

By the end of the week Abby had convinced me that Whitworth would be a wonderful place for me to heal and grow. She said classes were small, and they built community by sharing deep relationships in Christ with the students. Although it sounded good, I had no money and didn't know if my father would be angry with me for quitting school at the University of Hawaii.

When I called Dad, his heart had softened. "Things are going well here," he said. "I have your old room ready for you. Come on home." I was home a week when Abby called. "Gena, there's one bed left here at Whitworth. I know it's yours! You're supposed to be here. Promise me you'll pray about it and see what God says to you."

"Okay," I said, but I knew I'd never received a quick answer from the Lord before. Usually it took time for me to be sure of God's will. "God, I need to know if You want me to go to Whitworth, and it needs to be clear to me right now," I prayed. "School starts tomorrow." A sweet presence of God blanketed me. If I had not been sitting down, I would have fallen down as the very air felt like honey pouring over me.

Wow! I'd like to go to Whitworth.

Just then, Dad called out, "Gena, are you okay?"

"I just got a call from Whitworth College, Dad. Abby challenged me to pray about coming there and I did. I believe it's what God wants for my life."

"When does school start?"

"Tomorrow."

Dad's eyes brightened. "I'll pack the car, get you gas, and make sure you have a good map." Adventure grabbed both of us, and we raced to prepare. I called for my transcripts, left the next morning, and drove straight through to Spokane from Hayward, California.

Twenty-four hours later, after a short nap in the car, I strode into the school office to register. After I told the registrar the miraculous story of how God wanted me there, she asked, "Have you registered and been accepted?"

"No," I said. "Remember, I just found out that I'm supposed to be here."

"Do we have your high school transcripts?"

"No. I arrived before them."

"Do you have money for tuition?"

"No. I don't have that either."

Bewildered, she sent me to the financial aid officer who seemed important because his spacious carpeted office was at the top of the stairs. "Come in," he said. Now a little shaken by my less than enthusiastic reception downstairs, I quietly took a seat across from his massive desk.

I launched into my miracle once more. "Do you have financial provision to attend school here?" he asked.

"I don't have any money, but God wants me here."

"We could probably get you a student loan," he offered.

"I can't do that either; I probably won't live long enough to pay it back."

He smiled. "I'll talk to your dad later. You look tired. You've come a long way. Don't worry. We'll find you a job on campus." He called a student to escort me to the only bed left in the dorms so I could get some needed rest.

At nineteen, now at Whitworth, my life transformed. My facade of strength and confidence soon dissolved, exposing a lonely, grief-stricken girl with depression so deep the world seemed black and colorless. The lie I had believed that if I disappeared, no one would notice or care, dispelled.

SOMEONE did notice; He had brought me to this safe place with safe people to grow me into the knowledge of His unconditional love. That year God spoke to my heart, "Let Me father you." I began to learn what that meant and how to give my cares to Him by trusting in His provision and guidance. I met Penny, my spiritual mom and employer, at the college switchboard. She taught me how to pray when I was at the bottom of despair. I had only known how to pray when I felt acceptable to God.

"Tell Him how you feel," Penny said. "Be honest. He's in every valley. He's the eye of every storm." She gave me a new way to respond to the darkness by taking it to Jesus in prayer and letting Him lift it. I began to know the God of all comfort.

In the year of our day-by-day relationship, Penny taught me how to overcome despair with thanksgiving and praise to God. "You need to begin to thank God for something," she said. "The Bible tells us that we enter into His gates with thanksgiving and into His courts with praise. Depression can't follow you there."

I started with the small things. "Oh God, thank You for my feet and that I can walk. Thank You for grass and those flowers." The list began to grow. As one grateful response came forth another waited to run single file like a troop to battle. Depression lifted, and I could see the beauty of God's world and His love for me. Every tree had sunlit definition, every person a smile.

I met Lillian, another spiritual mom and Dean of Women, who was available for me when I needed to talk about my family, losses, and fears. She loved me unconditionally and believed in me even when I didn't believe in myself.

Through these relationships I began to learn about real love, and I realized that if I was honest with people—just being myself, not doing or performing for validation—they would genuinely love and accept me just as I am.

Lastly, I met Jack, my future husband and best friend. After discovering that I could talk to him about anything and that we could share our faith and future, we married at the end of the school year.

In this year at Whitworth, despair, depression, and loneliness disappeared, and I believed in my heart that God loved me. Whitworth, my new home and family, prepared me for the next stage of my life: marriage and career.

The golden thread began with my dad's career choice, which led us to Germany and ended at Whitworth College, where I received the grace and healing I needed. Thirty-eight years later I'm still married to my Whitworth sweetheart, and today we have four grown children (three are Whitworth graduates) and two beautiful grandchildren. We live in Spokane, and I continue to depend on Jesus to direct my steps. Depression-free all these years, I am grateful to God for His father-heart and cherish this abundant life of joy and peace He has given me and to all who call Him Father and Lord.

Gena Bradford is a college teacher, writer, and singer. She and her husband, Jack, have been married for over thirty-eight years and have four children and two grandchildren. Psalm 78 declares Gena's favorite thing in life: "That we will tell the next generation the praiseworthy deeds of the Lord, His power and the wonders He has done." Using her God-given musical gifting, she recently produced her first CD titled "Given Wings." Gena and Jack live in Spokane, Washington.

42

WHEN GOD SPEAKS TO MY HEART
by Rosalie Willis Storment

*My sheep that are My own hear and are listening to My voice;
And I know them, and they follow Me.*

JOHN 10:27 AMP

*A*fter receiving the baptism of the Holy Spirit in Newbury Park, California, it seemed that every time I turned around God would say, "Ask what you will, and you'll receive it." One day God spoke through a book I was reading: "Ask what you will, and you'll receive it." I didn't know it was possible to hear God's voice and didn't realize I was hearing His voice, yet I listened and responded.

In 1972 my husband, Dale, an FBI agent, had been transferred to Los Angeles, California, from Roswell, New Mexico. He disliked the smog and congestion in L.A. and was more accustomed to the mountains of Idaho where he had been raised. Responding to the Lord's prompting to *ask and receive,* I prayed, "I ask You to transfer us from Los Angeles to the state of Your choice, to the town of Your choice, to the house of Your choice, and to sell our home."

Shortly after I prayed the FBI approached Dale, who had been with the agency for two years, and said, "Where do you want to go?" Normally agents must have ten years of service to receive that kind of favor or to be asked where they want to go.

Dale requested Idaho, but learned that the way to Idaho was through Butte, Montana. Suddenly we were being transferred to Butte and had one month to sell our home. I told my friends, "God said He'll sell my house."

One neighbor came to my door and said, "Get a grip, it doesn't work this way!"

"No!" I said. "God said!" Nobody looked at our house except for a few couples with huge families, which wouldn't work in our three-bedroom home. The day the movers arrived, nobody had even considered buying our home. After the movers packed up and left, a car pulled in our driveway. "There's my buyers!" I said.

Although the real estate agent normally wanted me to disappear so she could show my home to potential buyers, this time she asked me to show my home. This was a gift, as I loved my home! When I finished the tour, the agent pulled me aside. "They really seem interested," she said. "Where will you be?"

"We'll be at Howard Johnson's to spend the night," I said. "Then we're headed for Butte, Montana, early tomorrow morning." When we pulled into Howard Johnson's, the telephone call was waiting. We drove to the real estate office, signed papers at 10:00 P.M., and left for Butte the next morning.

That began my adventure of hearing God's voice. God had said, and God had done! When we arrived in Butte, the FBI put us in a motel for a month. Six months later they sent us to Glasgow, Montana. I had told Dale that I'd go anywhere with him on the face of the earth *except Alaska*. Glasgow was colder than Alaska—49 degrees below zero the day we arrived!

We moved onto the Glasgow Air Force base, seventeen miles from town. Soon after I said, "God, I know You have a purpose for me here. So let's begin!"

The next day when Dale walked into the bank, Marge Forum, a real estate loan officer, said, "I'd really like to meet your wife." Marge invited me to lunch and told me of her desire to open a Christian bookstore. To me, nothing could have been more exciting.

Marge and I began working on this dream. The vice president of a bank in town said he had seven thousand bushels of wheat. "If you can sell it, you can have the money for the bookstore," he said. Wheat was then selling at $2.19 a bushel and profit meant anything over $3.00 a bushel. From that point on the price of wheat steadily climbed and sold at a price sufficient to provide the necessary capital to open the bookstore. Over seventy-five Christian friends came forward to help in any way they could—each one playing an important part in the formation of the store.

One day a greeting card company representative came in as we were ordering things and asked, "What are you going to use for fixtures?"

"God has provided everything else, He'll provide this too," we said. He drove over two thousand miles into Colorado to pick up fixtures for us and brought them back. God provided everything! The Good News Bookstore opened November 12, 1973.

When the vice president who had given us money to start the bookstore brought Bertha and Allan Phaup in one day, the Lord said, "This is important. Pay attention." Allan was the new deputy commander on the Glasgow Air Force Base. He and Bertha had moved there from Honolulu and had received the baptism of the Holy Spirit under Dennis Bennet in the Episcopal Church in Honolulu. As we talked about different merchants in town, they would say, "Oh yes, the Lord said we're supposed to meet them." The Lord said this and the Lord said that.

I had a personal relationship with the Lord, but I didn't know Him like *that*. The next night when I invited Allan and Bertha over for dinner, they told me how they had learned to hear His voice and how they documented everything He said in journals. For the next two weeks, whenever I wanted to know something from God, I'd call Allan and say, "Would you ask the Lord about this?" More than delighted, Allan would call me back and tell me the Lord's answer.

Two weeks later God told Allan, "She's potty trained; tell Rosalie to come to Me herself." That began my adventure of keeping journals, which I have done for thirty-two years. After learning to hear God's voice, the first thing I asked Him was, "When will we get transferred from Glasgow, Montana?" His caravan would move at His time and His bidding, He said, and my mind and heart was to be on His Word and His work.

When Allan and Bertha planned a trip out of town, I asked to borrow their journals. While they were gone I wrote down every word from their journals that spoke to my heart. When they returned the Lord directed me to do the same with my journals. He led me to put Allan and Bertha's journals first, mine second, and to title it *Glory to God*.

God directed me to take the manuscript for *Glory to God* to a man on the Air Force base at 10:00 A.M. on a particular day. He said that the man, who had a printing shop, would be happy to do the printing for me free of charge. Although I thought I would print three copies—one for me, one for a friend, and one for the Phaups—God said, "Make one hundred copies."

The man said he'd be happy to do it for me and wouldn't charge me anything, just as God said. He even included beautiful yellow covers without my asking. Then the Lord revealed each person who was to receive one of the copies. I gave the copies as directed, knowing they were either burned or thrown away. I said, "Lord, Why?" He said He wanted them to have the opportunity whether they took it or not.

Time passed and more journals were written by all of us. The Lord told me to do Volume 2 of *Glory to God*, this time putting my journals first and Allan and Bertha's second.

The time came when again I asked God, "When are You going to transfer us?" Learning that Dale's boss would retire on February 28, we knew our transfer would come soon as well. The Lord said our transfer would happen within the first fortnight of February. God expanded my vocabulary—I didn't know what a "fortnight" was!

One day Dale said, "You know, the first fortnight ends on Friday the 13th. He didn't want the transfer to come on Friday the 13th.

While I was in the shower on the morning of Thursday, February 12, 1976, the Lord kept saying, "Rejoice, rejoice, it's a wonderful day!"

I thought, *Can it be?*

That night Dale came home and didn't say a word until after dinner. "Did I tell you we got transferred to Coeur d'Alene, Idaho, today?" The government hadn't formulated the new budget, so nobody in the FBI was getting transferred—yet Dale was being transferred.

God led me to do a third volume of journals of Allan and Bertha's journals interspersed with mine, print one hundred copies of all three volumes, and take them to my new home in Coeur d'Alene. There He would show me where all one hundred sets were to go.

The Lord said, "Have you not been in the battlefield of the wilderness for forty months, and have I not led you every step of the way?" I counted the months we had lived in Glasgow: exactly forty months. From the wilderness of Glasgow, God sent us to the land of milk and honey: Coeur d'Alene, Idaho. Before we moved, I asked Him if I could own my own Christian bookstore, and He said I would.

After moving to Coeur d'Alene, I started job hunting because our daughter, Shanette, was about to start college and I needed to work to help pay for her education. My first job interview was with a real estate office. Because my family had been in real estate and I had been their secretary part of the time, the man said, "You're the perfect one for the job. I'll call you tomorrow."

When he called the next day, however, he said, "You *were* the perfect one. I don't know why I hired this other person!"

After my next interview at a bank, the banker said, "The job is yours."

"I need this job," I said. "But I can't take it, and I don't know why!" I went to my prayer group and asked them to pray.

When I returned home, I received a phone call from one in my prayer group. "I want you to call the manager at Beneficial Finance," she said. I called, interviewed, and landed the job.

The Lord had told me that when I opened the Christian bookstore, it must be on Sherman Avenue, with all windows to the street. Beneficial Finance was on Sherman with all windows to the street, but I didn't make the connection.

On January 28, 1980, God said, "Look forward to March 15, it's an important day." On March 15 a neighbor I didn't know well called. "I hear you're thinking about opening a Christian bookstore," she said. "Would you come over and talk to me about it?"

When I met with her and shared my testimony for over two hours, she said she wanted to give me $10,000—with no interest for ten years—so I could open the Christian bookstore. I now had about half of the money needed for the store. The Lord directed me to go on a 140-day bread and sugar fast. I was a sugarholic! He said the ship of His provision had set sail, and it would find safe harbor by September 1. On September 1, 1980, the last day of the sugar and bread fast, gifts of $10,000 and $5000 arrived. Now I had $25,000.

One year earlier on February 12, 1979, God had awakened me and said, "You only have two years left until the ministry I have for you begins." Right then I started ordering and collecting the things I would need for the bookstore and stored them in my basement.

One day my boss from Beneficial Finance told me his rent was being doubled. Suddenly it clicked! I had looked on Sherman Avenue for a bookstore location but had found nothing available. Now I realized why the other jobs didn't work out and why I had to work at a job I wouldn't normally enjoy. Calling people about getting their money in, working on a huge computer I had to figure out every day, and being unable to talk to people like I love to do—was like death—body, soul, and spirit.

Dale would say, "You could quit."

"No!" I'd say. "God placed me here! I don't know why, but I have to stay until He releases me." When I realized *this* was the site for the bookstore, I asked my boss if he would help me get the lease on the building. He agreed.

The following February 12, 1981—exactly two years from the day the Lord said my ministry would begin in two years and exactly five years from the day we had been transferred to Coeur d'Alene, Idaho—I flew to Boise and negotiated the building lease with the bank manager in a top floor conference room of a high rise building. Instead of doubling the rent, it increased only $25 a month. I flew back to Coeur d'Alene and gave my two-week notice to Beneficial Finance.

When the lease for this location on Sherman Avenue was firm, I was anxious to tell Jean Rainbolt, a dear friend I had known since 1976. After I shared the news Jean said, "Rosalie, I've had two special desires in life. One is to be a church secretary—which I am—and the other is to work in a Christian bookstore. I'd like to work with you, and I want no pay."

We gained access to the building on April 1. After our husbands built the bookshelves, painted, and put the whole store together, The Sonshine Bookstore opened May 1, 1981. Jean and I worked side by side and showed up even if we were sick because we didn't want to let each other down and wanted to play store together. Jean and I prayed together in the office every day. God's people visited our haven of peace, coming back into the office to be refreshed before returning to work.

After The Sonshine Bookstore had been open about two years, God said, "It's coming! It's coming! I'm going to open doors, and you're going to love it."

I said, "What's coming?"

One day while Shanette was home from college, Jean and I attended a Women's Aglow meeting while Shanette looked after the store. At the end of the meeting the pastor told us to break into twos to pray for one another.

Jean said, "I know what you want to pray for. God keeps telling you, 'It's coming! It's coming!' and you want to know *what's* coming."

"YES!" I said. So Jean prayed.

The next day Dale said, "Where would you like to go?" As an FBI agent he knew it was time for us to move on.

"There's no place better than Coeur d'Alene, Idaho," I said.

"How about Honolulu, Hawaii?" he suggested.

Shanette and I said, "Count us in!" Although his boss didn't like that idea, God said the transfer would come on the 28th of August and gave me the selling price for the bookstore. The next day I told Jean the news. Jean and her husband, Dick, had been planning to buy a motor home, but the night before the Lord told her, "No."

She thought, *How am I going to tell Dick?*

The next morning Dick said to Jean, "I don't think we're supposed to buy this motor home."

When Jean came to work the next day I said, "We're moving to Honolulu. Would you like to buy the bookstore?" The Lord told me the price the store would sell for, the day it was to sell, and the day our transfer would come—and it all happened exactly as He said, to the last detail. Dick and Jean Rainbolt owned the store from September 1, 1983, until May 1, 1992.

We moved to Honolulu in December of 1983. The Great Commission, an organization in Hawaii much like The Full Gospel Businessmen, met down the road from where I lived. I attended a Saturday meeting, where a chaplain from the Waikiki Beach Chaplaincy was speaking.

After the meeting I told the chaplain that I had just sold a Christian bookstore in Coeur d'Alene, Idaho. He said, "The Chaplaincy was just given money to open a Christian bookstore in Waikiki. Would you open it and manage it?"

Because God had told me I had come to Hawaii to sing, I said, "I'm going to have to pray about this. I thought I came here to sing."

After praying, the Lord directed me to manage the bookstore but to keep a loose hold on it and to let go when He told me to let go. I handled the ordering and setting up for *The Good News Bookstore*, working six days a week, then five, then four, then two, then one day a week.

I said, "Lord, how can I manage a store when I'm only here one day a week?"

"It's time to let go," the Lord said. "They don't need you anymore." It was a wonderful year.

The Waikiki Chaplainry, who acted as an agent for musicians, scheduled me to sing throughout the island—just like God said I would—during the two years we lived in Hawaii. From Honolulu we were transferred to Missoula, Montana, for seven years and then relocated to Post Falls, Idaho, near Coeur d'Alene.

Back in Coeur d'Alene, when Dick and Jean Rainbolt retired they closed the Sonshine Bookstore, and the building owners rented it as a used bookstore. Twelve years later the used bookstore closed, and I heard that a new business had opened.

In July 2005 I had lunch with my friends, Tex and Faye, at a new restaurant next door to the Sonshine Bookstore's original location. I bubbled with excitement during lunch. "This is where the Sonshine Bookstore used to be!" I said. I could hardly wait to finish eating so we could visit the new shop.

Walking over the threshold, I was delighted to find a beautiful gift store called *Possibilities,* taken from Matthew 19:26, "All things are possible with God." I made a beeline for the office, anxious to discover the wonderful things awaiting me. I found a wine tasting room, and Lee Kausen, the joint owner, sitting at a high table working on his lap top computer. His wife, Jill, was seated next to him.

After introducing myself, I asked, "Did you know there used to be a Christian bookstore here?"

"No!" Lee said.

"Yes!" I said. We both laughed for joy. Lee shared the miracle of God moving his family to Coeur d'Alene to open *Possibilities*, and I shared the miracle story of the Sonshine Bookstore. "I'm going home with Tex and Faye," I told Lee. "I'll come back with pictures of what it used to look like here as Beneficial Finance and as Sonshine Bookstore."

When I returned, Lee and I perused the pictures and talked animatedly until about 6:00 that night. I headed home full of excitement, knowing God had "re-dug the well" that He had dug twenty-five years before.

I gave Lee a copy of my book *A Walk With Jesus*, written from the first seven years of my journals, which document how God taught me to trust Him and His love. I also gave him *When God Speaks to My Heart*, published by White Stone Books and distributed through Harrison House Publishers. Lee loved them so much that they now sit on the wine tasting room table where customers can taste wine and read both books. Also tucked on shelves and in gift baskets throughout the store, they remind us of God's divinely orchestrated plans for the *Sonshine Bookstore* and the *Possibilities* that followed.

Raised in a Christian home, Rosalie doesn't remember ever not having Jesus in her life and loving God with all her heart. She is author of A Walk With Jesus, Walking on With Jesus, The Singing Bride *(Praise Publishing), and* When God Speaks to My Heart *(White Stone Books). After the Lord gave Rosalie music to the book of Psalms, word for word, she has recorded the first of twelve CDs. She is co-director of A Company of Women International, a family of Christian Women's Ministries, a network of "heart friends" around the world who love the Lord with all their hearts. A key part of A Company of Women is its International Prayer Network, the PraiseNet. On May 7, 2006, God joined Rosalie and Stormy Storment in marriage, truly a match made in heaven. Rosalie's greatest joy is being "a friend of God" and hearing His loving voice.*

43

MOM, ME, AND POSSIBILITIES
by Lee Kausen

With God all things are possible.

MATTHEW 19:26

*W*hen Mom's first pregnancy became toxic, doctors diagnosed preeclampsia, a condition characterized by hypertension, fluid retention, and in her case, severe kidney malfunction. On May 1, 1950, her pregnancy was terminated by C-section in Los Angeles, California, and my oldest brother, Marc, was delivered at 4 lbs., 11 oz. Marc, now fifty-five, is a healthy father of three.

In 1952 a normal, uneventful pregnancy blessed Mom and Dad with another treasured son, Scott. Early into another pregnancy in 1957, Mom developed high blood pressure and other medical problems. In spite of bed rest, a salt restricted diet, and medication, medical concerns persisted. When her blood pressure hit 240/120, kidneys again malfunctioned and swelling continued. Doctors diagnosed her with eclampsia, and an early C-section became necessary. Because of the problems during her first pregnancy and the severe complications of this pregnancy, the decision was also made to prevent future pregnancies through a tubal ligation.

Mom's C-section and tubal ligation were scheduled for March 13, 1957, at a Catholic hospital in Los Angeles, California. Although both parents' consent were required for tubal ligations at this hospital, the doctor forgot to obtain Mom's signature on the necessary papers before sedation for surgery.

Mom says that during the C-section she could hear the doctors talking with great concern because she had not signed the consent for sterilization. One doctor said, "We'll try to crush the tubes if we can." Mom was unable to speak or respond because of anesthesia. Because they failed to obtain her signature before administering the anesthetic, no tubal ligation took place. She delivered a baby girl weighing 2 lbs., 4 oz. Three days later the baby died.

Seven years later Mom became pregnant again. Both doctors Mom had seen since 1957 and an obstetrician told Mom to abort, but she refused. She searched for a doctor who would allow her to proceed with the pregnancy. Dr. Donald Willardson agreed to guide her through the pregnancy with the understanding that if severe adverse conditions developed at any time, she would terminate the pregnancy without dissent. Mom agreed.

The first eight months of the pregnancy proceeded smoothly with no complications. On August 25, 1964, about four weeks before term, fever, swelling, and elevated blood pressure developed so an early termination by C-section became necessary. On August 26, 1964, Mom says, "A healthy, beautiful baby boy was born!" That was me!

Mom says she forever gives thanks to an intervening heavenly hand that permitted me to come into the world. I grew up, married my gorgeous wife, Jill, had three children, a dog, a great job, and a beautiful home. Life seemed so good in the summer of 1996 that at the age of thirty-one I told a friend, "My life is perfect."

Unfortunately, my perfect life began to slide downhill fast. I lost a significant amount of money in the stock market, and work as a commercial real estate appraiser slowed. Within six months of saying, "My life is perfect," I looked in the mirror and saw a loser staring back at me. At the time I used to listen to sports radio regularly, but for some reason I tuned into a Christian station one day and left it there. When David Jeremiah, the preacher on the radio, invited listeners to turn their life over to God, I knelt and prayed with him.

I knew that something miraculous had happened to me, but didn't know *what* had happened. On February 20, 1997, I wrote on a piece of paper, "Live every second of every minute of every day of every year of the rest of my life for God. Pray that God will constantly help me with this. This is the day that will change the rest of my life."

For several years Jill and I tried and tried to open a store in the community of Fallbrook in San Diego County, California, and did not understand why it never worked out. We suffered great frustration, not realizing that God had other plans yet to be revealed. Little did I know He was about to change my career from a commercial real estate appraiser to a retail storeowner in Idaho.

In 2003 we traded in the twelve-year-old family car and planned a family vacation to Coeur d'Alene, Idaho. Some friends who travel frequently had told us that Coeur d'Alene, one of their favorite places, was beautiful. Jill's brother was considering a move from California and interested in Idaho as well.

When we arrived in Coeur d'Alene in August of 2003, the first place we visited was Big Dad-e, a café next to the store we eventually opened. We spent a few days exploring and enjoying family time. We met Tim, a born-again Christian, on Sanders Beach. When Tim told us that God had called him there, I asked him how we would know if we were called there. Tim said simply that we would know if Jill and I were in agreement about it.

When we returned to Fallbrook after our vacation, neither of us felt the same. Whenever we had left home for any period of time in the past, we were always glad to return home. This time, however, felt different for both of us. We flew into Coeur d'Alene one month later to celebrate Jill's birthday and spent some time investigating the area and real estate. We returned again in February 2004 to further check out the surroundings.

While eating lunch at a downtown restaurant, we spotted a vacant unit across the street and thought it would be a great place to open a gift basket store if we moved to the area. After lunch we walked across the street and spoke with the adjacent storeowner. The building owner was in the process of selling her unit and the four adjacent spaces, she said. All units had a buyer except for hers, and she was not planning to buy it. After she gave us the name and phone number of the broker, Jack Beebe, we visited him at his office.

With a handshake we verbally agreed to buy the building. Jack promised it to us; we only needed to have our house in Fallbrook, California, in escrow by August 1. We also entered into an escrow to purchase a home in Coeur d'Alene subject to our home selling in Fallbrook.

We returned to California and put our house on the market. We received an offer, but the deal fell through, and so did the deal for the house in Coeur d'Alene. August 1 came and went without a buyer for our Fallbrook home. Disappointed, I called Jack in Coeur d'Alene and left a voicemail message to tell him he could sell the store to someone else.

Three days later our home sold with a two-week escrow! I called Jack again to see if it wasn't too late to buy the store. He hadn't heard my other message yet because he had been on vacation. The deal was still on! Our home closed escrow, and we followed the moving truck out of the driveway, headed for Coeur d'Alene, Idaho.

After picking up the store keys, we started demolition and renovation in August. Our kids, Kyle, Kurt, and Haley, worked side-by-side with Jill and me, hoping to open up in time for the holidays. About halfway through the renovation the temptation was great to quit, but we couldn't quit and didn't quit. We opened the doors to *Possibilities,* on Sherman Avenue in Coeur d'Alene, Idaho, on November 11, 2004.

In July 2005 Rosalie Willis and her friends, Faye and Tex, ate lunch at Bella Rose (formerly Big Dad-e Café), the restaurant next door to *Possibilities.* Rosalie says she could hardly wait to finish lunch so she could come next door to see the new store.

After introducing herself, Rosalie explained that she used to own and operate the Sonshine Christian Bookstore on this property twenty-five years earlier. Hearing Rosalie tell us and show us photographs of the Christian history of this site further confirmed that God had ordained this specific store for us. As Rosalie says, "God is redigging the wells!"

Rosalie Willis's book, *When God Speaks to My Heart,* now sits on the table in the wine tasting room, blessing numerous customers who visit the store—and us. Now a mainstay at *Possibilities,* it reminds us of the long history of God's divinely orchestrated plans and purposes.

Lee Kausen lives in Coeur d'Alene, Idaho, with his wife, Jill, and their children, Kyle, Kurt, Haley, and Brodie. As Lee says, "God is sooooo awesome!" They are grateful to God for bringing them to the beautiful area of northern Idaho.

44

HAPPY BIRTHDAY, SHARON

by Sharon Morrison

This is the confidence we have in approaching God: that if we ask anything according to his will, he hears us. And if we know that he hears us–whatever we ask—we know that we have what we asked of him.

1 JOHN 5:14,15

In December 2000 my husband, Ron, and our three children and I went on holiday to Florida with Ron's brother, David, and his wife, Valerie. On Christmas Day I took ill while visiting Disney World. When my heart pounded and rapid palpitations continued for nearly two hours, Valerie, a registered nurse, encouraged me to rest and instructed me medically so I could continue my holiday.

When I arrived home to Belfast, Northern Ireland, I visited my doctor, who advised me to go straight to the hospital if I experienced these alarming heart symptoms again. A couple of months later, while working as a manager at a large utility company in Northern Ireland, the heart pounding and palpitations started again. Although my employer wanted to call an ambulance, we felt it would be quicker to drive. My nephew, Kristian Kennedy, who works in my building, drove me to Whiteabbey Hospital within five minutes.

At the hospital doctors and nurses sped around, attached me to heart monitors, and tried to stabilize my heart. I was given three injections to slow my heart rate and to normalize the heart rhythm. Although my heart eventually started to regulate, I remained in the hospital on a heart monitor, which had captured this episode on the machines and provided a print out. I was released from the hospital after two days, but I had to remain off work for a few more days—doctor's orders.

Doctors diagnosed my condition as rapid heartbeat, a dangerous illness that can strike anytime. With rapid heartbeat, the heart "jams," causing the heartbeat to increase—in my case at a rate of 240 beats. I was prescribed beta blockers (Bisoprolol), which slowed the heart rate, but even with this medication I experienced short bursts of rapid heartbeat. Because this heart condition can cause stroke, the doctor advised me to be very careful.

On Wednesday, June 25, 2003, Dr. Bruce Allen was ministering God's Word to the *Times of Refreshing* ministry team at The Ulster Temple in Belfast, Northern Ireland. He spoke about angels and prayed with those who wanted to see angels. When he came to me he said, "Oh, you've already started to see angels. Lord, enlarge her vision to see more."

I asked Dr. Bruce Allen to pray for my left knee. Being unable to kneel in prayer caused me great frustration spiritually. When Bruce and his wife, Reshma, prayed, the pain left instantly. I could bend my knee freely and was able to kneel for the first time in months.

Later, after Dr. Allen prayed for others on the team, I asked him to pray for me again because I wanted a new heart. I didn't want a *fixed* heart; I wanted a *new* heart. Because I believed God had plenty of spare parts available, I didn't want a reconditioned heart. Bruce laughed and said, "Why not!"

As Bruce prayed for me, out of the corner of my left eye I saw an angel approaching us with something cupped in his hands. The beautiful angel was dressed in a white robe from his neck to the floor and had a gold sash around his waist. I didn't see wings but saw his hands, which held my new heart.

I could scarcely breathe. I closed my eyes tightly and tried to concentrate on what God was going to do. When the angel seemed to put his hand into my chest, I felt my heart miss a beat then return to a normal rhythm. As the angel moved his hand down a little farther, Bruce said, "Oh! The angel is fixing something else." I nodded, unable to speak. I didn't dare open my eyes again. I sat down amazed, knowing something wonderful had happened.

The next morning, June 26, 2003, was my birthday. I woke up with an awareness of God's presence and sensed the Lord say, "Happy Birthday, Sharon. I have healed you!"

For the previous two years, I had taken my heart medication (Bisoprolol) in the morning, then Cimedine in the evening to treat a hiatus hernia I had suffered from for over six years. Looking at the prescription containers, I said, "Lord, do I need to take my beta-blockers?"

Instantly I sensed a strong inner witness—*No!*

God's direction delighted me, as I didn't want to damage my new heart with drugs. Throughout the day I experienced a wonderful sense of His presence. That night I asked the Lord again, "Do I need to take my medication for the hiatus hernia?"

Again I sensed an immediate inner witness—*No!* I thanked God repeatedly. Full of joy, I lay down and fell into a deep sleep. In the past, if I had forgotten to take my hernia medication, I would wake in the middle of the night with awful heartburn and painful burning in my throat. I woke the next morning with great excitement after sleeping like a baby throughout the night. I knew God had healed my hiatus hernia!

On August 7, 2003, the hospital sent me for a check-up. Hospitals in Northern Ireland schedule routine follow-up appointments and send letters of confirmation automatically. Preparing for my appointment, I wondered how I was going to explain my supernatural healing experience. On arrival at Dr. Mohan's Clinic in Belfast, a special clinic for heart patients, I went through the normal procedures: ECG, urine samples, blood tests, and blood pressure. At this clinic, after medical tests are done on site you wait for results, then see the doctor. The procedure usually requires a full afternoon.

After being shown in to see Dr. Armstrong, I waited while she checked my test results and read my medical notes. Satisfied, she said everything was perfect and tests were normal. Taking a deep breath, I told Dr. Armstrong that I had stopped my medication. I explained that after receiving prayer for healing, I believed God had touched me. Hearing my report, Dr. Armstrong immediately rechecked the notes and test results. After what seemed an eternity, she raised her head and asked me to describe the withdrawal symptoms I had experienced.

The doctor was amazed when I explained that I had not experienced any withdrawal symptoms. In fact, I didn't realize until then that people normally suffer severe withdrawal symptoms after stopping my medications. I praised God for keeping me from all withdrawal.

Dr. Armstrong said the fact that I had stopped the medication weeks ago with no side effects spoke for itself. She was pleased for me and took notes of everything I had said.

I have not experienced any physical problems since the day God healed me in June 2003. I thank God continually for His healing provision.

On January 20, 2004, I fell while going up some metal steps at the back of the building in which I work. I fractured my hand and a cast was put on for twelve weeks. Although I expected everything to return to normal when the cast was removed, the doctor put me in a special splint because I had damaged the tendons. After receiving two steroid injections, I learned that I needed an operation because I was suffering from synotendentious.

By September 2004 I continued to experience pain in my hand and became desperate for God's intervention. When I learned that Dr. Bruce Allen was going to minister at the Director of Times of Refreshing Ministries' home in Belfast, I knew God was going to heal me again. I was thankful that Bruce Allen was willing to be used by God as a vessel to minister the healing power of Jesus.

After waiting eagerly for an opportunity for healing prayer, God made a way when a small group of us met to pray for a conference Dr. Bruce was scheduled to speak at the next day. During the meeting, Bruce asked his wife, Reshma, to put her hand on my damaged hand, then asked God to completely heal all damage and to strengthen my wrist and fingers. As he prayed I felt heat going through my hand, and my fingers loosened. I was instantly healed!

Dr. Bruce asked me to do something with my hand that I hadn't been able to do previously. I couldn't wait to take off the splint! Removing the splint, I could hardly believe it when I felt my thumb bending easily. Although my hand had been idle for months, I could click my fingers, which was impossible prior to this prayer!

God had done it again! After months of constant pain and suffering, God healed me. No pain, no stiffness, and no weakness—our mighty God answered my prayer.

I am grateful to the Lord and to Dr. Bruce Allen for his impartation into my life and willingness to come to Belfast. I pray others will be blessed through this testimony and receive healing and encouragement. Jesus is still the same as He has always been, and He sends His mighty angels to minister to us.

We only need to ask.

Sharon and her husband, Ronnie, have been married for over twenty-nine years and have three beautiful daughters, Rebecca, Sarah, and Rachel. Sharon is employed as a manager with a large utility company. She is actively involved with Times of Refreshing Ministries (TRM) based in Belfast, Northern Ireland, that ministers through inner healing, deliverance, and teaching seminars. Sharon's burning desire is to see a mighty outpouring of God's power throughout the nations. She and her family have been members of the Ulster Temple Elim Pentecostal Church in Belfast, Northern Ireland, for the past thirty years.

45

BIG IN THE LITTLE
by Ron Hanson

And my God will meet all your needs according to his glorious riches in Christ Jesus.

PHILIPPIANS 4:19

*G*od's promise for provision has become increasingly clear and more real to me over the years. I especially needed to rely on God's provision from 1977-1980 while working as a full time missionary as Director for Child Evangelism Fellowship (CEF), based out of Rochester, Minnesota. CEF, an international ministry headquartered in Warrenton, Missouri, provides adults, teenagers, and churches with training and materials to reach children in their neighborhoods with the saving gospel of Jesus Christ and to bring Christian growth. While working for CEF was rewarding, it seemed like I was always scraping the bottom of the money barrel.

The area I directed for CEF was composed of ten counties in southeastern Minnesota. Covering this large territory required me to travel frequently to locations up to two hours away. While visiting various sites I conducted teacher training classes to promote CEF's work with supporters and churches. These classes were designed to help teachers make better preparations for the Good News Club (Children's Bible classes) that were held weekly at homes and churches after school.

On three different occasions between 1978 and 1980, I was scheduled to visit Mantorville, Minnesota, but had no money and not enough gas in my car to make the round trip. The car I was driving at the time was a gas hog. Because of a gas tank leak, I couldn't put more than four gallons of gas in the tank before gas started leaking out. What might have seemed to some as a little provisional need was a big need to me. And God cared about my need.

The night before each trip to Mantorville, I attended a normal Sunday evening service at Berean Fundamental Church in Rochester, the church I regularly attended. I didn't mention my need for money or gas to anyone, nor did I give any indication of my circumstances. Yet after service on all three occasions somebody walked up to me and without saying anything pressed five to ten dollars in my hand, plenty to fill up a tank back when prices were under sixty cents per gallon.

In another time of need I was on the verge of being late with my apartment rent payment. When the due date arrived, I did not have enough money to pay the bill. I talked to the Lord about the situation and expressed my need to Him. I reminded Him of Minnetonka Community Church, the church I was raised in and where I continued my membership while living in Rochester. This church had introduced me to CEF. Because Minnetonka Community Church was missionary minded, it had a large budget to support missionaries all over the world. As Missionary Director for CEF, I normally received $100 support per month from the church.

Minnetonka Community Church normally sent my support at various times during the month so I never knew when it would arrive in the mail. The day my rent came due, I said, "Lord, $100 would be enough to make my rent payment, and it sure would be nice if it would come today." When I opened the mailbox, the $100 check was waiting for me. Again, I knew God was interested in listening to me and interested in meeting my needs, big and little.

In 2001 God expanded my understanding of His provision by expanding my understanding of tithing. My parents, Ruth and Leonard Hanson, attend Anah Immanuel Church in Anah Township, near Spooner, Wisconsin, a small fellowship of thirty to forty people. During the annual meeting in November my mother spoke up and quoted from the book of Malachi.

> "Will a man rob God? Yet you rob me. But you ask, 'How do we rob you?' In tithes and offerings. You are under a curse-the whole nation of you-because you are robbing me. Bring the whole tithe into the storehouse, that there may be food in my house. Test me in this,' says the LORD Almighty, 'and see if I will not throw open the flood-

*gates of heaven and pour out so much blessing that you will not have
room enough for it. I will prevent pests from devouring your crops,
and the vines in your fields will not cast their fruit,' says the LORD
Almighty. Then all the nations will call you blessed, for yours will be
a delightful land,' says the LORD Almighty."*

MALACHI 3:8-12

Mom challenged the congregation to give above and beyond their
normal giving to see what God would do. The people responded to the challenge. And God responded too. A short time later, Anah Immanuel Church
received $30,000 from the will and estate of someone my parents had never
known, about twice the normal church's annual giving. Witnessing this
provisional miracle inspired me to increase my giving further.

In the past I had tithed 10 percent off my net income. I based the tithe
on my net income because I felt that money taken automatically out of my
paycheck for taxes and other miscellaneous deductions was never really
mine. In addition, I had convinced myself that I could not afford to tithe
off my gross income and pay my bills at the same time.

God prompted me, however, to tithe at least 10 percent of my gross
income. Although I hesitated because I had very little savings, I sensed
God say, "Obey Me and watch Me bless you." I again read in Malachi 3:10,
"'Bring the whole tithe into the storehouse, that there may be food in my
house. Test me in this,' says the LORD Almighty, 'and see if I will not throw
open the floodgates of heaven and pour out so much blessing that you will
not have room enough for it.'"

God had taken care of me in spite of my lack of understanding on
giving. However, now He wanted to take me to a new level. He showed me
that I was attempting to build up some personal savings through *my
method* of giving tithes and offerings—yet, where was the saving under my
plan? If I gave the way God directed me to give, would I really have any
less money? God challenged me to give His way and to watch Him work.
He didn't promise a big savings account, but He did promise to meet all my
financial needs and to give me a deeper understanding of Himself.

It became clear to me that the first 10 percent belonged to God—before taxes, before medical insurance, before any other deductions. I chose to obey God's command, giving at least 10 percent off the top of all income, whether I received it through employment or by gift. In spite of my concerns about not being able to pay my bills, I have watched God meet all of my needs—*without exception*. God has honored His Word, continuously supplying my every need, big and small, so I can enjoy the richness of His grace and mercy.

Once during a morning worship service at Fond du Lac Community Church in Duluth, Minnesota, the Lord prompted me to put an additional $50 in the offering. I knew that if I gave an extra $50, I would come up short in paying my bills for the week. Again I obeyed, in spite of my concerns of financial lack. A few hours later my dad called me to say that my sister Merrilee needed a ride to the airport. She unexpectedly paid me $50 for helping her!

A few months later God prompted me to put an additional $20 in the offering. The next day I opened the mail and found an unexpected $20 check from the mortgage company due to an overpayment.

God is big in the little, always proving Himself faithful to care for His own.

Ron was born and raised in Minnetonka, Minnesota, and is a graduate of Northwestern College in Roseville, Minnesota. Since 1994 Ron has been an announcer for WWJC Christian Radio located in Duluth, Minnesota. He is chairman of the deacon board at Fond du Lac Community Church, a church that is associated with Village Missions based in Dallas, Oregon. Ron and his wife, Marcie, have been married over ten years and live in Duluth, Minnesota.

46

NIGHT OF FIRE

by Evangelist Sammy Simon Wanyonyi

*Let no one despise your youth, but be an example to the believers
in word, in conduct, in love, in spirit, in faith, in purity. Till I come,
give attention to reading, to exhortation, to doctrine. Do not neglect
the gift that is in you, which was given to you by prophecy with the
laying on of the hands of the eldership. Meditate on these things; give
yourself entirely to them, that your progress may be evident to all.*

1 TIMOTHY 4:12-16 NKJV

For two years I worked as an airline manager with Air France based
at Nairobi International Airport, overseeing the catering operations in East
and Central Africa plus Madagascar and the Comoro Islands. I quickly
adjusted to the good monthly paycheck that placed me in the minority
Kenyan upper middle class, a status few of my peers, if any, enjoyed.

Given my newfound status I frequently was invited to international
dinners and parties, rubbing shoulders with the diplomatic communities
in Nairobi. On the ministry front I often visited high schools to speak to
students, organize youth rallies, and preach in small town evangelistic
crusades. I also led a weekly neighborhood Bible study and reached out to
children whose parents never attended church. By all standards, I was
serving the kingdom excellently and exhibiting unmatched zeal. I could
have easily continued on unfettered.

Yet, I felt a deep-seated dissatisfaction and mounting awareness that God
had wider horizons for me to explore. At my birth my parents dedicated me
to God as His special tithe, hence my name Samuel. Mom took every opportunity to reminisce over that fact while I grew up. This, along with the vision
God gave me at age nine of the perishing multitudes, hounded me.

At that time I read the story of missionary William Carey (popularly
known as the father of modern day missions). One of his exhortations felt

like God's direct missionary address to me: "God is calling you to a brilliant future. He is calling you to preach this gospel to the whole world. My friend, you need this wider vision." Although Bill had written this some two hundred years earlier, it was as powerful and vivid to me as though God was uttering the words to me. Deep beckoned unto deep, and the picture of what could be compared to what was could not be shoved aside, notwithstanding the lack of securities and tangible guarantees that would come with obedience to such a lofty call.

I felt nervous and terribly afraid. Then came my high school friend's letter with the quotation from Jim Elliot, "He is no fool who gives up what he can't keep to gain what he can't lose," echoed as a timely re-enforcement to Bill Carey's exhortation to attempt a step that my spirit was willing to take but my flesh was too weak to attempt. Bill further exhorted me to attempt great things for God and to expect great things from God. Eight months later I gathered the courage to accept the fact that there was more to come, however unknown the future seemed.

I call it the night of fire. On Tuesday, September 10, 1996, at 1:30 A.M. I lay prostrate on the floor of my apartment in Nairobi, Kenya, my heart vociferous with entreaties of surrender to God and His kingdom purposes. For three hours I lay flat, my belly kissing the floor as the deep groans from within the center of my spirit flowed outward through my mouth and into the realm of Omnipotence. This effusive emotion was an amalgamation of sorts, a climaxing of a deep work God had started eight months earlier.

Until then, though conscious of the call on my life, I vacillated between the desire for God and all He wanted for me and the fear that surrender might lead into the abyss of the unknown. Like any ordinary twenty-three-year old, between God and me stood the securities of the corporate world. The steady income that my job with the French airliner guaranteed had resulted in the nurture of dreams of self-advancement. In my dreams I had purchased a house, enjoyed a grandiose marriage to a gorgeous girl, and my love for travel had been nurtured. These, along with the insecurities of a dastardly background of having been raised by poor African village evangelists, brought the sense of unsuitability for global kingdom errands and crowded out any confidence of a positive response to the tugging of God. I reasoned that I was better placed to do His bidding while employed with an airline and given free travel advantages. In the natural it made more sense to approach ministry that way, then I would never become a "perpetual beggar" as seemed to be the case for most evangelists and missionaries.

As if to warn me of the transient nature of earthly dreams, in July of that year I found myself in a car crash that resulted in many deaths around me. During the accident, however, I was spared. In response to God's promise of protection in Psalm 91, His angel had come to my rescue. He literally pushed back the metals that would have hemmed me in and would have otherwise crushed and mangled my flesh.

Only seconds before the accident I had been silently meditating on Psalm 91 and reminiscing on verses 14, 15, and 16 when the taxi I was in collided head-on with another speeding taxi. Drivers of both taxis and two passengers were pronounced dead at the scene.

In what seemed like an eternity, I cried out loud to the Lord and with a stern voice rebuked the devil. I felt like an air bubble formed around me, and I spun as the wreckage rolled on and on. When it came to a stop in a trench, the windshield on my side of the car was shattered, and I heard a still, small but firm voice command me to drop down through the shattered windshield. I did so and crawled away into the grass as I continued loudly praising God and making mockery of Satan. After I had crawled away, the car landed on the very side I had dropped out of.

In the middle of nowhere, it took a while before emergency help arrived. Amazingly I had escaped unscathed with just a small bruise on my hand. As I recovered, the proceeding days were full of contemplation of the vanity of dreams apart from God and served to deflate my high stake on the same.

Besides this dramatic event, heaven seemed to deposit and amplify at every corner of the Kenyan capital the explicit message to leave all and follow Jesus into the unknown future. Entering a taxi one day, I found a scripture stuck on the side conveying that very message. Entering someone's house, I found hanging on their living room wall a message about God's call to forsake all and follow Him. My fellowship with other saints often culminated with them talking about how God calls people to specific ministry. Even more surprising was the day my non-professing boss, who also doubled as the French diplomat to Kenya, called me into his office to inquire about my faith. After three hours of heated discourse, he, along with two other senior diplomatic staff, stated that I was meant for the world of Christian philanthropy.

That September morning—the night of fire—marked the turning point in my conflicted interior that resulted in the aligning of my heart, mind, and spirit with what I had known was the tugging of God to forsake all and follow Him.

Heavy with emotion and exhausted from indecision, I poured out my heart to God mostly in groans, barely managing to articulate the deeper desire and sense of surrender. As I made supplication over the course of three hours, I felt warmth around me that engulfed me from within and seemed to embrace me from without. It felt like thin-spreading ointment over my body. My spirit was zoomed in, absorbed in the delightful interchange with the Center of Heaven Himself. Amidst these interchanges and feelings of warmth, I sensed Him speak to me and assuage any reservations.

With this interchange peace descended over me like a river. I lay down and slept like a child for the night, relieved from the exhaustion of spiritual flight that had dogged me for eight months. My joy was restored, even though it still remained uncertain to me how everything would unfold. I was for the most part satisfied with the decision following the tremendous peace I felt in my heart. God, however, needed to solidify the affirmation in one deeper way that would once and for all assuage any lingering doubt and to establish me on His pre-determined course.

A couple of weeks later, as I prayed more regarding my decision, the Lord seemed to re-emphasize that I was to serve Him as a missionary, evangelist, and pastor and not as a Kenyan minister as my personal preference would have been. The thought often knocked over my center as I contemplated what it all meant. On this particular night of September 28, 1996, the words of Bill Carey, uttered two centuries earlier, reverberated again and again with a strange yet authentic authority that appealed to my own deep and persistent quest: "God is calling you to a brilliant future, He is calling you to preach His gospel throughout the earth. My friend, you need this wider vision."

"Lord, You don't use people like me to do this kind of ministry! I'm a farm boy, remember? And not *just* a farm boy. I'm an African farm boy!" I marveled to the Lord. "Indeed, You use people like Billy Graham from America, Reinhard Bonnke from Germany, David Cho from South Korea, and Dennis White, my "mega church" Pentecostal pastor who comes from Canada. I'm too ordinary for You to do anything significant with my life that would affect people beyond the boundaries of my nation."

I told God all this, unaware that He would sovereignly arrange for me to meet one of these servants and that I would learn my lesson of ordinariness from him.

Amidst such feelings of inadequacy I often sat in my office with the map of the world stretched on one side of the wall. Deep inside my heart I was drawn by a strange attraction and passion for the nations that seemed unbearable. *Could it be that God wants me to take His gospel to the ends of the earth, a young man who at one time treaded the village barefoot carrying the same gospel? I wondered. How can that be? My background is too humble and my way of life too ordinary!*

I recalled an incident when I had first arrived in Nairobi five years earlier, raggedy except for the dignified heart full of zeal to obey God. One day I had left the house and ventured into the city's business district on my own to do some sightseeing and familiarize myself with the city. As I walked on the streets enthralled by everything I saw, two plain-clothed police officers stopped to arrest me. Their charge: I looked too raggedy and posed a security risk for the city businesses.

When I protested their arrest and told them where I lived, they did not want to believe me. Unintimidated, I gave them an articulate gospel message and challenged them to come to Christ for the forgiveness of their sins. Surprised by what they heard, they realized that I was no ordinary teenager on the street and released me immediately.

Now, of course, I was a different young man who dressed well, had a little status, and carried some money in my pocket. I interacted with the international community and had befriended diplomats of foreign nations, lawyers, and doctors, among others. But even that could not prevent the overwhelming sense of ordinariness. The thought of serving as an international evangelist and missionary was intimidating.

"Lord, wherever You want me to go, will the people there respond to me with respect?" I prayed. "If I no longer have guaranteed income and colorful dreams of personal advancement, but instead am totally committed to preaching the gospel 'throughout the earth' as You're asking me to do, will they think it worthy to listen to what I have to say? Won't they consider me a welfare case? What will I eat? What will I wear? What will I drink? And who will watch for me peradventure I fall sick?"

These issues inspired a continuous sense of trepidation. The only thing keeping me from their paralyzing capacity was the quest to spend time alone with God in prayer. The more I prayed and sought the Lord, the greater the burden for the nations grew in my heart and with it the courage to face the challenges of the call. God showed me the complacency and religious oppression in European and American churches, charging me to stand and proclaim His gospel in these places. He directed me to bring a message of renewal and deliverance to His church and salvation to the lost around the world.

This night as I prayed, the Holy Spirit moved over me with heaven's burdens for countries like Haiti, Guyana, and Jamaica. The Holy Spirit spoke through my mouth, "I want My people! I want My people from the ends of the earth! I want My people from Haiti, Guyana, and Jamaica who are bound up in voodoo! I want My people from the ends of the earth!" I had never heard of voodoo practice before, hence when I later matched up these island nations with the actual practice of voodoo, it startled me.

Still feeling inadequate as I arose from my knees, the Holy Spirit whispered to my spirit saying, "Sammy, I will show you something today." That evening as I sat in my office at the Jomo Kenyatta International Airport, I sensed a commanding tap on my spirit, "Arise and go to the aircraft!"

Obediently I arose, entered my car, and drove off to the tarmac area inside the airport. A colleague standing by the door of the Air France plane waved and called me over. "Sammy, do you know that your brother is on this flight?" he asked.

"What brother? None of my brothers are traveling," I responded.

"No, your brother is traveling, I mean your brother Reinhard Bonnke. I'm sure you want to talk to him. He's in first class! Upstairs, hurry! The crew will soon shut the doors, but you might be able to say hi to him!"

Hearing this I was at first surprised by the exuberance in my colleague's voice, considering he was not a believer. I hesitated for a moment, quietly pondering the implications of the invitation. The same gentle instruction arose in my spirit again, "Go, talk to Reinhard Bonnke! That's why I asked you to come!"

The command terrified me. How could I talk to Reinhard Bonnke, a man who has brought entire cities and nations to Christ in a single day? Presidents of countries, leaders, and great men alike acknowledge that perhaps since the days of Paul, no other evangelist has preached to greater masses with greater fervor and a demonstration of the *gospel* than he. No other evangelist or preacher has ever taken on African nations like he has with such success.

The first time I heard Rev. Bonnke preach was via national radio in 1987. At fourteen years of age, after hearing him preach, I prayed to God, "Lord, when I grow up I want to preach Your Word like that man." Up to 200,000 people gathered to hear him preach daily at his evangelistic crusades in Nairobi's Uhuru Park. Innumerable others across East and Central Africa listened to him on Kenya's then only licensed radio station while others watched on television. I was in the remote villages of western Kenya, four hundred miles away, when I tuned in to listen. My heart had been strangely attracted to that kind of preaching. All my days, however, I never imagined that I would one day come face to face with the man.

"Go talk to him!" the Holy Spirit persisted.

Trembling, I went to the first class passenger cabin where Reinhard was immersed in a newspaper. *Ah Lord, so he's ordinary!* I prayed in my heart. *He's reading the same newspaper I read in my office earlier today!*

"Yes, I don't use extraordinary people to do My work," the Holy Spirit whispered. "I use ordinary men and women to accomplish My purposes."

Even so, Lord, I can't talk to him, I protested for the second time. I proceeded past him to the catering service area and casually asked the hostess if everything was okay. After she affirmed that everything was in order, I descended the stairs without speaking to Reinhard who was still engrossed in the newspaper.

When I reached the door, conviction arrested me. *I just disobeyed God!* "Oh Lord, forgive me," I prayed. "Please Lord, I'm sorry. I know that the crew are about to close the doors, but if You create another opportunity I'll gladly go back and talk to him."

At that moment the station manager called on the walkie-talkie, asking if any ground staff were near the aircraft. I responded. He asked me to let the crew know that one passenger hadn't boarded and they should wait a few minutes, as he was on his way.

"There's your opportunity again. Go back. Don't blow it this time," the Holy Spirit warned me. Relieved, I sprung upstairs one more time.

As I approached, Reinhard lowered the newspaper and looked straight at me as if he had been notified of my presence. As our eyes met, his smile was broad and inviting. Before I could say a word, he spoke with his raspy preacher voice, "God bless you! God bless your ministry. God bless you!" I shook his hand, short on words after being hit by the pronouncement, "God bless your ministry!"

Astounded, I wondered how in the world he knew God was talking to me about ministry since I was in my airline uniform. *Could it be that God had just spoken through him to affirm the very things He was speaking to my heart?* I wondered. I headed down the stairs, overcome with joy knowing that God would go to this effort to create an appointment with one of His choicest servants to confirm His call on my life.

As if one appointment were insufficient, exactly a year later to the date, time, and circumstances, at a time when I was discouraged and questioning whether the Lord had indeed called me since everything seemed to work against the whole process, God brought the same man again.

This time, kneeling on the plane in the presence of many surprised passengers, Reinhard laid his hands on my head and prayed, saying, "Father, in the name of Jesus Christ, I lay my hands upon this young man to release Your anointing in his life. In the name of the Lord Jesus Christ, Holy Spirit, move in his life and ministry. Use him to touch many nations with Your Word. I release God's blessing over his life. I release the Spirit of life over his speech. In Jesus' name I pray." He then charged me, "As from today henceforth, you will no longer be with the airline, but you will be in the pulpit. Next time I see you, I want to see you in the pulpit."

That night of September 29, 1997, I left the Air France plane leaping, rarely noticing the surprise on the faces of those I met. I determined that with such obvious confirmation, I would obey God and walk in the destiny set before me. The next day I submitted my resignation letter to the Air France management and committed to God the rest of my days.

These two meetings with Reinhard Bonnke did three things for me. First, God confirmed through an authoritative, respectable human vessel His specific call on my life to preach the gospel to the nations. Secondly, I believed the laying on of hands affirmed the special anointing of God to carry on the apostolic message of the kingdom of God. It was a sign of how meticulously personal and accurate God is in dealing with us as His servants. Finally, in observing Evangelist Bonnke read the same newspaper as I had read in my office, not holding a huge Bible on his lap as I had expected, God taught me the lesson of the ordinariness of His ministers. My ordinariness was no longer valid ground for refusal to follow through with the call of God on my life.

From that point forward I was done with low living, sight walking, small planning, smooth knees, colorless dreams, tame visions, mundane talking, cheap giving, and dwarfed goals. I no longer needed preeminence, prosperity, position, promotions, plaudits, or popularity. I didn't have to be right, first, tops, recognized, praised, regarded, or rewarded. The time had come to live by faith, lean on His presence, love with patience, live by prayer, and labor with power. I became a disciple of Jesus, compelled to go until He comes, give until I drop, preach until all know, and work until He stops me.

Paul's exhortation to Timothy in 1 Timothy 1:18 has since become so true for me, ringing with authenticity and authority as I proclaim Jesus Christ both in North America and around the world as the Lord leads me.

Still in his early thirties, Sammy Wanyonyi is an international evangelist whose ministry currently spans three continents: North America, Asia, and Africa. He is founder and president of Sammy Wanyonyi International Ministries (S.W.I.M.), an evangelistic and teaching ministry based out of Minneapolis, Minnesota. His passion is to reach entire communities with the Good News of salvation through Jesus Christ by holding citywide evangelistic festivals, leadership seminars, and revival, evangelism, and mission conferences as a way of strengthening the Church of Jesus Christ. In addition to his global travels, he is currently completing his master's in divinity at Bethel University Seminary in St. Paul, Minnesota.

47

HI HO, HI HO, OFF TO AMERICA I GO!
by Christel Bresko

There is a time for everything, and a season for every activity under heaven.

ECCLESIASTES 3:1

I arrived in Hamburg, Germany, in 1965 as a missionary intern from the Berea Bible School in Erzhausen/Darmstadt Germany. Although I had planned to stay only for the summer, Pastor Rabe, Senior Pastor of Elim Gemeinde Pentecostal Church, kept me on as nurse for his congregation of nine hundred members.

Preparations were in full swing for a November 6, 1967, revival meeting at Elim Gemeinde. Dr. Charles Butterfield, revival evangelist and President of Northwest College in Kirkland, Washington (USA), was scheduled as the main speaker. Although Dr. Butterfield had his own living quarters, he joined the trainee pastors, assistant pastor, nurses, and other helpers for meals in the dining room. At the breakfast table one morning, Dr. Butterfield asked if I wanted to serve on the staff of a medical ship traveling to the Virgin Islands in the South Seas. The door to my missionary calling opened wide.

With a nursing license in my pocket, I wanted to see the world. Dr. Butterfield encouraged me with my missionary journey ahead and while in Hamburg visited the U.S. embassy to arrange a green card for me. He and Northwest College committed to being my sole U.S. sponsor. This meant that they agreed to be responsible for my time in America, assisting me with a job and keeping a close eye on me.

A delay in obtaining my passport made it impossible for me to travel to the Virgin Islands when the medical ship of mercy sailed in January of 1968. However, the same month the Northwest College Dean of Women wrote me a letter telling me about the Missions Department and invited me to the college as a missions student. Not only did her proposal sound interesting to me, but I sensed a great pull in my heart to go.

By law I could not purchase my airline ticket until my visa was processed and finalized. Yet when Dr. Butterfield informed me of my departure date for America—Frankfurt Airport on Tuesday, March 22, 1968—I went against all odds and secured a one-way ticket to the U.S.

Dr. Butterfield and his wife, Edith, departed from the United States to the Scandinavian countries for special meetings. We planned to meet in Frankfurt, Germany, on my scheduled departure date of March 22. On Thursday, March 17, a letter arrived from the German Embassy. "Come and pick up your visa with your sponsor's signature," it read. *With my sponsor's signature? I thought. Impossible!*

My adventurous spirit suddenly slid to the verge of collapse. My sponsor, Dr. Butterfield, was out of the country on the evangelistic tour. Writing to Northwest College for a signature would have taken at least two weeks, and fax machines did not exist at the time.

How can I possibly do it? I wondered. In order to make my March 22 departure, I would have to pick up my visa by Monday, travel home to my folks—about a five-hour train ride—pack, then travel two more hours to Frankfurt to catch my flight to America. Darkness engulfed my dreams. My trip, my ticket, and world missions all washed away. "Lord," I said, "it's up to You. It's out of my hands, so I'm trusting You!"

Every Thursday night at 7:30 P.M. we held a Bible study and prayer meeting in Hamburg in the lower level of the church. But that evening I told Pastor Rabe that I would not attend the Bible study. Instead, I sat at the top of the stairs, next to a table with a telephone. In a somber mood I felt drawn into a cocoon, wondering if all of my plans had fallen apart.

When the phone rang at 7:45 I picked it up. "Miss Christel Decker, please," the familiar sounding man said.

With confidence I spoke up. "This is Christel Decker."

"Christel, this is Charles Butterfield. Edith and I are here in Hamburg, in your fine city."

"But you're supposed to be in Stockholm, Sweden!" I said. "What are you doing in Hamburg?"

"Yes," he said. "We left for Stockholm to fly into Copenhagen, Denmark, but the airport was all fogged in so we couldn't land," he explained. "Somehow we were rerouted and landed in Hamburg."

I couldn't believe it. "I need your signature to get my visa!" I told Dr. Butterfield, trying to catch my breath.

Dr. Butterfield invited me to the Alster Hotel, where he and his wife were staying. I sped to his hotel by taxi, obtained his signature, and without a minute to spare my visa was processed on Friday.

On Saturday, March 22, I travelled home for a short visit with my family, then arrived in Frankfurt to catch my flight to America—*just in time!*

Leaving Germany the weather was cool, the trees bare, and early spring flowers had popped their heads out only to be nipped by night frost. On the long flight to America I pondered the previous stressful months and God's plan for my life.

When we touched down in Seattle early in the morning, springtime had arrived with a lovely fragrance and warm fresh air. Magnolia trees were flowering and pink cherry trees lined the streets. Everything seemed magnified. The cars looked much bigger, the streets wider, even the sun seemed brighter. I needed time to take it all in!

I arrived at Northwest College in March 1968 and attended classes until June, taking English and missions courses. After Christmas Bill Bresko, a missions candidate, invited me to a candlelight dinner at the Flame Restaurant in Kirkland, a basketball game, and an outing at the Seattle ice rink—all the same night! We could not make it up the hill to get back to campus because it had snowed all day in the Seattle area, so we took the long way around. As Bill pointed something out to me, he kissed me on the cheek as I turned.

I couldn't wait to get to my room so I could write my family a letter and ask them to take a vote on what I ought to do about Bill. Mom told me I was old enough to make my own decision, and we were married June 14, 1969.

Bill wanted me to see Alaska before we made a long-term commitment as missionaries. After a stopover in Medical Lake, we headed to Alaska to enjoy the summer, then returned to the college in September after a two-week stay in Germany with my folks.

Bill, who grew up as a Catholic orphan in Pennsylvania, had made a promise to the Lord. His dad had signed him up for the Navy, and at seventeen he was a soldier in Korea. During that time he prayed, "Lord, if You get me out of this country alive, I'll serve You in Australia or Alaska." Although we had made plans for visa passports, especially for Australia, our plans changed when B.P. Wilson, the Alaskan superintendent, interviewed us.

When a village in Fort Yukon, above the Arctic Circle, asked for a missionary couple to fill in for Mr. and Mrs. Lance and their daughter Elaine while they vacationed in Florida, B.P. Wilson arranged for us to fill the void. We had never seen or heard about this village during the summer we had stayed in Alaska, but off we went. At summer's end, Mr. and Mrs. Lance and their daughter returned from Florida, and after investigating our arctic abode we found a cabin built in 1916 next to Black River.

In September 1970 the Assembly of God in Alaska arranged for us to do pioneering and live in Chalkyitsik, a small Indian village that is a thirty-minute flight northeast from Fort Yukon flying in a Cessna. We departed in a thick snowstorm, chartering two airplanes to carry our staples, belongings, two dogs, and a cat. The snow continued to fall after we landed. Darkness coming, we pitched two tents and loaded our belongings into our tent, then Bill ventured out to find our cabin.

When he approached some children they ran away. Someone pointed and showed him the place: a sod roof, doors and windows missing, years worth of garbage piled up, dirt floor, and Penny's/Sears catalogs for wallpaper. We did not even own a broom!

Bill hauled our belongings using a borrowed wheelbarrow, and I found a broom. After warming the cabin with a trash fire in a barrel stove we got a good sleep, staying close on our Army cot bed. Everything looked better in the morning.

As missionaries, our purpose was to preach the Word of God. Athabaskan preacher David Salmon preached in the Indian language on Sunday morning, and we held Sunday school. On our first day of Sunday school we counted thirty-five children. To this day God's Word is still being preached.

After four years we felt in our heart that we needed a change, so we served seven more years in small multiple culture villages. Bill became the pastor in Anderson Alaska, south of Fairbanks. We filled in when needed, enjoying our stay at Little Beaver Lake near Wasilla. It had a Bible Camp used by different denominations like Women's Aglow, Royal Rangers, men's ministries, and Kid's Camp—especially the snow camps.

In 1984 Bill and I returned to Silverlake Camp in Medical Lake, Washington. After accepting an invitation to visit Chalkyitsik in 2003, we were welcomed like a king and queen. Seeing the evidence of the God-filled village, I pondered His divine orchestration in my life—and remembered how He changed the course of an airplane headed to Copenhagen and brought it to Hamburg so I could begin my journey as a missionary.

In Germany Christel's father became a follower of Hitler in his youth because at the time families were expected to train up their children to be part of the Nazi party. When her dad became a Christian before getting married in 1935, he realized that Nazism and Christianity did not mix well. With great difficulty and threats, Christel's father turned his back on the Hitler regime and became a follower of Christ. Today all of Christel's family serve the Lord: her brother Guenter Decker is a pastor, her sister Inge Decker Tietz is a dedicated pillar in her church, and her dad served on the German Mission board. Her mom cared for many missionaries who stayed in the family home, a haven for many visitors and friends. Christel and her husband now live in Medical Lake, Washington.

48

FROM PRISON CAMP TO PRAISE
by Karola Anna Manessah Brownfield

*You are standing here in order to enter into a covenant with the
LORD your God, a covenant the LORD is making with you this day and
sealing with an oath, to confirm you this day as his people, that he
may be your God as he promised you and as he swore to your fathers,
Abraham, Isaac and Jacob.*

DEUTERONOMY 29:12,13

$\mathcal{M}$y grandfather, Joshua Balaam Zukerman, rabbi to the Rhineland
Jewish Community, was married to Regina Uymarka. I, Karole Anna
Manessah Reisman Brownfield, was born June 28, 1935, in Hassen,
Deutschlaand, to Rabbis Thomas Moshe and Fegila Borta Reiseman. I was
the third child of seven. There were three boys: Thomas Bertram, the
oldest, Benjamin Michael, and Konel Abraham. There were four girls:
Johanne Serah, Nanet Mirian, Barata Mariette, and myself.

Raised in the strictest religious order of Judaism, we observed the
seven Jewish holidays and other Jewish rituals. We resided in one of three
Jewish communities where the people worked together as a team. The
elderly did not work and the children had their place in the nursery under
the care of an appointed lady. These appointments could change from week
to week as the rabbinical leaders so desired.

My mother began working in the fields only hours after I was born,
harvesting vegetables for the winter season. Mira, an attendant, cradled me
and tended to my every need, calling mother only when I needed to be fed,
rocked, or given tender loving care. Other women in the community were
assigned to clean the temple and cook for the holidays.

My father worked with the men fixing the gates, harvesting hay, and
other hard labor. At the end of the day all returned to their individual

homes to study religion, eat, play, and enjoy one another. The children knew that Jehovah Adonai gave them to their parents.

None of us could have known what would befall our well-loved and established community. But Hitler, a man to whom the Jews gave little credence, had plans for our community and many others as well. Because the economy was in a lapse, the Germans needed a union to insure benefits as they labored in the factories. This was the ticket Hitler used to gain power. After the people voted him in, he made good on his promises for a brief time but that ended when he focused on a plan to destroy the Jews.

Hitler was a mad man. He wanted an Arian race of people and the Jews were not a part of his plan. Because he hated Jews he forced a census on the country, forcing every Jew to report and wear the Star of David as an armband—so humiliating, as the star was a religious symbol to the Jews.

Nazi army tanks began moving in, crowding the roads of Bavaria. Then the Hitler Youth Movement was established in the schools. When the Hitler Youth became informants, those whom they accused were arrested, imprisoned, and in some instances shot on the spot. The Gestapo infiltrated the country, leaving us no safe refuge. Speaking against the government or a government official put one's life at risk.

Nazis confiscated and burned all Jewish people's records. They torched the synagogues. Throughout Germany anything representing the Jewish people or Jewish religion was destroyed. One night Nazi soldiers arrived at my grandfather's house, rummaged through his house, and burned everything in sight—clothes, hats, and jewelry.

The German government took possession of the money in banks. Fortunately my parents sent some money to England, yet most of their money was stolen according to Hitler's orders. Fearing for our family, my father and mother escaped to Holland before Hitler could harm us. They had friends who lived in Amsterdam and thought it would be safe, as many Jews were fleeing there to find refuge.

In time Amsterdam was not safe, as Hitler's soldiers surrounded the country to box us in. After arresting us, they stuffed us on a train bound for a detainee camp in Poland. Later, another train transported us to the Bergen-Belsen Interment Camp in Germany.

I well remember the train ride where they packed us in like sardines. The straw-covered floor felt ice cold. An awful stench pervaded the train as only one bucket was provided for elimination. The few people with food would not share. Some died from starvation while others perished from asphyxiation.

At the camp guards played a game, directing us to stand in line where we received a number. One number meant death, another number meant you would live—for a while. They were so cruel. While I stood in the hellish camp with my mother and nine-year-old twin brother, guards told mother she could not have two children. They forced her to pick one of us and let the other die. Mother dropped to her knees and pleaded for Konel's life. But alas, they grabbed Konel, threw him to the ground, and shot him to death.

Because I didn't understand what was happening, I asked my mother to explain. Mother said Konel was now in heaven. She told me not to cry, but I did cry, as I loved my brother with all my heart. I witnessed many being murdered that dreadful day.

Once past the gates we were showered and deloused. Guards accused us of being filthy, an insult as we had been clean people all our lives. We had lived right, eaten right, and rarely were ill. They gave us skimpy dresses, but our feet remained bare. When I complained to mother because of the cold, she cried, not only for me but also for her dead children.

I will never forget the barracks with row after row of barbed wire on the windows. No one was allowed outside, and we knew if we tried to get out we would be killed instantly. Bright light surrounded the camp, and armed guards in towers positioned themselves all the way around.

Our barrack was filled to capacity, and we slept on the frigid floor. A few people had beds, if you can call a hard board a bed. Trying to find a bit of warmth, we huddled close to one another. Many elderly people died from the freezing cold and sickness.

Several months after we arrived at the prison camp, officials decided to transfer men from our barracks to work camps. My grandfather, my father, and my last two surviving brothers, Thomas and Benjamin, were all chosen for the work camp. When allowed to see them I asked my daddy why he was leaving. Father said he was going to work at another camp and that I would see him again. He urged me to be strong for my older sister, Johanne, and my mother. After I promised him I would take good care of them, Daddy and Grandfather kissed me then were pulled away. I never saw them again.

On a freezing cold day Johanne died of starvation. I watched mother holding back her tears. She didn't want me to be scared, but I *was* scared. That same day they took my grandmother and my younger sisters, Nanet and Barata, to "a shower"—the gas chamber. They hugged me before they walked to their death.

Now only Mother and I were left. But they took my mother to a hospital for experimental purposes. She knew that she would never see me again. Before leaving she gave me her wedding ring and a necklace, telling me I would need them to gain passage out. Holding me, she said, "I'll see you in heaven." They murdered her in the most vicious way.

One might wonder how I hid the necklace and ring so I would have them when needed. Mother had told me to hide the jewelry in my rectum. It was so painful, but it meant my life, so I endured the pain.

Soon after my mother's death I sat on the barrack floor sobbing my heart out. An older woman crouched down beside me, enfolded me in her arms, and then whispered in my ear words I could hardly believe.

"I know someone who can get you out of this camp," she said.

This terrified me, as I knew that if anyone heard us talk they might tell the guards, and we'd both be killed on the spot. I really didn't trust her or anyone in the camp, for that matter. I knew they could sell me short for as little as a hard piece of bread. Hunger in the camp cannot be described. Everyone was hungry. It wasn't safe to turn one's back on food or it would be gone, just like that.

Within a couple of weeks our escape plan was worked out and began. The guide, who posed as a Nazi soldier, entered the gate and gave orders to kill more Jews. He announced his plans to spend a few days in our camp before returning to his headquarters. Then he secretly met with us and revealed his plan to help us. We paid him, and wonder of wonders, several days later we were on our way to freedom. Our journey took us through an underground tunnel, a stinky pipe filled with rats, water, and fecal matter. We crept through the pipe keeping our heads down and remaining totally silent. Knowing the guards might hear something terrified us.

We crawled out of the tunnel so dirty. My hair looked as if someone had dumped motor oil over me, my clothes were wet, and I felt like vomiting. But unlike some, I made it out. Others were too weak, but we could not stop to help them along.

We were hurried to a small wooden boat and rowed across a lake. Guards had been alerted and shot at us but missed. Guides rushed us into a house where food and shelter awaited us. After spending the night there, early the next morning we were escorted to a cart and told to lay flat on the truck bed after being covered with hay. Instructed to remain absolutely quiet, we didn't move a muscle as the farmer drove us to another house, where we stayed for a week or two. Again they cautioned us to be still, to never look out the windows, open the door, or leave the hiding place. We were warned not to try to escape on our own, as it was too perilous.

After arrangements were made for our relocation to the Kinderdorf Children's Transfer in England, we were transported to a seaport by train where we boarded a ship for England. Although I became seasick and felt sad leaving my country, the journey was a blessing, and I looked forward to becoming a citizen of Great Britain. Because I knew no English, the interpreter told me I must study and learn English.

The first sights I remember seeing upon arrival in England were The Tower with Big Ben and the London Bridge. What awesome sites! While still on board, however, doctors had examined me and had determined that I needed further care. So I was immediately admitted to a makeshift hospital, along with others, to tend to my health problems.

When deemed well enough, we were introduced to government employees working with the German consulate then taken to our new homes. As I travelled by train to Summerset, I saw the ravage of war everywhere. Arriving at my new home, I cried at my gray and dormant surroundings. Summerset was a small English town inhabited by people who hated Germans. After all, we had been their enemy.

My new family told me I must work for my keep and attend school where I would learn English. They frightened me by saying that if I did not do as I was told the government might send me back. I promised to be good. And I was.

Everything I remember about my life in England was terrible, but I didn't have any other choice. Daily children at school ridiculed me and at home adults forced me to work as a slave. Nightly I sought relief in my dark, cold room. I was denied another blanket and told, "Shut up and be grateful. Don't you know how lucky you are?"

My strategy was to put my all into school. Being an avid student—the one thing I had going for me—I enjoyed learning anything I could about English history and culture. English culture was very different from German culture. The English seemed solemn, a bit cocky, and honest almost to a fault. This was a source of hurt to me for I was a very sensitive child and found forthright speech hard to digest. My love for music was a counterbalance. The family loved music and took me to church, where young girls and women were allowed to sing. In my synagogue life only boys and men had been allowed to sing.

The tension arising in my mind between Christianity and Judaism became heavy. Thus, when I attended the Christian church I felt it needful to perform the "smutches," a Jewish ritual to cleanse me from any evil the Christians forced on me. It seemed Christians were robbing me of my free will and making me a slave to their beliefs. In the end I hated them; I hated their God and most certainly hated Jesus.

I wanted to run away, but at the mercy of the German Consulate I had nowhere to go. Being warned that any trouble reported concerning misbehavior would lead to deportation back to Germany, I lived deep in fear and conformed to everything I was told to do, even when it went against what I wanted.

Although some orphans in foster homes were well treated, it was not my fate. The adults in my home treated their biological children so differently than they treated me. My clothes were shabby while their children were nicely dressed, their children ate better than I did, and they assigned to me the dirty work to spare their children.

I had little time to play with friends, and since my enjoyment centered in singing temple music and dancing Jewish dances, even my playtime was spoiled. They called me a Christ killer, an unbeliever, and a sinner. How these taunts tormented me! The English children mocked and chided me, making it clear that I was their enemy, which scared me. I saw these children as uncaring and cruel. Though I never understood English children, I had some adult friends who encouraged me to work hard to remain in the German Consulate's favor. Those friends sowed the seed in my little mind to apply to immigrate to the United States.

Two years after arriving in England I received my papers and passport to board a ship headed for New York. On my way to the United Sates, I felt happy and frightened. I wanted to think that something better awaited me on the other side of the ocean. Deep down I knew it must be better than what I had experienced in England. There would be no more war and bomb destruction and no more hate for Germans and Jews.

That day of departure many of us Kinderdorf children were taken to the ship in a London port. We had been provided a small suitcase, a passport, and other documents. After an official questioned me, I boarded ship. Again terror reigned in my heart. My English was poor and my customs had been unacceptable in England. Would they be accepted in America? Would Americans like me? Amidst my fears, the awful death of my family played a relentless tune in the back of my mind.

The crossing was a daze. Seasick, I gobbled the good food, then became sick. Soon we would all be placed in foster homes and in the care of the new government. I arrived in New York harbor on a gorgeous day and remember seeing the beautiful lady standing tall, holding her torch high. I later learned she was the Statue of Liberty given to America by

France. Then the outline of New York's tall buildings took my breath away. That day all of us Kinderdorf children forgot our sadness. I smiled and laughed—just for a while. I had made it to freedom and fulfilled my mother's hopes and dreams for me.

Those who were cleared to go after an onboard doctor's examination left the ship and were greeted by the County Welfare. I trembled at the thought of another foster home, wondering what type of people would take me into their home and what kind of treatment I would find in the United States.

I had hoped for a Jewish family but was placed in a home where I suffered abuse for being a Jew. Beaten and sexually molested, I lived in hell. Again I wanted to run away, but where would I go? I feared that only jail awaited me if I ran. When I tried to tell the county welfare department about the abuse, they did not believe me. After asking to be sent to another state and requesting placement in a Jewish home, I was granted a move to San Diego, California.

In America I moved from foster home to foster home and from state to state where I suffered continual physical, emotional, and sexual abuse. At the time few laws existed to protect children, so foster homes got away with much. As years passed resentment and bitterness from my past filled my heart.

Many told me about Jesus over the years. I remember renting a room above a Pentecostal church in Los Angeles. For seven years I cleaned the church, and every evening when I tried to sleep, I could hear church services in the sanctuary below my room. The floors were so thin I heard everything: the loud singing and praise, the dancing—and preaching about Jesus.

"Karola," they'd tell me, "you need Jesus." But I told them repeatedly that I had my own faith. Although Jesus had spared my life and given His life for me, I continued to reject Him and didn't want to know Him. I was a Jew, and Jews didn't believe in Jesus.

Filled with rage after being mistreated by so many mean people in my past, over time I developed into an extremely angry person. One day in

2004, when I arrived at the end of my limit, I hurried to the synagogue in search of peace. I found no peace and, in desperation, I ran out. Hopeless, I decided to end my dreadful life. I planned to drown myself at Richmond Beach, Washington, intending to walk into the water and end it all.

Before I carried out my plan a thought entered my mind. *Before I die, I'll talk to a minister.* Taking the phone book, I randomly picked a church and dialed the phone. Pastor Bunn from North Seattle Alliance Church answered the phone. "I don't know you, and you don't know me," I said. "I don't even know why I'm calling you." I explained that nobody loved me or cared about me, I had no friends, and I had nothing to live for.

"Everything you need, Karola," Pastor Bunn said, "is in Jesus." He talked to me about Jesus for almost two hours and so lovingly answering my every concern. If Pastor Bunn hadn't taken my phone call or hadn't spoken to me in such a loving manner, I wouldn't be alive today.

God, through Pastor Bunn, connected me with several people who ministered love and hope to me. Lisa Hoover talked to me more, further turning my hopelessness to hope. When I met Pastor Grace, we talked some more, and I found more hope. I started attending church where I received unconditional love and acceptance.

In spite of my anger, hostility, and fears, Pastor Grace visited me repeatedly and patiently walked me through my issues. Finally, one day after many years of people sowing seeds of Jesus into my life, I said, "I want to receive Jesus. He saved my life." Dropping to my knees, I invited Jesus into my heart. And I've never been the same since.

Karola, a German Jew and holocaust survivor, lives in Shoreline, Washington. Karola speaks fluent Hebrew and is deeply loved and cherished by many, including the compiler of Extraordinary Miracles in the Live of Ordinary People.

49

IN SPITE OF MYSELF

by Pastor Randy Klein

The Lord isn't really being slow about his promise to return, as some people think. No, he is being patient for your sake. He does not want anyone to perish, so he is giving more time for everyone to repent.

2 PETER 3:9,10 NLT

One fall weekend in 1998 my wife, Gwen, attended a women's retreat in northern Spokane sponsored by Rock of Ages Church. During the retreat she injured her lower back severely. Although the women's group prayed for Gwen's healing, her pain worsened. On Sunday they brought her down the mountain from the retreat center to the chiropractor's office, where I met them. When the chiropractor was unable to help Gwen, I took her to Holy Family Hospital where she was examined and admitted.

The next day I planned to visit Gwen at the hospital. After working all day on a construction job, exhaustion plagued me. "Lord," I prayed on the way to the hospital, "when I get to the hospital, I just want to see Gwen. I don't want to talk to anybody, I don't want to see anybody else or do anything else. I only want to see Gwen and go home." I must admit that I had a bad attitude.

Walking into the hospital I headed to the elevator and pushed the up button. When the elevator door opened, I found Gary Laursen, a gentleman I knew from Northern Park Racquetball Club but hadn't seen in a few years. Because I was so bushed and didn't want to talk to anybody, I thought to myself, *Maybe he won't recognize me.* But as I stepped onto the elevator, Gary said, "Hello, Randy. How are you?"

"Well hello, Gary," I said. "I'm here to see my wife tonight. Gwen was admitted because she hurt her back and is in severe pain. What are you doing here?"

"My father-in-law is here to die," he answered. "He was flown here from Montana by a medical helicopter."

"I'm a minister, so if I can help, let me know," I told him. We got off on the third floor, where I headed to Gwen's room and Gary headed the other direction to his father-in-law's room. While I visited with Gwen and prayed for her, the Lord kept saying over and over again, "Go down and see Gary." When I knew the Lord wouldn't let me ignore His prompting, I said, "Gwen, I have to walk down the hall to see Gary. I'll be back."

I started down the hall and found the room of Gary's father-in-law, Wilbur. When I peeked into the room I spotted Gary and some nurses who were attending to Wilbur. Gary saw me and came into the hallway to introduce his wife. "This is my wife, Leslie," Gary said.

"It's nice to meet you," I said. Leslie was in tears seeing her father suffer. She knew he was dying. Not only did Wilber have liver cancer, but complications also caused fishers in his esophagus to rupture, making him bleed out of his throat. As we spoke the nurses were cleaning him up from a current rupture episode.

"Leslie," I said, "while I was visiting my wife down the hall, the Lord wouldn't leave me alone about coming down here to see your father."

"Three other people, including hospital chaplains, came to see Dad," she said. "He wouldn't receive any of them." Still in my work clothes after a long day, my dirty hands and roughed up appearance must have been obvious. "Go ahead and see him," she said. "But it's not a very pretty sight in there."

"I'm not concerned about that," I told her. "I'm concerned about your dad's salvation." Gary and I entered Wilbur's room, where the nurse was completing Wilbur's medical care.

"Wilbur—Dad, this is my friend Randy," Gary said. "He's a minister, and he wants to talk to you about Jesus."

"I don't want to talk to him," Wilbur answered.

I leaned back against the window and prayed silently, "Lord, You asked me to come down here to see Wilbur, and You're going to have to make it possible for me to talk to him alone."

About that time Gary said, "Well, I'll leave you two alone." After the nurse checked a few things, she left the room too. Wilbur was facing away from me, looking toward the door. Reaching out I touched his shoulder. "Wilbur," I said, "I came here tonight to talk to you about Jesus."

"Who?"

"Jesus."

Wilbur turned his head toward me and listened. "I want to tell you about Jesus and why He came into this world," I said. I shared God's plan of salvation with Wilbur and explained how Jesus died on the Cross and rose from the dead, paying the price for our sins. I told him that if we accept Jesus and ask for forgiveness of our sins, He cleanses us of all unrighteousness and enables us to stand before God without any blame.

"Wilbur," I said, "would you like to pray a simple prayer and ask Jesus Christ to forgive your sins?"

"Yes, I would," Wilbur answered.

After leading him in the sinner's prayer, I said, "Praise the Lord, Wilbur! I'll see you in heaven!"

"Praise the Lord!" Wilbur answered.

When I saw Leslie and Gary, I thanked them for letting me visit Wilbur. They were ecstatic to hear that Leslie's dad had received Christ.

After returning to Gwen's room to finish our visit, I left. The next day, September 28, my son, Ben, and I drove to the hospital after lunch. After visiting Gwen we felt led to see Wilbur. As we came through the door, Leslie and Gary said, "Pastor Randy, come on in here." After we entered Wilbur's room, they said, "We're not sure how much time he's got. Is there anything you'd like to say to him?"

Going to Wilbur's side, I said, "Wilbur, God has a plan for you. He must have something for you to do in heaven. Everyone here is going to be okay." Then I told family and friends, about ten people, "Go ahead and say good-bye to him." One by one they came to Wilbur's bedside, kissed him, and said good-bye.

As this emotional scene unfolded in Wilbur's room, two airplanes in the sky crossed, leaving a vapor trail in the sign of the Cross. Everybody in the room witnessed the cross in the sky and marveled. Leslie and Gary said that from their position it looked like it was above Wilbur's head. At that moment, Wilbur passed away.

I asked Leslie and Gary, "Did you talk to Wilbur after I left last night?"

"No," they said. "After you left, he never said another word."

The last words out of Wilbur's mouth before he entered glory were "Praise the Lord!" which he spoke after receiving Jesus. His funeral service was held in Montana.

Gwen improved and was released from the hospital. They never discovered what had caused the severe pain in her lower back. At the hospital, however, something had puzzled me. I had prayed, "Lord, where is Wilbur's wife?" I didn't want to ask the family because if she had passed away recently, my question might bring more pain. Although Wilbur's passing was a great miracle, it also brought the pain of loss to loved ones.

The following Sunday evening I preached at Hilliard Assembly of God, where I had been helping out on Sunday evenings after Brother Hunter, the Senior Pastor, had passed away. During my message I shared the story of how God had brought Wilbur to Spokane from Montana, how Gwen hurt her back and was taken down the mountain to the hospital, how Gary and I met in the elevator—so we could all be in the right place at exactly the right time to bring forth a soul for the kingdom.

After the service a woman named Ruth Bates came forward to talk to me. "I know Wilbur, and I know Leslie," she said. "I take care of Wilbur's wife, Leslie's mother, at a rest home called Royal Courts Plaza. She's an Alzheimer's patient." God had answered my prayer, telling me exactly where Wilbur's wife was!

A month had passed when I woke up one day hearing the Lord say, "I want you to go see Wilbur's wife." I told Gwen about God's prompting me to visit Wilbur's wife, then we made arrangements to see her.

When we arrived, Ruth Bates told Wilbur's wife, "A pastor friend of mine is here to see you. He talked to Wilbur before he died. His name is Randy."

In a deep guttural voice, she said, "I know Randy."

Although she suffered from Alzheimer's, she was able to converse easily with us and listened as I shared God's plan of salvation with her. Only God knows if she accepted Christ, but I knew God had performed another great miracle.

God loves us so much that He would orchestrate such a scenario so a person can come to the saving knowledge of Jesus Christ. If we could see the miracle of how God dealt with us when He brought us to Him, it would be a miracle in the same way. Above all, it's a miracle to receive eternal life, and it is also amazing when we see how far God will go to give it to us!

Pastor Randy Klein is Senior Pastor of Living Water Christian Fellowship. He owned and operated Handy Randy's as a contractor for twelve years and now works in real estate. Randy and his wife, Gwen, have been married for twenty-nine years. With their son, Ben, they perform an Elvis tribute show incorporating the gospel message. Ben is an award-winning tribute artist. Randy, Gwen, and Ben live in Spokane, Washington.

50

PRAYING FOR MORE OF
THE MIRACULOUS

by Robert Weston

It is my pleasure to tell you about the miraculous signs and wonders that the Most High God has performed for me.

DANIEL 4:2

From the depths of a Soviet concentration camp a message was smuggled out to the West: "Yes, our main need is for prayer—but lead such lives that God can answer your prayers." What a challenge to ponder and to take to heart! This is something I learned early in my walk with the Lord.

As a student of modern languages, I spent a year in France. I wrote on my application form, "Anywhere but the Paris region," but a few months later I found myself in the French capital. One day I returned to my lodgings from a Bible study. For whatever reason, my contributions had been poorly received. I flopped despondently to my knees, feeling overwhelmed and useless, and poured out my heart in repentance to God.

There was nothing new about this; the closer we draw to God the more profoundly we may find ourselves mourning the many ways in which we fail Him, whether for specific opportunities missed or for repeated character failings. *This* time of repentance felt particularly deep that night, however.

Suddenly I found myself praying the most outrageous prayer, "Lord, let me go to heaven tonight!" And in a sense I did! It was not so much that I went to heaven as that heaven came to me. Unexpectedly, gloriously, the presence of the Lord filled my room. I could hear the inexpressibly beautiful sounds of heavenly worship, exquisite melodies entwined with soaring harmonies of such sublime subtlety that no words can do them justice.

I could see neither shape nor form, but was overwhelmed by the certainty that the Lord Jesus Himself was right there with me in the room. He told me that the Father had specifically accorded this time, and that I was free to ask Him questions. With the touching naivete and dazed incredulity of a very young Christian, I asked whether He could appear to people on the other side of the world at the same time as He did to me. When He said that of course He could, my awe knew no words.

Caught up in the Lord's sweet presence, we communed together for what turned out to be about three hours, though never have hours passed so swiftly. I asked the Lord how I would be able to be sure in the future that I had not imagined this intimate encounter. He directed me immediately to read a passage in Deuteronomy that perfectly summed up that momentous evening. "Today we have seen that a man can live even if God speaks with him" (Deuteronomy 5:24).

When the Lord Jesus finally said that our time together must come to an end, He told me that I would not meet Him again in quite so full a way until He called me home to heaven. I felt an immediate grief at the thought of being separated from such perfect love, but He promised that He would send me the fullness of the Holy Spirit, the Comforter. In an outpouring of love and worship I was baptized in the Holy Spirit and received the gift of a heavenly language. This wonderful awareness of the Lord's presence continued unabated for several weeks.

Through this encounter I learned a truth I have never forgotten since. Heaven is not far away; it is just another dimension. At any point, into any darkness or despair, the power and presence of the Lord can break through. In my case profound repentance was a key to this release. As surely as I yielded to the spirit of repentance on that glorious night in Paris, God broke through.

It is not that the Lord has favorites who are on the right side of miracles, while others are destined to remain less favored sons and daughters. Perhaps it would be nearer the mark to say that just as *we* respond more easily to grateful children than to sullen, surly, and rebellious ones, so the Lord is able to give Himself more freely to those with eager, trusting hearts. The more willing we are to yield *all* that we *are,* all that we *do,* and all that we *have* to the Lord, the easier He finds it to demonstrate His miraculous power through and on behalf of us.

We can never lose out by yielding completely to Him—even if, as happened to Abraham, He asks for our "Isaacs"—the things that He

Himself has promised us. If we hold on too tightly to these activities, positions, or treasures, it may be a sign that our work *for* God rather than God Himself has subtly become the all-consuming focus of our life. I learned this in my relationship with my future wife.

Over a period of many months my relationship with Rosalind, whom I had met as a student nurse, developed into a prayer partnership and then into something still more precious. In contrast to earlier whirlwind romances, the Lord reined back our emotions in order to develop this strong bond of prayer and friendship. One evening, however, just a week before we were due to move to separate towns, the Lord spoke to us simultaneously. He told us to neither see, write, or even telephone each other again until He specifically permitted us to.

The Lord's edict to us was our mini Mount Moriah. Offering up our "Isaac" on the altar, we had no choice but to die to the hope that God was giving us to each other. So far as we could tell, He had brought our relationship to an untimely end. All He encouraged us to do was to keep a journal during our separation.

The pain of being separated from Rosalind softened my emotions to the point where I could feel more sensitively for people in need. Although I often chafed against the sense of loss, God was beginning to forge a new and deeper intercessory calling in my heart. The outcome was one of abundant mercy. Having genuinely handed over our feelings for each other (and lived through the turmoil that this brought), the Lord released us some three months later to see each other again. We discovered then through our journals how closely our prayers had been tracking as we prayed for people and countries around the world. Twenty-two years later we still track closely together and are immensely grateful to the Lord for giving us back to each other.

The Lord is an eminent psychologist. If He asks us to surrender something and subsequently restores it, we are much less likely to take it for granted or treat it as being ours by right. Rather, we treasure it as His special gift. What we cannot afford are any "no-go" areas in our lives. Rather than trying to dodge His searchlight, think how good it is to face the worst in ourselves and find not the condemnation that we dread but rather the loving embrace of the Lord, who has nothing but our best interests at heart.

When God is going to do something special He often allows us to see the difficulties first. But when He is going to do something really magnificent, He often allows it to appear completely impossible! That is why two key characteristics will help us to flow in the miraculous: strong perseverance and a willingness to humble ourselves under the chastising hand of our heavenly Father. For just as surely as high calling attracts strong opposition, so serious and prolonged testing usually precedes great fruitfulness.

In the early 1980s I was leading a powerful young ministry team. In certain key areas, however, we were heading off course and allowing our flawed vision to become more important than anything else. The Lord loves us too much to allow us to go off course without taking whatever steps are necessary to bring us back on course. The day came when I heard the Lord say quite clearly to me, "You're going to find this hard to hear, but your ministry team no longer exists."

It was as though one of the "watcher angels" of Daniel 4:13-17 had spoken. Like Nebuchadnezzar, it was time for us to be "cut down to size" (Daniel. 4:23-27). Shortly after this members of our team went their separate ways, but in His mercy God did not take away either the vision or His power in my ministry. "Between the idea and the reality...Falls the shadow," warns the poet T.S. Eliot.* All who have experienced the greyness of a "dark night of the soul" know what he meant. During painful times of relationship difficulties and times of testing we may often be more conscious of God's absence than of His presence. The most important thing is not to give up when the bottom falls out and the roof caves in!

When our initial attempts do not work out as we had hoped—even those we had felt so confident God was in—we are bound to be left with egg on our face and questions in our heart. *Did we get it all wrong, Lord? Were we too presumptuous?* If the pain and confusion drive us to seek the Lord more (as opposed to giving up altogether) we will rejoice all the more when the real thing comes through—even if God has to take us from A to B via C, D, E, F, and even G.

It is by no means always easy to discern whether a vision is a dummy run or the real thing. It often takes time and testing for the matter to become clear. God, as pure Spirit, does not experience waiting in the uncertain and often anxiety-laden way that we do. When He summons us to something, His call meshes sooner or later into Greenwich Mean Time with split-second precision—but it *originates* in the altogether different time scale of heaven. God, give us grace to make whatever adjustments may be necessary on the way—and above all to persevere until the time scales line up!

Sometimes in a woman's labor, there comes a phase when she feels so disoriented that all she wants to do is to stop the whole process and go back home. It is a great relief when she moves beyond this phase. The most intense pain still lies ahead, but now it is pain that is going somewhere. Beyond the transition phase comes the "crowning"! It is much the same in the spiritual realm. God can always find ingenious ways to use all that we go through, and all that we offer Him. When He sees that our deepest desire is to honor Him (rather than develop our own empire) and persevere through testing and trial, He often moves with immense speed to manifest the answers to many months and even years of praying.

In the case of the painful and disorientating time I recorded above, God did the same for me that He did for Nebuchadnezzar: He left the stump in the ground. Through intense heart-searching and repentance, the Lord worked sovereignly to put together a far more experienced team and relaunched us as an entirely new ministry team that preserved the best of the old. The ground had been tilled and was able now to bear much healthier fruit.

Jesus taught a lot about the need for perseverance in prayer. We should never fall into the trap of equating the miraculous with a quick-fix short cut. Britain was saved from defeat during the Second World War by two things. On the one hand were God's miraculous deliverances—the flat sea at Dunkirk, the change of strategy in the Battle of Britain at the crucial moment, and other key divine interventions. But there was also the inspired doggedness of Winston Churchill. Speaking at Harrow, his old school, after the war, he stood to address the boys in his famously stentorian voice. "Young men, I say to you: Never give up. Never, never, never give up." It was surely the shortest speech of all time, but one that nobody present will ever forget. May the Lord help us to take its message to heart at the times we need it most.

We should not confine miracles to specific events like a healing or a financial breakthrough. The way God equips and commissions people for their ministries can also be miraculous. During my experience in Paris, when the Lord Jesus appeared to me, He asked me three times whether I was prepared to serve Him. In the presence of such perfect peace, how could the thought of refusing enter the head? There and then He called me to be His witness wherever I went. After some years as a parish evangelist, I received a further call that made me realize that being a "witness" involved more than telling sinners about their need for salvation. It also meant being a watchman for the Lord, sensing the things on God's heart, and directing the body of Christ to respond accordingly.

It all started one evening when the Lord told me to lay aside my plans and read the book of Amos. As I did He opened my eyes to the true condition of both our church and our nation. He warned in particular how grieved and angry He was when people set up other gods and then presented them as being equal to Himself. From that moment on the concept and burden of praying for nations moved swiftly from my head to my heart. A prophetic call gradually emerged that has ultimately inspired many others to cry out to God together for the future of our country.

Just as surely as the enemy sends *counterfeit* messages that lead to the founding of cults and to great deception (Matthew 24:24), so the Lord confirms His call by signs and wonders. Shortly after I had begun to take the message God was giving us to wider audiences, I had an experience that dramatically confirmed the substance of the message I was sharing. We were praying one day in the company of a converted Iranian, who became very animated when he heard me praying in tongues. "Do you realize what you are saying? You are speaking in Farsi!" Some of the sentences were perfectly formed, while others were more fragmented, but the substance was clear. God was warning us about the state of the nation and calling us to cry out to Him together.

My first attempt to encourage people to pray for the nation produced unexpected results. While attending a large campmeeting, the Lord impressed on me the need to harness the potential of so many thousands of Spirit-fired Christians to call on the Lord together for the future of the country. When I shared this with the leadership, they agreed in principle but were most unwilling to allow anything to be added to their scheduled program.

I returned despondently to my tent, only to hear the still, small voice telling me quite distinctly, "This time next year you will be leading your own conference." I doubt I would have dared believe such a radical word had it not been for the fact that the first thing the next morning one of our group came bounding up to knock on the door of my tent (as much as you can ever knock on the door of a tent) and burst out, "Guess what? The Lord showed me last night that this time next year you will be leading your own conference!"

The Lord had called and exactly as He promised a movement was launched that drew Christians together from across the denominations to seek His face in worship and pray for the nations. He has given us much favor and beginner's grace precisely, I think, because we were so concerned to make the things on His heart a higher priority than the meeting of our own needs. As a result He took care of them as well, often supernaturally. For example, as we prayed one day against the spread of Islam in our nation, a lady's ear was healed!

Over the years the message has matured and deepened, but its substance can still be summarized by the well-known verse from 2 Chronicles 7:14, that if *only* God's people will seek His face and live for Him with all their hearts, there is still hope for our all but hopelessly backslidden nation.

Music has also played a big role. Rightly described as the language of heaven, it draws us in powerful ways into His throne room and touches our hearts in ways that words alone cannot always reach. From considerable experience we can say that there are few things more likely to release God's miraculous power than when music and worship combine with intense longing in prayer.

It requires openness to God and to each other to experience the level of breakthrough that releases His power into situations, however. Once when we were praying in the New Year, we felt as though our prayers were hitting the ceiling. I even had a picture of a drum skin stretched tight across the top of the room. "Okay, Lord," I asked. "What's wrong?"

"You're not being honest enough with each other!" came His immediate answer. We thought we knew and related closely to each other. As we repented, one particularly anointed singer began to sing an exquisitely beautiful song in the Spirit. Later, the Lord gave her the words for it—a lament from the Lord's heart to open up the way to deeper things. Her openness and obedience to sing the song of the Lord changed the course of our ministry that evening.

We witnessed another similar miracle in a dear friend. A few years ago someone had given him a prophecy that he was going to lead worship from a keyboard. Not only was he not a worship leader, he couldn't even play the piano! When he confessed to his complete lack of musical sensitivity, the seminar leader gently pulled him by his trouser turn-ups and prayed for a gift of creativity to be released in him. The results have been startling. He has not only learned to play the keyboard but is now writing wonderfully anointed music. When I think how easy it would have been to dismiss that initial prophecy as being wrong!

The way the Lord has developed a musical gift in Steve also reminds me of a seventh-century cowman called Caedmon, who became England's first English singer-poet. Totally ungifted by nature, an angel appeared to him one night and commanded him to sing. Overcoming his protests that he was no musician, Caedmon stepped out in obedience and began to sing beautiful and thought-provoking songs that quickly became known across the north of England as the Christian faith swept through the land.

Inspired music enables us to reach new depths in prayer, just as the themes the Lord gives us in prayer draws forth music that matches the situations we are praying for. Sometimes this will be primarily of a declaratory nature, as when we joined the worldwide prayer push to pray down the Iron Curtain. At other times we will experience more of His minor key lament, as we cry out for the unreached and the suffering. All that matters is to be sensitive to the mode God wants us to be in rather than sticking rigidly to our prepared lists of songs.

Once we have known this level of intimacy, we can never be satisfied with keeping prayer and worship as completely separate parts of our meetings. It is so much richer when we learn to let them flow in and out of each other. We have also seen miraculous breakthroughs come about when our musicians have walked out among people in the congregation and begun to play over them.

Worship is right at the forefront of what God is doing—and it is only common sense to realize that it will be opposed. Once, when I was ministering on the theme of spiritual warfare, the atmosphere was feeling unbearably heavy. My fellow leaders slipped quietly out of the room, and I wondered if they were deserting me in my hour of need. But they had gone to phone our wives to round up extra prayer support.

As the worship continued, several people commented on the beautiful flute playing. One even identified it specifically as a *wooden* flute. The only thing was—there was no flute player present! Unknown to us, a hundred miles away the wife of one of our leaders was playing a wooden flute in the Spirit as she interceded for us! The atmosphere in the meeting changed completely. When I divided the conference into groups to pray as the Spirit led, later we discovered that four of them were led to pray for precisely the same thing!

It is a great joy and a wonderful gift when God gives us dreams and visions, or when Bible verses stand out to us and important doors are opened for us. We should expect such things and be confident in His leading. At the same time, we must be aware that if God wants us to make a major decision, He will usually confirm it to us by several strands. Most of the mistakes I have made in matters of guidance have stemmed from placing too much emphasis on one strand alone.

For example, outside Scalloway Harbour in Shetland lie numerous rocky reefs. As fishing boats approach it, they can see three harbour lights (green, red, and white). It is only when all three line up so that they show as one white light that it is safe to proceed. Spiritually we must often wait for things to line up before a call from the Lord becomes a commission and it is safe for us to proceed.

After three years of intense busyness, the Lord called me to resign as an evangelist in Oxford and to go wherever He led me. It was during that transition period that I had a dream of black and white houses and felt convinced that the place referred to was Chester, a city I knew nothing about.

As I waited on the Lord He showed me from Deuteronomy 18 that I was to be a Levite, set apart without title or income to minister to Him. I asked the Lord for more details. As I was going to bed a few nights later, He whispered the names of two Anglican churches into my ear. On the strength of this word, I paid the city a flying visit. Feeling more than a little foolish, I asked a news agent whether she had heard of these churches. To my amazement, they turned out to be neighboring parishes.

On the principle that every leading needs testing, it wasn't enough that I had found the churches the Lord had told me about through a word of knowledge. The clinching factor came when I met to pray with the leaders of the church in Chester about the possibility of my coming to join them. The vicar was given a clear conviction that our lives had been proceeding, as it were, along parallel lines, and that the Lord now wanted to bring our paths together. Within a few months I was based at one church and leading a prayer group in the other, which some years later enabled the four main churches in the city to work effectively together.

God loves to lead His children, but may I encourage you first to take time to let Him *confirm* His plans. Secondly, do not settle for an easier course of action once the Lord has called you to attempt something unconventional. Such temptations test your willingness to pay the cost to see God's highest vision through to completion.

The most effective framework I have discovered to welcome the Lord's miraculous works is as simple and as challenging as saying, "Let's pray together." Even experienced Christians often hold back from taking such a step because the flesh is concerned for appearances. However, the devil fears the power of prayer, for he has had only too much experience over the centuries of being clobbered by praying saints. Just think how many issues we come across in the course of a day that we can turn into prayer if we will but learn to train and tune our spirits to do so. Such action truly will honor God and release His power.

The history of the church is of God opening a window in heaven, and the church, after some initial blessing, putting the window firmly back on its catch. The Bible calls this quenching the Spirit. But if we are prayerful and careful not to limit God, there is no limit to what He can do. Heaven with all its beauty, resources, and power is close at hand.

Many times in meetings we have been led into times of praying all together which have led to seeing His power released into many situations. On one occasion, as we were doing so, the Lord suddenly gave me the burden to cry out loud for bombs to be defused. That very night, an IRA bomb was discovered in London and safely defused.

Occasionally the Lord has told me He is taking the leadership right out of my hands. On one occasion when He did this, such a sense of His presence came on the meeting that one experienced leader described it afterwards as the nearest he had ever known to revival. I could see the Lord meeting with people in depth, but as time went on I could also see half the congregation beginning to get bored. Pastorally, everything inside me longed to bring the meeting back to safer realms, but for the sake of those who were being touched I knew I must not quench the Spirit.

This has immense implications for our top-down, agenda-laden church services and programs. Jesus did not rise from the dead just to give us the grace to listen to pastor-dominated sermons. He wants us *all* to contribute and to receive. How determined we must be not to revert to safe and trusted ways of doing things when He wants to do something entirely new.

Increasingly our aim has been to develop body ministry and to get real people doing real things! This is the note I will close on because, like the Acts of the Apostles, it is more a starting point for fresh adventures than a conclusion in itself. God wants us to be drenched in His Spirit so that it is He who controls our hearts and minds rather than the lusts of the flesh or the over rationalizing of the mind quenching His Spirit. He wants us to see, as it were out of the corner of our eyes, what He is doing. And then, with faith and courage, to allow Him to lead us where He wills. Then there is no quota of blessing we can ever exceed and no limit to how many miraculous things the Lord can do in our midst.

Robert and his wife, Rosalind, have led numerous prayer and worship conferences over the past twenty-five years, including two national days of prayer: Fight for this Nation and Britain and Ireland United in Prayer. Writing is Robert's main calling and passion. He is the author of numerous books including Ravens and the Prophet, Intimacy and Eternity, and Praying Together. His latest book, The Still Small Voice, draws people into God's presence and helps them make sense of the many ways He speaks to us. You can order this interactive experience in listening to the Lord from the home page of www.ruachmnistries.org. Robert and Ros live in Canturbury, Kent, following a three-year sojourn in the Shetland Islands, where Robert led Fire From the North in 2005, an international prayer conference for Europe. It drew together representatives from more than twenty nations.

* http://www.cs.umbc.edu/~evans/hollow.html

CONCLUSION

*H*ave you ever wondered why you don't witness more miracles? Knowing that God performs miracles and displays His power among the people (Psalm 77:14), have you wondered why miracles seem to be the exception and not the norm? I've wept before the Lord countless times, desperate for answers to these often unspoken questions. Maybe you have too, especially after reading these remarkable miracle stories.

Pondering these questions, I thought of Gideon, a man who felt grossly underqualified to deliver Israel from enemies that had ravaged them for seven years. When the angel of the LORD appeared to Gideon, he said, "The LORD is with you, mighty warrior" (Judges 6:12).

"But sir," Gideon replied, "if the LORD is with us, why has all this happened to us? Where are all his wonders that our fathers told us about when they said, 'Did not the LORD bring us up out of Egypt?' But now the LORD has abandoned us and put us into the hand of Midian" (Judges 6:13).

I can relate to Gideon! I've read the miracles of the Bible. I've heard, documented, and preached about God's miracles. Yet when I scan my surroundings, even in the body of Christ, I see lives ravaged by the enemy as Israel was in Gideon's day. Countless people are desperate for a miracle and are weary from waiting for their breakthrough.

You don't have to look far to find people entangled in bondage. Many suffer with debilitating sickness. Some are stuck in the rut of poverty, unable to put food on their tables. And multitudes are desperate for a supernatural miracle because all alternate options have expired.

If God is a supernatural God who performs supernatural miracles, one might ask as Gideon asked, "If You are with us, Lord, then why has all of this happened to us? Where are all of the wonders that the Bible tells us about? Have You abandoned us and left us in the hand of the enemy?"

I've pounded heaven's gates about this subject repeatedly.

"Why, Lord, are so many sick when Isaiah 53:4-5 says that Your Son already bore the stripes for our healing and wholeness?"

"Why do some of Your children die prematurely when You promised long life in Psalm 91:16?"

"Why are many of Your faithful servants struggling to pay their bills when You promised to meet our every need in Philippians 4:19?"

Have you asked God questions like that? I've asked because I, too, need a miracle or two! When those questions tumble from my mouth, the Holy Spirit reminds me of God's biblical promises that address all issues of life.

After meditating on God's promises, I asked myself, *What do I expect? When was the last time I laid hands on the sick and believed that God would heal them?* I admitted that I sometimes listen to people's ailments and say, "I'll be praying for you." Yet later I either forget to pray or don't *expect* God to answer.

When God brings people across our path needing a touch from heaven, we can approach the throne of grace through prayer, wherever we happen to be. God doesn't need the perfect atmosphere in which to perform miracles. If we do our part—to believe, obey, and trust—God does His part! The results are up to Him.

Although the Bible instructs us to lay hands on the sick (Mark 16:17-18), God does not ask us to do the healing. If you pray for the lame and they do not recover immediately, it is not *your* problem. Likewise, if you pray for the sick, and they leap out of their wheelchair, it is not because *you* prayed the perfect prayer or because *you* are a spiritual powerhouse. You were simply a tool in the Master's hand, the willing and obedient vessel *through* whom God moved.

It amazes me that God can use us in spite of a bad attitude, as we saw in Pastor Randy Klein's story. And God can accomplish life-changing work when we are seeped in cow dung as we read in Jennifer Rees Larcombe's story. God doesn't require a theology degree or a perfect life to be used by Him. Every great man and woman of God in the Bible—used mightily by God—made mistakes and failed in many ways. God wants to use *you* too—in spite of your weaknesses, failures, or mistakes. You only need to be *available* to Him and willing to *trust* Him and His promises.

God's response to our petitions may arrive in timing we don't understand or like. His answers may come in ways that make no sense. Yet He says, "Trust in the Lord with all your heart and lean not on your own understanding" (Proverbs 3:5-6). Unwavering trust in God and His unchanging Word leads us to a place of rest where we know that He has a plan and is working out that plan—even when we don't understand.

I pray you will allow God to draw you to a deeper place of trust and rest in Him, as He did me, where you can say, "I *know* my God will deliver me...*and even if it takes a long time* I will NOT bow down to sickness, disease, lack, depression, strife, danger, or anything else! I will *not* quit!"

The Bible says that God confirms His Word with miraculous signs and wonders. (See Acts 14:3.) God's Word is preached across the globe every day. Are we expecting God to confirm His Word with signs and wonders? Or are we yawning and waiting for the service to end so we can feed our flesh at the local restaurant?

Passionate pursuit of God, not the miracles we want *from* Him, will break the dams of revival and flood the earth with His glory. The miracles we cry out for are *in Him* and flowing from His flood of glory!

The true stories you've read in this collection are only a peek into what God is doing in the earth today. Much more is yet to come! God has set the stage to shake the earth with a mighty move of the miraculous.

In your hot pursuit of God, raise your *expectation for* the miraculous because He *is* on the move doing the extraordinary in the lives of the ordinary!

DO YOU KNOW THE MIRACLE WORKER?

Do you have a personal relationship with the God of miracles through a personal relationship with Jesus Christ? Because "all have sinned and fall short of the glory of God" (Romans 3:23), we were without hope for a future, unable to enter the presence of a Holy God. Yet God, the Creator of the universe, out of His unfailing love for you and me, offered His Son Jesus as a sacrifice for sin. Although we deserve eternal separation from God, He offers us life—the *gift* of eternal life through Christ Jesus (Romans 6:23).

God provided eternal life—*salvation*—through the sacrifice of His only Son Jesus, but it's up to you to personally receive His gift. God will not force Himself into your life. He will come into your heart to cleanse you from sin by invitation only. He offers you the gift of eternal life. Will you receive His gift and make Jesus Lord of your life?

Jesus is the *one and only* way to heaven and the Father. No one can see the Father except through Jesus (John 14:6). No person will ever see the kingdom of God unless they are born again (John 3:3). The *only* way to eternal glory is through Jesus. Alternate routes to heaven are nonexistent.

Jesus stands at the door of your heart knocking. If you open the door, He promises to come in (Revelation 3:20). If you have never repented of your sin and accepted Jesus as Savior, I invite you to make Jesus Lord of your life right now. If you want to accept God's gift of forgiveness and eternal life, pray this prayer out loud.

> *Father, I come to You in the name of Jesus. I believe Jesus Christ is the Son of God. I know I'm a sinner and need your forgiveness. I'm sorry for my sin and want to turn from my sin. I believe Jesus died and was raised from the dead for my justification. I invite You to come into my heart right now to be Lord of my life. I believe with my heart and confess with my mouth Jesus as my Lord and Savior. Heavenly Father, fill me with Your Holy Spirit. I receive everything You have for me in Jesus' name. Amen.*

You are now a part of the kingdom of God! You are a child of the King of Kings, the Master of Miracles! You are born again and all heaven is rejoicing (Luke 15:10). A party is going on in heaven right now!

If you prayed this prayer to receive Jesus Christ as your Savior for the first time, please contact us on the Web at **www.harrisonhouse.com** to receive a free book.

Or you may write to us at

Harrison House
P.O. Box 35035
Tulsa, Oklahoma 74153

CONTRIBUTORS' CONTACT INFORMATION

Niki Anderson (Chapter 2)
E-mail: Nander1405@aol.com
Phone: 509-448-2277 for speaking or
   teaching engagements (women's
   retreats, cat or gardening events,
   writers' conferences)

Stephen Bennett (Chapter 22)
Stephen Bennett Ministries
P.O. Box 2095
Huntington, CT 06484
(203) 926-6960
E-mail: office@SBMinistries.org
www.sbministries.org

Tom Blossom (Chapter 17)
P.O. Box 4660
Spokane, WA 99220

Gena Bradford (Chapter 41)
www.genabradford.com
E-mail:gena@genabradford.com

Christel Decker Bresko (Chapter 38)
10604 S Lakehurst Dr.
Medical Lake, WA 99022-8824
Tel/Fax 509-299-3144
E-mail: noapples@centurytel.net
www.theredhatsite.com

Karola Brownsfield (Chapter 48)
P.O. Box 55063
Shoreline, WA 98155-0063

Terry Charlton (Chapter 29)
E-mail: terry.charlton@mission-
   africa.org

Jan Coates (Chapter 21)
www.jancoates.com

Russ Doyl (Chapter 11)
c/o Destiny Church
4017 E. 21st Ave.
Spokane, WA 99223
509-443-8677
www.destinychurchinfo.org
pastor@destinychurchinfo.org

Michael Drynan (Chapter 25)
2428 Woodglade Blvd.
Peterborough, Ontario, Canada
K9K-2K9
1-705-749-2554

Flo Ellers (Chapter 31)
P. O. Box 3
Aberdeen, Washington 98520
360-532-0490
Ph/Fax: 360.532.0490
floellers@comcast.net
www.floellers.org

Jeri Erskine (Chapter 40)
E-mail: jcerskine1@juno.com

Carla Estes (Chapter 19)
215 Grant St.
Hoquiam, WA 98550
360-533-7765
kcestes4kids@hotmail.com

Julie Greenfield (Chapter 26)
E-mail: dmtc@hotmail.com

David Gurno (Chapter 13)
1508 E. 26th St.
Apt 2
Minneapolis, MN 55404
612-729-9574

De-Bora Gurno (Chapter 14)
1508 E. 26th Street
Apt 2
Mpls, MN 55404
612-729-9574

Ron Hanson (Chapter 45)
WWJC Radio
1120 E McCuen St
Duluth, MN 55808
218-626-2738
E-mail: romahanson@juno.com
Home address: 510 101st Ave. W.
Duluth, MN 55808
218-626-4784

Carol Harrison (Chapter 5)
P.O. Box 86
St. John, WA 99171
E-mail: landch@hotmail.com

Tami Hedrick (Chapter 8)
P.O. Box 370
Valley, WA 99181
Phone: 509-937-2129
Fax: 509-937-2554
E-mail: dovefinan-
   cial_tami@hotamil.com

Roger Helle (Chapter 23)
Teen Challenge of the Mid-South
1108 W. 33rd Street
Chattanooga, TN 37410
(423) 756-5558
E-mail: point.man@charter.net

Dorothy Faye Higbee
   (Chapter 6 and 39)
E-mail: prazmag@roadrunner.com

Gail Justesen (Chapter 32)
422 W. Cascade Way
Spokane, WA 99208
E-mail: encouragers2@juno.com

Samjee Kallimel (Chapter 9)
E-mail: samjeepk@satyam.net.in
Action for Asia Outreach
108, Venvan Colony
Katol Road, P.O. Nagpur – 44013
India
Tel: 091-712-2570633

Lee Kausen (Chapter 43)
Possibilities
211 Sherman Avenue
Coeur d' Alene, ID 83814
(208) 665-9166
www.cdagifts.com
fax: 208-676-8062
lee@cdagifts.com

Laurie Klein (Chapter 7)
E-mail: laurieklein@wildblue.net

Randy Klein (Chapter 49)
3327 W. Indian Trail Road
PMB 176
Spokane, WA 99208
509-710-0704

Therese Marszalek
   (Chapter 3, 16 and 30)
Kingskids5@comcast.net
www.breakingoutministries.com

Sharon Morrison (Chapter 44)
E-mail: rsmorrison1@excite.com

Pastor James Mutahi (Chapter 27)
3076 Lexington Ave. No. A1
Roseville, MN 55113
651-204-0210
jnmutahi@hotmail.com

Jennifer Rees Larcombe (Chapter 4)
www.beautyfromashes.co.uk
jen@beautyfromashes.co.uk

Carol Miller McCleery (Chapter 37)
Contact Info:
   carole@healingsandmiracles.org
www.healingsandmiracles.org

Marta Nelson (Chapter 34)
509-483-2574

Raven Nelson (Chapter 10)
P.O. Box 1099
Kettle Falls, WA 99141
E-mail: Ravennelson@hotmail.com

Pat Oberstar (Chapter 12)
651-636-1532

Lydiah Parkinson (Chapter 35)
11835 Fillmore St. NE
Blaine, MN 55434

Suzanne Pillans (Chapter 2)
Standlake Equestrian Centre
   and Ranch
Downs Road, Standlake
Witney, OX29 7UH
Phone: 01865 300099
E-mail wpillans@aol.com
www.standlakeranh.co.uk

Art Pope (Chapter 18)
Phone: 208-318-3445

Jim Preston (Chapter 24)
E-mail: Kingskid4@gmail.com

Jake and Theresa Raven (Chapter 15)
Box 2835
Grand Forks, BC Canada V0H 1H0
250-442-8016
E-mail: tjraven@telus.net
USA Address:
Box 426
Danville, WA 99121-0426

Sue Reeve (Chapter 33)
Phone: 208-667-5780
E-mail: suer@my180.net

Kay Ritchey (Chapter 38)
Kay_ritchey@yahoo.com

Arnie Suntag (Chapter 20)
Rationalchristian@earthlink.net
www.rationalchristianministries.com

Della Walton (Chapter 36)
TimWalton@hotmail.com

Pastor Sammy Wanyonyi
   (Chapter 28 and 46)
10410 Normandale Blvd.
Bloomington, MN 55437
612-220-7779
Fax: 952-224-7301
E-mail: samsimo@msn.com
www.sammywanyonyi.org

Robert Weston (Chapter 50)
Glebe House
Military Road
Canterbury, Kent CT1 1PA
England
Phone: 00+44+(0)1227-463505
Mobile: 07760 1382 10
rrweston@rrweston.f9.co.uk
www.ruachministries.org

Rosalie Willis Storment (Chapter 42)
P.O. Box 324
Post Falls, Idaho 83877-0324
praisenet@acompanyofwomen.org
www.rosaliewillis.com
www.acompanyofwomen.org
PraiseNet International Prayer
    Network: cwpraise@oregontrail.net

MIRACLES CAN STILL HAPPEN FOR YOU!

Are you aware that miracles are happening every day, at almost any time, everywhere on earth? God isn't dead, nor is He sitting back and watching events play out here on earth. He is actively involved and sending His angels to help people. People like you.

This powerful, inspiring book is a compilation of nearly seventy stories of God's miracle power in action. Gathered from around the world and compiled by two women who were compelled to document and publicize eye-witness accounts of God working miracles on our behalf, this book will encourage, uplift, and energize you that God is alive and very active in the world today!

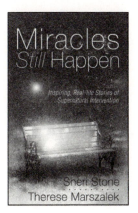

Miracles Still Happen
By Sheri Stone and Therese Marszalek
ISBN 13: 978-1-57794-573-4
ISBN 10: 1-57794-573-5

Available at bookstores everywhere or visit **www.harrisonhouse.com**.

Fast. Easy. Convenient.

For the latest Harrison House product information and author news, look no further than your computer. All the details on our powerful, life-changing products are just a click away. New releases, E-mail subscriptions, Podcasts, testimonies, monthly specials—find it all in one place. Visit harrisonhouse.com today!

harrisonhouse

THE HARRISON HOUSE VISION

Proclaiming the truth and the power
Of the gospel of Jesus Christ
With excellence;

Challenging Christians to
Live victoriously,
Grow spiritually,
Know God intimately.